CRIMINAL PROFILING

The LAW AND PUBLIC POLICY: PSYCHOLOGY AND THE
SOCIAL SCIENCES series includes books in three domains:

> *Legal Studies*—writings by legal scholars about issues of relevance to
> psychology and the other social sciences, or that employ social
> science information to advance the legal analysis;

> *Social Science Studies*—writings by scientists from psychology and
> the other social sciences about issues of relevance to law and public
> policy; and

> *Forensic Studies*—writings by psychologists and other mental health
> scientists and professionals about issues relevant to forensic mental
> health science and practice.

The series is guided by its editor, Bruce D. Sales, PhD, JD, University
of Arizona; and coeditors, Bruce J. Winick, JD, University of Miami;
Norman J. Finkel, PhD, Georgetown University; and Valerie P. Hans,
PhD, University of Delaware.

* * *

The Right to Refuse Mental Health Treatment
    Bruce J. Winick
Violent Offenders: Appraising and Managing Risk
    Vernon L. Quinsey, Grant T. Harris, Marnie E. Rice, and
    Catherine A. Cormier
Recollection, Testimony, and Lying in Early Childhood
    Clara Stern and William Stern; James T. Lamiell (translator)
*Genetics and Criminality: The Potential Misuse of Scientific Information
in Court*
    Edited by Jeffrey R. Botkin, William M. McMahon, and
    Leslie Pickering Francis
The Hidden Prejudice: Mental Disability on Trial
    Michael L. Perlin
*Adolescents, Sex, and the Law: Preparing Adolescents for Responsible
Citizenship*
    Roger J. R. Levesque
Legal Blame: How Jurors Think and Talk About Accidents
    Neal Feigenson
*Justice and the Prosecution of Old Crimes: Balancing Legal, Psychological,
and Moral Concerns*
    Daniel W. Shuman and Alexander McCall Smith

*The Psychology of Rights and Duties: Empirical Contributions
and Normative Commentaries*
    Edited by Norman J. Finkel and Fathali M. Moghaddam
*The Causes of Rape: Understanding Individual Differences in Male Propensity
for Sexual Aggression*
    Martin L. Lalumière, Grant T. Harris, Vernon L. Quinsey, and
    Marnie E. Rice
Preventing Sexual Violence: How Society Should Cope With Sex Offenders
    John Q. La Fond
Homophobia and the Law
    Amy D. Ronner
Experts in Court: Reconciling Law, Science, and Professional Knowledge
    Bruce D. Sales and Daniel W. Shuman
More Than the Law: Behavioral and Social Facts in Legal Decision Making
    Peter W. English and Bruce D. Sales
Laws Affecting Clinical Practice
    Bruce D. Sales, Michael Owen Miller, and Susan R. Hall
Constructive Divorce: Procedural Justice and Sociolegal Reform
    Penelope Eileen Bryan
Violent Offenders: Appraising and Managing Risk, Second Edition
    Vernon L. Quinsey, Grant T. Harris, Marnie E. Rice, and
    Cathering A. Cormier
Reforming Punishment: Psychological Limits to the Pains of Imprisonment
    Craig Haney
Criminal Profiling: Developing an Effective Science and Practice
    Scotia J. Hicks and Bruce D. Sales

CRIMINAL PROFILING

Developing an Effective Science and Practice

Scotia J. Hicks
Bruce D. Sales

AMERICAN PSYCHOLOGICAL ASSOCIATION
WASHINGTON, DC

Published by
American Psychological Association
750 First Street, NE
Washington, DC 20002
www.apa.org

To order
APA Order Department
P.O. Box 92984
Washington, DC 20090-2984
Tel: (800) 374-2721
Direct: (202) 336-5510
Fax: (202) 336-5502
TDD/TTY: (202) 336-6123
Online: www.apa.org/books/
E-mail: order@apa.org

In the U.K., Europe, Africa, and the Middle East, copies may be ordered from
American Psychological Association
3 Henrietta Street
Covent Garden, London
WC2E 8LU England

Typeset in Goudy by World Composition Services, Inc., Sterling, VA

Printer: United Book Press, Inc., Baltimore, MD
Cover Designer: Berg Design, Albany, NY
Technical/Production Editor: Genevieve Gill

The opinions and statements published are the responsibility of the authors, and such opinions and statements do not necessarily represent the policies of the American Psychological Association.

Library of Congress Cataloging-in-Publication Data

Hicks, Scotia J.
    Criminal profiling : developing an effective science and practice / Scotia J. Hicks and Bruce D. Sales.
        p. cm.— (Law and public policy)
    Includes bibliographical references and index.
    ISBN 1-59147-392-6
    1. Criminal behavior, Prediction of. 2. Criminal investigation—Psychological aspects.
    I. Sales, Bruce Dennis. II. Title. III. Series.

HV8073.5.H53 2006
363.25'8—dc22   2005026517

British Library Cataloguing-in-Publication Data
A CIP record is available from the British Library.

Printed in the United States of America
First Edition

CONTENTS

CRIMINAL PROFILING

1

INTRODUCTION: THE ROOTS OF MODERN PROFILING

In recent years, the American public has become increasingly fascinated by criminal profiling. This interest has been both evidenced, and capitalized on, by the popular media in movies such as *The Silence of the Lambs* (Bozman & Demme, 1991) and *Copycat* (Fiedler & Amiel, 1995); television shows, including *Millenium* (Carter, 1996), *Profiler* (Kronish, 1996), and *The X-Files* (Carter, 1993); and fictional novels such as *The Alienist* (Carr, 1994) and *The Angel of Darkness* (Carr, 1997). Although the profilers in these movies, television programs, and mystery novels typically have academic backgrounds and law enforcement experience, their methods center primarily on intuitive knowledge and the occasional psychic vision. These portrayals continue to encourage a view of profiling as an art rather than a science.

Behavioral profiling historically has always been an art. Its roots are not in scientific, academic, or applied criminological pursuits—instead, many of the ideas central to profiling first emerged in works of fictional literature. Literature's first criminal profiler was C. Auguste Dupin, the hero of Edgar Allan Poe's (1814/1982) tale "The Murders in the Rue Morgue." Dupin was an amateur detective, an analyst imbued with a keen understanding of human nature. In this story about a series of unsolved murders, Dupin "throws himself into the spirit of his opponent, identifies himself therewith, and . . . sees . . . the sole methods by which he may seduce [the perpetrator]

3

into error or hurry into miscalculation" (Poe, 1814/1982, p. 76). Although Dupin lacks the specialized training of today's FBI profilers, his methods continue to be the basis of the current art of profiling. He uses bits of evidence and other elements of the crimes to draw larger conclusions about the unidentified perpetrator, eventually solving the mystery. In addition to providing the first profiling prototype, Poe may have been the first to expose the American public to the lore of "profiling intuition"—the sixth sense that modern profilers are popularly thought to possess. Poe (1814/1982, p. 75) wrote of Dupin, "His results, brought about by the very soul and essence of method, have, in truth, the whole air of intuition." Dupin's skill, therefore, has the appearance of being analytical and methodical combined with an element of mystery in his ability to profile the offender. Poe provided the first characterization of analysts as an elite who are born with rather than taught this intuitive sense: "The analytical power should not be confounded with simple ingenuity; for while the analyst is necessarily ingenious, the ingenious man is often remarkably incapable of analysis" (Poe, 1814/ 1982, p. 77).

By the mid to late 19th century, other authors began to write mystery novels whose protagonists were, like Dupin, a new hybrid of amateur detective and armchair psychologist. Wilkie Collins's (1862/1985) novel *The Woman in White* features Walter Hartright, a young man who begins his pursuit of an elusive woman by "gathering together as many facts as could be collected" and "as much additional evidence as [he could] procure from other people" (Collins, 1862/1985, p. 389). Using his intuition and informal knowledge about human behavior, Hartright's first profiling task is to attribute the authorship of an anonymous letter. After conducting a brief interview in town, he concludes that the local schoolmaster has "unconsciously told" his colleague the identity of the writer (Collins, 1862/1985, p. 75). Combined in Hartright's conclusion are his careful attention to the schoolmaster's responses and demeanor, and his inferences about human behavior. *The Woman in White*, like "The Murders in the Rue Morgue," demonstrates one of the first attempts by a detective/psychologist to flush out a perpetrator. In the novel, Hartright insists, "I can force him from his position of security, I can drag him and his villainy into the face of day" (Collins, 1862/1985, p. 402). Like a modern-day profiler, Hartright considers the evidence and assesses how to best persuade the villain to reveal himself.

Collins is also credited with authoring the first modern detective novel. Whereas Poe's Dupin and *The Woman in White*'s Hartright were only amateurs, Collins's (1868/1994) novel *The Moonstone* introduces a law enforcement agent who tries his hand at profiling. Scotland Yard's Sergeant Cuff is a professional detective employed by a family to locate a stolen diamond. He proceeds in his investigation by collecting witness statements and using crime scene evidence to infer the behaviors and motives of the unidentified perpetrator. He then uses this information to identify a potential suspect and suggest a strategy for recovering the stolen diamond. This is perhaps the earliest example of bringing in an expert to consult on a criminal case. By the end of the 19th century, however, expert consultation would be the hallmark of mystery literature.

The detective novel may have been invented by Wilkie Collins, but it was popularized from the late 19th century to the early 20th century by Sir Arthur Conan Doyle, in his *Complete Sherlock Holmes* (1892–1927/1992). In contrast to the previous early profilers, Holmes is considered by colleagues to be more of a scientist. In describing Holmes to Dr. Watson before their introduction, a mutual acquaintance describes him as "an enthusiast in some branches of science . . . well up in anatomy, and . . . a first-class chemist" (Doyle, 1892–1927/1992, p. 16). The same acquaintance also says "Holmes is a little too scientific for my tastes—it approaches to cold-bloodedness" (Doyle, 1892–1927/1992, p. 17). His methods are even referred to as "the science of deduction" (Doyle, 1892–1927/1992, p. 19). However, the reader is also introduced to the intuitive, nonobjective element of Holmes' expertise. "He is a little queer in his ideas," Doyle wrote; "His studies are very . . . eccentric, but he has amassed a lot of out-of-the-way knowledge which would astonish his professors" (Doyle, 1892–1927/1992, p. 16). Holmes describes himself as "a consulting detective" (Doyle, 1892–1927/1992, p. 24). He explains how, when government detectives cannot solve a case, they "lay all the evidence before me, and I am generally able, by my knowledge . . . to set them straight . . . I have a kind of intuition that way" (Doyle, 1892–1927/1992, p. 24). In Sherlock Holmes, therefore, Doyle provides the public with the most popular and enduring example of what is now called a *profiler*: an expert called in when traditional investigative methods are inadequate. A profiler possesses some knowledge of science but relies on practical experience and intuition.

JACK THE RIPPER

During the same time that Sherlock Holmes was solving fictional London murders, a very real series of still-unsolved killings was being perpetrated in the Whitechapel district of London. Between August and November of 1888, an individual who would come to be known as "Jack the Ripper" slit the throats of five prostitutes. Although crime, even the murder of prostitutes, was hardly uncommon in 1880s Whitechapel, these particular murders created considerable public fear. Not only were the victims attacked on public streets; their bodies were left somewhat brazenly out in the open. The victims were generally found quite soon after death, their bodies still warm, which implied that the killer—after he had violently killed these women and even mutilated four of them after death, in some cases disemboweling them and removing organs from their bodies—had very likely walked down the street, and even passed through the crowds, completely undetected.

In response to the murders, many people volunteered their speculations and tips about the unidentified perpetrator. These opinions came from the lay public as well as from witnesses, journalists, and law enforcement officers. The only "profile," however, came from Thomas Bond, who performed autopsies on two of the Ripper's victims. Bond was a specialist in forensic medicine and was the first to offer speculations about the psychology of the offender, contained in an 11-point report to the head of the London Criminal Investigation Division (CID):

> The murderer must have been a man of great physical strength and of great coolness and daring. There is no evidence that he had an accomplice. He must in my opinion be a man subject to periodical attacks of Homicidal and Erotic mania. The character of the mutilations indicate that the man may be in a condition sexually, that may be called Satyriasis. It is of course possible that the Homicidal impulse may have developed from a revengeful or brooding condition of the mind, or that religious mania may have been the original disease but I do not think either hypothesis is likely. The murderer in external appearance is quite likely to be a quiet inoffensive looking man probably middle-aged and neatly and respectably dressed. I think he must be in the habit of wearing a cloak or overcoat or he could hardly have escaped notice in the streets if the blood on his hands or clothes were visible.
>
> Assuming the murderer to be such a person as I have just described, he would be solitary and eccentric in his habits, also he is most likely to be a man without regular occupation, but with some small income or pension. He is possibly living among respectable persons who have some knowledge of his character and habits and who may have grounds for suspicion that he isn't quite right in his mind at times. Such persons would probably be unwilling to communicate suspicions to the Police for fear of trouble or notoriety, whereas if there were prospect of reward it might overcome their scruples. (Rumbelow, 1975, p. 138)

This report thus represents the first departure of profiling from the realm of fictional literature. For the first time, a criminal investigation was informed by a medical professional. Bond extrapolated from the available medical evidence to offer speculations about the unknown offender's behavioral and psychological characteristics. And, as with Sherlock Holmes, Bond's conclusions went beyond those that could be directly substantiated by the evidence, thus using a certain degree of intuition. Unfortunately, because the Ripper murders were never solved, the accuracy of Bond's predictions cannot be evaluated today. The value of his report at the time of the crimes is also unclear. Although it was found among the confidential files of the head of the London CID, it is not certain how much credence investigators gave the report, or whether they used it at all in their investigation.

MILITARY USES OF PROFILING

Since Bond's offering to the Ripper investigation, it is certainly likely that other medical and mental health professionals continued to offer their opinions at various times to law enforcement agencies investigating crimes. However, it was military agencies that first came upon a practical application for profiling. Toward the end of World War II, as Adolf Hitler asserted his power in Nazi Germany, the U.S. military became interested in the nature of his influence over the German people and concerned with the future course of his behavior. In 1943, Walter Langer, a psychoanalyst, was asked to create a personality profile of Hitler for the Office of Strategic Services. In general, the United States needed a "realistic appraisal of the German situation" (Langer, 1972, p. 10). This not only required Langer to construct a biography of Hitler's life and rise to power but also entailed an analysis of Hitler's psychological makeup. The U.S. officials wanted to know "the things that make him tick" (Langer, 1972, p. 10). In addition, Langer was asked to predict how Hitler was likely to respond if he began to fail in his military efforts.

Langer applied a psychoanalytic approach to the task of profiling Hitler. He relied heavily on speeches and literature written by Hitler, searching for the symbolic meaning behind the words:

> In every utterance a speaker or writer unknowingly tells us a great deal about himself of which he is entirely unaware . . . the figures of speech he employs reflect unconscious conflicts and linkages, and the incidence of particular types or topics can almost be used as a measure of his preoccupation with problems related to them. (Langer, 1972, p. 141)

From Hitler's words, as well as from documents and interviews with informants close to Hitler, Langer constructed a profile that portrayed Hitler as a repressed and antisocial individual who had projected his own feelings of inadequacy and disgust onto the Jews. Langer examined the various choices that Hitler might face if the Nazis were to face defeat and correctly concluded that rather than fail before the entire world, Hitler would most likely retreat to his safehouse and commit suicide (Langer, 1972, p. 212).

Similar to Langer's task with Hitler, the military has relied on profiling to assess the weaknesses and likely reactions of major enemy figures (Watson, 1978). However, in addition to profiling military foes, psychologists were also asked to profile American soldiers by using personality tests. Up to and including the Vietnam and Korean Wars, these profiles were conducted to identify which soldiers were likely to be successful soldiers and which ones had vulnerabilities that would make them unsuitable for combat or likely to avoid conscription, run from combat situations, or experience emotional breakdowns if placed in stressful situations. In addition, profiling techniques were used to predict the dependability and success of criminals who were paroled into military service and to identify individuals with certain abilities that might be of use in specialized military operations (e.g., bomb disposal, piloting, code-breaking, and counterintelligence operations). Personality profiling also was used to find those soldiers who could withstand sensory deprivation, interrogation, and pain; individuals who could survive adverse conditions, including isolation and continuous operations; and individuals who had personalities suitable for commando killing and counterintelligence operations.

It is difficult to elaborate in great detail on the military's profiling practices because much of the research involved has been classified or was otherwise conducted in secrecy (Watson, 1978). On the basis of interviews of soldiers conducted after the Korean War, it appeared that at least certain findings regarding soldier behavior and personality profile characteristics were consistent. Even though these claims could not be verified in real combat, the fact that individuals' personalities could be profiled before they were sent into combat as soldiers theoretically provided an advantage that did not previously exist for the military. Profiling conducted in the military used links among language, appearance, lifestyle, personality, and deviant behavior—factors that would later constitute some of the basic criminal profiling components.

BIRTH OF LAW ENFORCEMENT PROFILING

Profiling expertise was first called on by law enforcement in 1956, when James A. Brussel was asked to consult on the Mad Bomber case. The Mad Bomber was an elusive perpetrator who set off more than 50 homemade bombs in New York City over the course of 17 years, beginning in 1940. Although he often left forensic evidence at the scenes of the bombings, and even wrote several letters to newspapers and businesses describing some of his motivations for the bombings (to avenge what he considered to be mistreatment—"'dastardly deeds'" (Brussel, 1968, p. 17)—at the hands of his former employer, Con Edison), the police were unable to identify or apprehend him. In 1956, Inspector Finney, the director of the New York Police Department's crime laboratory, consulted Brussel, a psychiatrist who had experience with criminal offenders. Although Brussel had no investigative training, the police were under pressure to solve the case and were desperate for leads. The captain of the New York Bureau of Missing Persons had arranged the consultation between Finney and Brussel and encouraged Brussel to evaluate the evidence. "Give it a whirl, doctor," he told Brussel; "Sometimes the difference between failure and success is a new thought" (Brussel, 1968, p. 5).

Brussel reviewed the letters and crime scene photographs that Finney provided. After considering the available facts, he produced a profile of the unidentified bomber. Brussel described the perpetrator as a paranoid, symmetrically built, middle-aged man. He would be a skilled mechanic of Slavic descent and would live either alone or with an older female relative. He would have a chronic illness (heart disease, cancer, or tuberculosis), which he would believe he had contracted on the job at Con Edison. Brussel predicted that the offender would be a high school graduate, a loner, a regular churchgoer, and impeccably neat. "When you catch him," he told the inspector, "he'll be wearing a double-breasted suit . . . buttoned" (Brussel, 1968, p. 46). Parts of Brussel's profile were actuarial predictions. For example, he predicted the symmetrical body type by referring to Ernst Kretschmer's informal survey of 10,000 patients, which revealed that "85% of paranoiacs have . . . an 'athletic' body type" (Brussel, 1968, p. 32). He also based the age range of the offender on averages, adding the average age of onset of paranoia (early 30s) to the 16 years of the perpetrator's bomb-making. In both of these cases, Brussel wrote, "The laws of probability were on my side" (Brussel, 1968, p. 33). As was the case with Collins's fictional character Walter Hartright, Brussel suggested a proactive strategy to flush out the offender. He suggested publicizing the profile:

> By putting these theories of mine in the papers, you might prod the Bomber out of hiding . . . It'll challenge him . . . He'll say to himself "Here's some psychiatrist who thinks . . . he can outfox me . . ." and then maybe he'll write to some newspaper and tell how wrong I am. He might give . . . other clues. (Brussel, 1968, p. 45)

The profile was published in *The New York Times*, and the Mad Bomber did in fact respond with more letters and a threatening phone call to Brussel. Meanwhile, a review of Con Edison's employee records revealed a "'troublesome'" (Brussel, 1968, p. 62) case involving a disagreement with a generator wiper named George Metesky, who had been injured on the job and blamed this injury for causing a subsequent illness. In one of the letters written by Metesky to Con Edison appeared the phrase "dastardly deeds," the same one that had been used in several of the Mad Bomber's letters to the press. The police investigated Metesky and eventually arrested him for the bombings. Metesky was a 54-year-old man of Polish descent, living with his two older sisters. He was "well-proportioned" (Brussel, 1968, p. 67), at 5 feet 9 inches and 170 pounds. His neighbors characterized him as aloof and unfriendly; his former employer described him as meticulous in his work—he was a trained electrician. He rarely missed Mass at St. Patrick's Cathedral, and he had tuberculosis, which he blamed on his accident at Con Edison. When police arrested him, Metesky was wearing "a blue pin-striped double-breasted suit. It was buttoned" (Brussel, 1968, p. 69).

Brussel went on to consult in other high-profile cases, most notably that of the Boston Strangler. He acknowledges that he sometimes made errors; however, there is no information in his *Casebook of a Crime Psychiatrist* (Brussel, 1968) on his accuracy rate. On the basis of anecdotal success, however, police departments and attorneys frequently asked for profiles from him. Ultimately, Brussel was asked by the "father of FBI profiling" (Kessler, 1993, p. 217), Howard D. Teten, to tutor him in his profiling methods. Teten independently began developing ideas on profiling as an evidence officer in California, where he was also earning a degree in criminology at the University of California, Berkeley. On the basis of his observations about the relationships between crime scene evidence and the perpetrators of those crimes, he concluded that patterns could be recognized and compared with patterns from other cases to narrow down lists of suspects. He believed that crime scene patterns could be associated with particular mental disorders. Teten joined the FBI in 1962 and began teaching a course in applied criminology in the late 1960s. In teaching, he offered suggestions and conclusions on unsolved cases that police officers brought to class. When some of these profiles were successfully used to solve some difficult cases, the FBI "recognize[d] we had a contribution to make" (Kessler, 1993, p. 222). Teten's class evolved into a series of courses and eventually into the training program that has become the FBI's Investigative Support Unit, which is discussed in more detail shortly.

Teten's early partner in these endeavors was Patrick Mullany, an agent in New York who had a degree in psychology and was interested in the work that Teten had been doing. He transferred to the FBI Academy, and the two began consulting privately on unsolved murder cases. In 1974, they were joined by Robert Ressler and, 3 years later, in 1977, by John Douglas.

During this time, profiling in the FBI was enjoying some initial success. The first case that was solved using Teten's systematic profiling techniques was a kidnapping that took place in 1973. Seven-year-old Susan Jaeger had been abducted from her tent while on a camping trip with her family. Teten and Mullany profiled the offender as a young, White, male loner who lived locally in the Bozeman, Montana, area. The local FBI office had identified an individual, David Meierhofer, who matched Teten and Mullany's profile, but there was no evidence to tie him to the crime. Early the following year, a woman who had been associated with Meierhofer was also reported as missing. Although there was still no evidence to link the two crimes with Meierhofer, this second crime allowed Teten, Mullany, and now Ressler to "refine the profile" (Ressler & Shachtman, 1992, p. 154). They determined that the offender would be the type of person who would enjoy reliving his crimes and might telephone the families of his victims. On the basis of this, the lead agent on the case in Bozeman recommended to the Jaeger family that they keep a tape recorder near their telephone. On the anniversary of Susan Jaeger's abduction, the Jaegers received a phone call from the kidnapper. An FBI voice analysis identified Meierhofer as the caller, but this was insufficient for obtaining a search warrant and arresting him. Mullany then suggested to Mrs. Jaeger that, on the basis of the profile, Meierhofer "could be woman-dominated" (Ressler & Shachtman, 1992, p. 155). He recommended that she go to Montana and confront the suspect. She did so, and shortly thereafter the kidnapper called the Jaeger home again. This time, Mrs. Jaeger was able to identify the voice as that of Meierhofer, and the FBI was then able to arrest him and search his home, where they discovered remains of both victims.

Word began to spread about Teten's and Mullany's success with profiling unsolved crimes, and with the end of the J. Edgar Hoover era, profiling was becoming a more accepted practice within the FBI. Teten, however, wanted to add a research component to the Behavioral Science Unit and needed a larger database of information on criminal behavior to improve on the unit's profiling capabilities. Academic research was not thought to be helpful to this end: "By and large, academics study crime from afar. They generally focus on theories and would not think of asking criminals how they did their crimes" (Kessler, 1993, p. 222). So, Ressler and Douglas began to supplement the needed database by interviewing incarcerated serial rapists, murderers, and assassins around the United States.

Ressler and Douglas traveled the United States, collecting 57 pages of data on each of 36 incarcerated offenders. They noted similarities and differences in the offenders' responses, including information about motives, planning of crimes, and the disposal of evidence. "By the time Ressler and I had done ten or twelve prison interviews," Douglas reported, "It was clear to any reasonably intelligent observer that we were onto something. For the first time, we were able to correlate what was going on in an offender's mind with the evidence he left at a crime scene" (Douglas & Olshaker, 1995, p. 117). Of particular interest to them were serial sexual offenders, whose repeated crimes provided a wealth of crime scene and victim information. Collaborating with Ann Burgess, of the University of Pennsylvania School of Nursing, Ressler and Douglas began to direct their interviews in an attempt to create a taxonomy of these sexual offenders. Funded by the National Institute of Justice, this study, called the Criminal Personality Research Project (CPRP), culminated in the publication of *Sexual Homicide: Patterns and Motives* (Ressler, Burgess, & Douglas, 1988), a handbook of characteristics of sexual killers.

Douglas and Ressler subsequently collaborated with Burgess once again (and with Allen Burgess) to author the *Crime Classification Manual* (Douglas, Burgess, Burgess, & Ressler, 1992). On the basis of data from the CPRP and other FBI studies of sexual murderers, rapists, child molesters and abductors, and arsonists, this manual was intended to provide an empirically derived taxonomy for organizing and classifying serious crimes by behavioral characteristics. Finding the academic literature on these subjects to be lacking, Douglas and Olshaker (1995) wrote that this manual provided a system to "explain [crimes] in a way that a strictly psychological approach such as the *DSM* has never been able to do" (p. 354).

Ressler and Douglas are perhaps the best-known FBI profilers in the popular media today, having contributed significantly to the popularization of the art of criminal profiling. Both went on to speak in seminars and write books about their experiences as profilers. Both consulted with Thomas Harris (1991), author of *The Silence of the Lambs*, when he was doing research to construct his plot. In fact, one of the characters was modeled after Douglas, who went on to consult in the making of the Academy Award-winning film version of Harris's novel.

Douglas eventually became the head of the Behavioral Science Unit (later renamed the *Investigative Support Unit*) and continued to do intuitive profiling, while Ressler became an innovator in the research and training arm of the unit. As early as 1981, Ressler suggested establishing the National Center for the Analysis of Violent Crime (NCAVC), a research and training center that would encompass the CPRP, police intern training, and programs that applied results of research projects to law enforcement tasks such as interrogation and warrant applications. Eventually, the NCAVC would encompass most of the behavioral science programs at the FBI. Ressler also helped to establish the Violent Criminal Apprehension Program (VICAP), a nationwide computer system designed to allow law enforcement agencies in one area to cross-reference data from their unsolved cases with data from other unsolved cases in other areas. Since retiring from the FBI, both Douglas and Ressler have continued to stay active in profiling, providing consulting services in the private sector.

Developments in criminal profiling were not limited to the United States. David Canter, an academic in England, made his contribution to British profiling soon after Ressler and Douglas conducted their interviews of incarcerated offenders. Canter was asked by the London police to consult on a series of rapes and murders that plagued London in the mid-1980s. By compiling witness descriptions and applying some of his early profiling theories to the case evidence, Canter assisted police in apprehending the Railway Rapist (Canter, 1994, p. 54). In the resulting criminal trial, John Duffy was convicted of five rapes and two murders in 1988, following the "largest police investigation since the Yorkshire [R]ipper inquiry" (Canter,

1988, p. 14). Although Canter's approach to the Duffy case was certainly not a complete departure from that of Teten and Mullany, he did apply some additional theories and statistical analyses to an equally successful end. Canter's work is considered again in chapters 4 and 5.

PROFILING IN THE CRIMINAL JUSTICE PROCESS

Criminal profiling is currently used in three phases of the criminal justice process: criminal investigation, apprehension, and prosecution. Although some of these involvements are explicitly stated by FBI profilers (Douglas, Ressler, Burgess, & Hartman, 1986) or by other, individual profilers (Turvey, 1999), others are simply inferred from the fact that profiling techniques are consistently used in a manner that furthers such goals (e.g., Turco, 1990). Within the criminal investigation phase, profiling still seems to be used after traditional investigative methods have been unsuccessful. In this phase, the goals of profiling are to link offenses together as part of a series, to identify physical, psychological, and lifestyle characteristics of unknown offenders; to suggest the pre- and postoffense behaviors that an offender is likely to exhibit; to evaluate the potential for certain criminal behaviors to escalate to more serious, violent crimes; and to suggest proactive tactics to flush out or lure an unknown offender into revealing his identity. Within the apprehension phase, the goals of profiling are to suggest items to include on search warrants as well as locations to be searched, to predict an offender's reactions or behaviors on arrest, and to suggest interrogation techniques that are likely to elicit a confession. Finally, in the prosecution phase, the goals of profiling are to provide expertise in the courtroom to demonstrate the linking of multiple offenses to one individual and to match a particular individual to the relevant crime(s) by virtue of his or her fit with the profile.

GOALS AND ORGANIZATION OF THIS BOOK

Despite the popularity of criminal profiling, evidence of its accuracy and utility in serving the previously discussed phases of the criminal justice process has not been scientifically demonstrated. Although historically portrayed as an art, profiling has increasingly been represented as a science. For example, the efforts of the FBI have been characterized as a "science of profiling" (Jeffreys, 1995, p. 45), even though this "science" has over the last 20 years consisted mainly of descriptive work.

The purpose of this book is twofold. First, the state of criminal profiling today is critically examined. This examination includes a discussion of the scientific and practical limits of existing approaches and the scientific and practice implications of these limitations for the field of profiling. To accomplish these goals, Part I of the book is organized into five chapters. Chapter 1 introduced a brief history of the roots of modern profiling. Chapter 2 then reviews the nonscientific models of criminal profiling, and chapter 3 presents the problems with these nonscientific profiling models. Chapter 4 reviews the one current model of scientific profiling, and chapter 5 critically evaluates this model as well as the attempted use of science in the nonscientific models of profiling covered in chapter 2. Taken together, these chapters demonstrate that criminal profiling is still an art, not an established science, and that profilers will differ in their conclusions and recommendations given the lack of scientific base for their judgments, a problem that vitiates any claim that profiling is an effective law enforcement tool.

Next, to address this problem and need, Part II is devoted to a discussion of building a science of profiling. Our approach is comprehensive and new but builds on existing practice and research, recognizing that empirical information can lead to better practice strategies and techniques. This discussion comprises eight chapters. Chapter 6 discusses goals for a science of profiling and the development of a theory with which to guide that science. Specification of goals is critical to keep new scientific work focused on testing that which will be important for the development of accurate profiling techniques. Theory is essential because it provides a body of principles to explain how and why the profiling process works, which can then be tested scientifically. Chapter 7 discusses crime scene evidence and its relationship to a science of profiling. This evidence is all that is available to investigators at the start of the profiling process, and thus it is essential to building a profile. Chapter 8 describes the constructs of the three offender characteristics essential to profiling: the perpetrator's motive, personality, and behavior. By describing the offender's motive for committing the crime, personality traits, and behaviors, the profile will narrow the field of persons that investigators need to consider. Chapters 9 and 10 discuss the study of motive and behavior, and personality and behavior, respectively, using examples from the psychological literature. Part II of this book argues that crime scene evidence is predicted by offender behavior, which in turn is predicted by the perpetrator's motive and personality or other offender behaviors. Chapter 11 describes a scientific model of profiling based on our theory relating the components of crime scene evidence, motive, personality, and behavior to each other, and chapter 12 discusses strategies for testing this model. Finally, chapter 13 offers conclusions and recommendations for profiling practice, as the field awaits the development of a new science of profiling. Collectively, these chapters should enable profiling to emerge as a credible and respected field that ultimately will significantly advance law enforcement investigations.

I

PROFILING TODAY

2

CURRENT NONSCIENTIFIC MODELS OF PROFILING

Both the nonscientific and the scientific models and procedures for criminal profiling have been described by their creators and discussed in textbooks (Turvey, 1999), the professional literature (Holmes & DeBurger, 1985; Holmes & Holmes, 1992, 1996; Homant & Kennedy, 1998), and the popular literature (Douglas & Olshaker, 1995; Jeffreys, 1995; Kessler, 1993; Ressler & Shachtman, 1992). The presentations of these models, however, have been too cursory to be relied on for scholarly analysis. This chapter presents each of the current nonscientific models of profiling as they have been described by their creators. Each model's components, therefore, will become accessible for the critical scrutiny to which they are submitted in chapter 3.

Note that in this book, the word *model* is used broadly to incorporate heuristics, guidelines, or approaches recommended for constructing profiles. Each was developed to be used in profiling, so they are all worthy of consideration. The models discussed in this chapter are labeled *nonscientific* because, although they may refer to principles of science in varying degrees, each model implicitly or explicitly relies on an artful component to complete an offender profile.

DOUGLAS ET AL. MODEL

To date, the most detailed description of profiling procedures comes from Douglas, Ressler, Burgess, and Hartman (1986), who categorized these procedures into six stages: Profiling Inputs, Decision-Process Models, Crime Assessment, Criminal Profile, Investigation, and Apprehension. Each stage is described in detail in the following sections. Much of the terminology used by these authors is also used by law enforcement agents and other authors writing about profiling. Thus, for the purposes of this book, the Douglas et al. (1986) terminology serves as the standard unless otherwise noted.

Stage 1: Profiling Inputs

The basic goal of this stage is to collect information and evidence and organize it into the following categories.

Crime Scene

This category contains information about the physical evidence, pattern of evidence, body position, and weapons. The *physical evidence* includes blood spatters, footprints, tools and paraphernalia left at the scene, information about weather and traffic patterns in the area, information about the ease of access to the location, and even factors such as the social and political climate of the area. The *pattern of evidence* requires the integration of this evidence into a synopsis of the crime. *Body position* refers to the positioning of deceased victims at the crime scene, and *weapons* refers to any murder weapons as well as any weapon used to subdue the victims.

Victimology

The goal of this category is to collect evidence about the victim. If the victim is deceased, the profiler must rely on informants or records for this information. If the victim is living, he or she may be interviewed directly. According to Douglas et al. (1986), however, the profiler should still consult informants and records for a more complete assessment. First, information about the victim's background should be gathered. This would include information about his or her personality, reputation, and possible criminal history. Second, inquiries should be made regarding the victim's habits, hobbies, and social conduct. Third, information about the family structure should be gathered. This includes information about the nature of the victim's relationships with family members as well as his or her domestic situation. Fourth, it is important to ascertain where the victim was last seen. Fifth, information about the victim's age and physical condition should be obtained. Finally, the victim's occupation, employment setting, and situation should be described.

Forensic Information

The primary source of forensic information will be the autopsy conducted on the deceased victim. Although forensic evidence may still be collected from a living victim, the nature of this evidence may differ from that collected at a murder scene. The autopsy report should provide the medical examiner's findings regarding the cause and time of death, the type of weapon used, and the sequence in which wounds were delivered. It is also important to ascertain whether wounds and/or sexual assault were inflicted pre- or postmortem. The report should make note of any sexual acts that took place and should include a full toxicology screen in the laboratory report.

Preliminary Police Reports

The police reports will include some of the same information present in the crime scene and victimology sections. In addition, it should include any observations made by officers on the scene, such as descriptions of the behavior and demeanor of witnesses, the time of the crime, information about who reported the crime, and a description of the neighborhood in which the crime was committed. This neighborhood description would include maps, directions, distances, the socioeconomic status of the residents, and the crime rate in the area.

Photographs

Three types of photographs should be included in the Profiling Inputs section: aerial photographs of the neighborhood; 8-inch × 10-inch pictures of the crime scene; and pictures of the victim, including photos of the victim's cleansed wounds.

Stage 2: Decision-Process Models

In this stage, information from the Profiling Inputs stage is integrated into various classification categories.

Homicide Type and Style

There are six types of homicides included in this model.

1. A *single homicide* is defined as one event with one victim in one location.

2. A *double homicide* is defined as one event with two victims in one location.

3. A *triple homicide* is defined as one event with three victims in one location.

4. A *mass murder* is defined as one event involving four or more victims in one location. There are three kinds of mass murders. A *classic* mass murder involves one perpetrator operating in one location over one period of time (which can be minutes, hours, or days). The perpetrator is typically a mentally disordered individual who releases his[1] frustration and hostility by acting violently against a group of people otherwise unrelated to him. A mass murder is described as a *family* mass murder if four or more victims are family members. If a perpetrator commits a mass murder and then takes his own life, then the classification is *mass murder/suicide*.

5. A *spree murder* involves killings at two or more locations, with no "emotional cooling off period" (Douglas et al., 1986, p. 409) in between attacks. The killings are all part of a single event, which can be of a short or long duration.

6. A *serial murder* consists of three or more victims in three or more separate events with an emotional cooling-off period (lasting days, weeks, or months) between homicides. These murders are typically premeditated and planned.

Primary Intent

There are three basic types of intent in the commission of homicides. In each of these cases, the perpetrator can be acting individually or as part of a group. In the *criminal enterprise* category, there is no personal malice toward the victim. The primary motive is likely to be financial gain, and criminal activity is viewed by the perpetrator as essential to his or her livelihood. Examples of murders in this category include drug murders, felony murders (indiscriminate or situational), political murders, insurance-motivated murders, product tampering, gang murders, criminal competition, and contract murders. The intent in *emotional/selfish/cause-specific* types of murders can include erotomanic murders; argument-motivated murders; hostage murders; hero killings; mercy killings; revenge murders; self-defense; murders caused by family disputes that result in infanticide, matricide, patricide, or spouse and sibling killings; murders precipitated by paranoid reactions; murders committed by individuals with mental disorders, in which

---

[1] Because the vast majority of violent offenders are male, *his* is used, rather than *his or her*, throughout the book.

the crime is symbolic or the result of a "psychotic outburst" (Douglas et al., 1986, p. 410); assassinations; and murders caused by religious, cult, or fanatical motivations. The third category, *sexual intent*, encompasses situations in which murder is committed as a result of, or to engage in, sexual activity, mutilation, dismemberment, evisceration, or other activities that have sexual meaning only to the offender.

Victim Risk

Factors such as victim age, occupation, lifestyle, physical stature, resistance ability, and location are considered to make a determination about how likely the victim was to be targeted. Victim risk should be classified as high, moderate, or low. High-risk victims are typically sought out where people tend to be more vulnerable, such as in isolated areas, bus stations, or high prostitution areas. Low-risk victims are those whose occupations and lifestyles do not typically lead them to be targeted for violent crime.

Offender Risk

Offender risk refers to the degree of risk undertaken by the perpetrator to commit the crime and is related to victim risk. For example, abducting a child from the playground of his or her school in broad daylight with other children and teachers present would be high risk for the offender. If a low-risk victim is taken under high-risk circumstances (as in the preceding example), it may imply certain beliefs held by the offender—a belief that he will not be caught, a need for excitement during the commission of the crime, emotional immaturity, and so on.

Escalation

Another issue to be addressed is whether there is a significant potential for the offender to escalate in his criminal activity or repeat the activity with another victim. Information about the sequence of acts, as well as information from other sections of the Decision-Process Models stage, is used to make this determination.

Time Factors

An important aspect of the crime(s) to note is the length of time required by the offender to kill the victim, commit additional acts (if any) with the body, and dispose of the body. This can also assist in the evaluation of offender risk: The longer an offender spends with a victim, the higher the risk that he will be caught. Another time factor to consider is whether the crime(s) took place during the day or night. This may provide information about the offender's lifestyle and occupation.

Location Factors

It is important to obtain information about where the victim was approached, where the crime occurred, and whether the crime scene and death scene are in the same location. In addition, one should determine whether a vehicle was used to transport the victim from the death scene to the crime scene or whether the victim was killed at the point of abduction.

Stage 3: Crime Assessment

In this stage, information from the first two stages is further integrated into categories requiring more judgment on the part of the profiler.

Reconstruction of the Crime

This category requires the profiler to reconstruct the sequence of events and the behaviors of both perpetrator and victim. This would include information about how things happened, how the encounter was planned or organized, and any verbal or nonverbal techniques used to gain control of the victim.

Crime Classification

The primary determination to be made here is whether the crime scene and offender are organized or disorganized. There are three factors to be used in making this determination.

1. *Victim selection.* Organized offenders typically target a particular victim, or a specific type of victim. Disorganized offenders usually happen upon their victims by chance.
2. *Strategies used to control the victim.* Organized offenders tend to obtain victims by using a con or ruse, such as openly approaching the victim under the pretext of asking directions. These offenders also may use physical force, however, to maintain control over the victim. Disorganized offenders typically use physical force to immediately incapacitate the victim in a "blitz" style of attack (Ressler & Shachtman, 1992, p. 136). They also behave haphazardly during the commission of the crime, and the crime scene will usually reflect a lack of control over the victim.
3. *Sequence of crime.* Organized offenders typically plan the sequence of acts in a crime, according to long-standing fantasies. Disorganized offenders do not act according to fantasy scripts, and the sequence of events is typically unplanned.

Staging

Sometimes, perpetrators will attempt to mislead police by altering the crime scene. For example, an offender might remove some valuable items from a crime scene to make it appear as though the murder was motivated by robbery. It is important to ascertain whether a crime scene has been staged (Douglas et al., 1986, p. 413) and to include the presence of staging in the assessment of the offender.

Motivation

Motivation typically is difficult to identify with disorganized offenders because they often act without any specific plan or motive. The motivation of organized offenders, however, may be easier to ascertain. Their crimes are typically fantasy driven, and the crime scene may reflect elements of those fantasies.

Crime Scene Dynamics

It is also important to note the relationship of various pieces of information to each other. An assessment of this relationship might include factors such as the location of the crime scene, cause of death, method of killing, positioning of the body, presence of excessive trauma, and location of the wounds.

Stage 4: Criminal Profile

At this stage, all of the available information and professional judgments are integrated into a profile, which is submitted to the investigating agency. The statements in a profile are considered to be hypotheses, and it is not expected that every statement will be accurate.

Demographics

The profile should include predictions about the offender's level of intelligence, schooling, military experience, job status, living circumstances, interpersonal style and relationship to others, and (if applicable) the make and color of his vehicle.

Physical Characteristics

This section should include the perpetrator's ethnic background, age, height, weight, and build.

Habits

Here, the profile would include factors such as neatness or disorganization; drug and alcohol use; and hobbies and interests such as metalworking, athletics, and so on.

Beliefs and Values

This section could include predictions about the perpetrator's beliefs about women, sexual relationships, family, politics, and so on.

Pre- and Postoffense Behavior

In this section, predictions would be made about any unusual behavior the perpetrator might have exhibited before the commission of the crime, speculation about stressors that may have triggered the act, and information about what to look for in the offender's postoffense behavior (e.g., excessive drinking, bragging).

Recommendations

In this section of the profile, recommendations are made about how best to proceed with the investigation. One piece of advice might be to plant information or "traps" in the news media to encourage the perpetrator to reveal him- or herself. An example of this would be to publicize the funeral or anniversary of the victim's death and then monitor the cemetery for any unusual visitors. Another example would be to issue a challenge to the offender through news coverage in the hopes that it would anger the perpetrator and lead him to write a letter to a newspaper or otherwise provide more behavioral evidence. A second piece of advice would be tips for interviewing suspects. This would include suggestions about whether to interview the suspect late at night or early in the morning as well as whether to adopt a "soft" or "hard" interrogation style.

Feedback Filter 1: Validation of Profile

Between Stages 4 and 5 there is a *feedback filter* (Douglas et al., 1986, p. 401) that serves as a check between the elements of a written profile and the information used to construct it. In this stage, the profiler is looking for congruence between the profile and the information collected. Specifically, the written profile should be evaluated with attention to the crime scene and death scene information, evidence, decision models, and recommendations. If there is a lack of congruence, the profile may need to be modified.

Stage 5: Investigation

In this stage, the profile has been submitted to the investigating agency, which proceeds with its attempts to identify the perpetrator.

Feedback Filter 2: New Evidence

The investigation stage may result in the emergence of new evidence. There is a second feedback filter to provide an opportunity to check and modify the profile on the basis of new evidence.

Stage 6: Apprehension

Ideally, the profile will assist in achieving this final stage, in which the investigation leads to the capture and prosecution of the offender.

HOLMES AND HOLMES MODEL

Holmes and Holmes (1996) presented a model of profiling that, similar to Douglas et al.'s (1986), is an intuitive analysis of crime scene evidence. They described proficiency in profiling as "in part a gift reserved to certain individuals who can reach inside the criminal mind and understand it" (Holmes & Holmes, 1996, p. 166). Their basic approach is to match case evidence to various criminal typologies, which are discussed in more detail below. These typologies are derived from various sources, including the work of Douglas, Burgess, and Ressler in the Criminal Personality Research Project (see chap. 1) and Holmes and Holmes's own research. Holmes and Holmes (1996) did not include a section in their model that integrates these various typologies; however, they did discuss the importance of accounting for geography and victim characteristics in the profiling process.

Typologies

Disorganized Asocial Versus Organized Nonsocial Offenders

This typology comes directly from the work of Ressler, Burgess, and Douglas (1988). The *disorganized offender* is described as being disorganized in all facets of life: appearance, psychological state, domestic situation, and criminal activity. The asocial component reflects the offender's probable segregation from society because he is a "loner" (Holmes & Holmes, 1996, p. 49) and is perceived by others to be strange. In contrast, the *organized offender* is organized in his lifestyle, home, and appearance. He is described as having a character disorder (unspecified) and a "masculine personality" that results in his dressing in a "flashy manner" and driving a car that "reflects his personality" (Holmes & Holmes, 1996, p. 54). The offender is nonsocial in that he chooses to avoid social contact because he feels that "no one else is good enough to be around [him]" (Holmes & Holmes, 1996, p. 52).

These categories are the most general ones presented in Holmes and Holmes's (1996) book. Note that although the FBI has dropped the terms *asocial* and *nonsocial* (Holmes & Holmes, 1996, p. 60), Holmes and Holmes (1996) retained them in their description because they believed them to be important dimensions.

Serial Murderers

The following typology is based on interviews and case studies conducted by Holmes and DeBurger (1985). It is not clear from Holmes and Holmes' book (1996), or from the cited publications, exactly how this typology was derived from these interviews. No data are presented on the number of offenders interviewed, and no information is provided on how their statements were generalized into creating the categories of the typology.

Spatial Mobility. Holmes and Holmes (1996) argued that there is a meaningful distinction to be made between serial murderers who live in one area and kill in that same area, or a nearby area, and those who travel to commit their murders. The former type is termed *geographically stable*, and the latter is labeled *geographically transient*.

The Visionary Serial Killer. This type of killer is induced to murder because he sees visions or hears voices telling him to do so. His victims are typically strangers, and he is usually psychotic (Holmes & Holmes, 1996, p. 64), resulting in him often being declared incompetent or insane in court.

The Mission Serial Killer. These killers are described as feeling "a need on a conscious level to eradicate a certain group of people" (Holmes & Holmes, 1996, p. 64). Unlike the visionary serial killer, the mission killer is not psychotic and is typically of the organized nonsocial type of offender described earlier in this section. The drive for these offenders is to eliminate some identifiable class of people (e.g., prostitutes, Jews).

The Hedonistic Serial Killer. This type of serial murderer either derives sexual pleasure or some personal gain from the act of killing. In the former case, the offender will typically prolong the killing of the victim to commit further acts of mutilation, torture, dismemberment, domination, or necrophilia. In the latter case, termed *comfort-oriented serial murder* (Holmes & Holmes, 1996, p. 66), offenders kill because there is some profit to be realized from doing so. This category can include professional assassins as well as individuals who murder family members for financial gain.

The Power/Control Serial Killer. The power/control killer derives sexual pleasure from exerting power, control, and domination over a helpless victim.

This type of offender prolongs the killing scene and kills with "hands-on weapons" (Holmes & Holmes, 1996, p. 67), often strangling victims.

Arsonists

Holmes and Holmes (1996) cited research that seems to establish arsonists as conceptually distinct from other types of offenders (Kolko & Kazdin, 1992; Sakheim, Vigdor, Gordon, & Helprin, 1985). Indeed, the setting of fires is not a behavior typical of other kinds of criminals unless it is done to conceal a crime or produce some secondary gain. Holmes and Holmes (1996) further argued that personalities, motives, and behaviors differ within arsonists as a group. To illustrate this, they described two typologies of arsonists.

Rider (1980a, 1980b), who presented the first typology, believes that there are four types of arsonists. The first is the *jealousy-motivated adult male*, an arsonist who sets fires in reaction to incidents that "impair his vanity and impugn his personality" (Holmes & Holmes, 1996, p. 97). The second type is the *would-be hero*, who sets fires and then rushes to the scene to save lives and appear to be the hero. Third is the *excitement fire-setter*, who sets fires out of a need for personal excitement. Fourth is the *pyromaniac*, an arsonist who sets fires compulsively for sensual satisfaction and tension reduction.

The second typology is that suggested by Douglas, Burgess, Burgess, and Ressler (1992) in the *Crime Classification Manual*. Similar to the jealousy-motivated arsonist in Rider's (1980a, 1980b) typology, Douglas et al. (1992) identified a category of *arson for revenge*. The fires set by this group of arsonists are usually precipitated by some sort of real or imagined insult to the offender. There is typically only one fire set, targeted at the individual or organization that is the source of the perceived injustice. Other characteristics of revenge arsonists include setting fires on the weekend, near their homes, having a lower-class background, and using alcohol to lower inhibitions for fire-setting. A second category, similar to Rider's (1980a, 1980b) excitement fire-setter, is that of *arson for excitement*. Typical targets for this type of arsonist include vegetation, trash cans, and construction sites. The excitement arsonist sets fires for attention—he will often observe the fire and ensuing chaos from a safe distance. This type of arsonist usually has an arrest record and commits his crimes alone. There are four subtypes of the excitement arsonist: the thrill seeker, the attention seeker, the recognition seeker, and the sexually perverted arsonist. These subtypes are not defined or discussed by Holmes and Holmes (1996) or in the *Crime Classification Manual* (Douglas et al., 1992). The third category in this typology is *arson for vandalism*. These arsonists are typically juveniles, and the targets are typically schools. Vandal arsonists come from lower-class backgrounds, live with their parents, and set fires at times when school is not in session. After setting fires, these arsonists typically flee the scene. The fourth category is *arson for crime concealment*. This type of arsonist sets fires to destroy evidence or mislead law enforcement. The offender is likely to be a single adult male from a lower-class background, living alone. The crime-concealment arsonist typically operates late at night or early in the morning and flees the scene once the fire is set. Finally, there is the *arson for profit* category. This type of arsonist sets fires solely for material gain, such as collecting insurance money, and is usually a single male, living alone, and not living near the crime scene. He is of average intelligence and may have had extensive contact with the criminal justice system. Douglas et al. (1992) also applied the organized–disorganized typology to these categories of arsonists. Organized arsonists are more likely to use elaborate incendiary devices (e.g., bombs equipped with timers), leave less physical evidence at the crime scene, and set fires with a more methodical approach. Disorganized offenders are more likely to use common incendiary devices and accelerants, such as matches and gasoline; use materials that happen to be available; and leave more physical evidence at the scene.

Rapists

Citing Groth, Burgess, and Holmstrom (1977), Holmes and Holmes (1996) argued that the elements of power, anger, and sexuality present in rape "lend themselves well to psychological profiling" (p. 117). They proposed a largely psychodynamic model of the etiology of rapists, focusing on the presence of a rejecting, controlling, and seductive mother as influencing the development of a rapist's behavior. A rapist's hostility toward women is therefore the product of the "pain he suffered at the hands of . . . his mother" (Holmes & Holmes, 1996, p. 118). The authors asserted that "the professional literature suggests that parental rejection, domination, cruelty, and seductiveness are important factors in the early life of the rapist" (Holmes & Holmes, 1996, p. 118).

The typology endorsed by Holmes and Holmes (1996) for the profiling of rapists is a taxonomy based on Groth et al.'s (1977) research and further elaborated on by Knight and Prentky (1987), who divided rapists into four categories: power reassurance, anger retaliation, exploitive, and sadistic.

Power Reassurance. The power-reassurance rapist is a passive social loner with feelings of inadequacy. He is single and nonathletic and lives with his parents while working at a menial job. He may be involved in other inappropriate sexual activities, such as exhibitionism and voyeurism. This type of rapist rapes to "elevate his own self-status" (Holmes & Holmes, 1996, p. 120). He attacks victims in his own neighborhood in the early morning hours, travels on foot, and believes that the victim enjoys the rape.

For this reason, he may contact victims at a later date to inquire about their well-being. Interviewing strategies for this type of offender include appealing to his sense of masculinity, playing a sympathetic role to allow him to feel "understood," or both (Holmes & Holmes, 1996, p. 122).

Anger Retaliation. This type of rapist has a "general overarching purpose to hurt women" (Holmes & Holmes, 1996, p. 123). He is typically socially competent and athletic, with an action-oriented occupation. He is likely married, but he hates women and frequents bars. Characteristics of the rapes include a sudden, unplanned attack; use of profanity; selection of victims near his home; use of weapons of opportunity; anal and oral sex; and an intent to harm the victim. Interviewing recommendations specify that the interviewer should be male, owing to the suspect's hatred of women. The interview should be businesslike, and the interviewer may attempt to ally himself with the suspect against a female officer or against women in general. This is designed to lead the suspect to increase his cooperation with the interviewing officer.

Anger Exploitive. The anger–exploitive rapist believes he is entitled to rape in an expression of dominance. He is typically athletic, with a "macho occupation" (Holmes & Holmes, 1996, p. 126), flashy car, and a series of unsuccessful marriages. He frequents bars and may have a history of property offenses as well as a dishonorable discharge from the military. His rape offenses contain both verbal and physical assault. He tends to commit rapes in a 20- to 25-day cycle, which Holmes and Holmes (1996) described as "strangely similar to the length of a menstrual cycle" (p. 127). This type of rapist picks his victims up at bars and does not attempt to conceal his identity from victims. He plans his attacks and uses aggression to force the victim's compliance. Holmes and Holmes (1996) described this type of rapist as being sociopathic/psychopathic. Thus, interview strategies are not likely to be successful if they are geared to appeal to the suspect's emotions or sense of remorse or if they focus on intimidation. Instead, it is suggested that interviewers be familiar with the details of the case and maintain a professional demeanor.

Sadistic. This type of rapist is considered the most dangerous. He has "made a vital connection between aggression and sexual gratification—in other words, he has eroticized aggression and violence" (Holmes & Holmes, 1996, p. 128). The sadistic rapist is typically a married, middle-class family man between the ages of 30 and 39. He has a white-collar job and no arrest record. His offenses are characterized by stalking the victim; use of excessive restraints; increasing violence that eventually results in killing victims if he is not apprehended; ritualistic behaviors; and the use of a "rape kit," consisting of weapons, bindings, and other items that the offender brings with him to commit the rape. According to Holmes and Holmes (1996), interviewing this type of rapist is difficult and may require a variety of strategies. For example, they contended that this type of offender is unlikely to cooperate if the interviewer appears unprofessional; however, they did not explain why this is likely to be the case or how best to elicit cooperation (Holmes & Holmes, 1996).

Pedophiles

Holmes and Holmes (1996) used the terms *pedophile* and *child molester* interchangeably in their typology of pedophiles. Note that whereas the term *child molester* connotes that an illegal act has been committed, the *Diagnostic and Statistical Manual of Mental Disorders* (4th ed.; American Psychiatric Association, 1994) definition of *pedophilia* requires no such act. Relying primarily on the child abusers typology created by Burgess, Groth, and Holmstrom (1978), Holmes and Holmes's (1996) typology categorizes pedophiles as either *situational* or *preferential*, with various subtypes.

Situational Child Molester. This type of offender is described as not having a "true sexual interest in children" (Holmes & Holmes, 1996, p. 136). He will typically molest children when under stress and may also victimize other "vulnerable persons, such as the elderly or the physically or mentally impaired" (Holmes & Holmes, 1996, p. 137). There are four subtypes of situational child molester. The *regressed pedophile* molests children in response to some situational stressor that "challenges his self-image and results in poor self-esteem" (Holmes & Holmes, 1996, p. 137). He has no obvious difficulty relating to adults and engages in normal personal and sexual adult relationships. However, under certain kinds of stress (e.g., divorce, work related) he "experiences the child as a pseudoadult" (Holmes & Holmes, 1996, p. 137), which leads to the victimization. This type of molester tends to have poor coping skills and abuses female children he does not know. He may also abuse alcohol and typically obtains victims through coercion. The second subtype of situational child molester is the *morally indiscriminate* type. This type of offender does not prefer children as sexual partners but instead abuses children as part of a more general pattern of victimizing others. He is likely to collect detective magazines and bondage-related pornography, and he obtains victims by lure, force, manipulation, or some combination of these. The third subtype, the *sexually indiscriminate* molester, also has no particular preference for children but abuses them as part of a more general pattern of sexual experimentation. He may be involved in a wide variety of sexual practices, including "tyndarianism (mate swapping), bondage and discipline, triolism [becoming sexually aroused by watching one's partner engage in sex with another person] and other unusual practices" (Holmes & Holmes, 1996, p. 138). These practices may also include the offender's biological children or stepchildren. This type of offender is also highly likely to collect pornography. Finally, the *naïve/inadequate* child molester "suffers from some form of mental disorder . . . that renders him unable to make the distinction between right and wrong concerning sexual practices with children" (Holmes & Holmes, 1996, p. 138). He is typically noticed by others as being a strange or bizarre loner and is motivated to victimize children because he finds relating to adults more threatening. He exploits his size advantage to obtain victims and is likely to collect pornography not of the "child porn genre" (Holmes & Holmes, 1996, p. 139).

Preferential Child Molester. These offenders prefer children to adults as objects of sexual interest and gratification. There are three subtypes in this category: sadistic, seductive, and fixated. The *sadistic pedophile* "has made a vital connection between sexual gratification and fatal violence" (Holmes & Holmes, 1996, p. 139). He victimizes strangers, typically young boys, first stalking and then abducting them from playgrounds, schools, and other areas frequented by children. He inflicts physical harm and mutilation on the child, which eventually results in the child's death. His crimes are premeditated and "ritualized" (Holmes & Holmes, 1996, p. 140), and he often uses some kind of weapon to induce fear. The sadistic offender is described as having an "aggressive and antisocial personality" (Holmes & Holmes, 1996, p. 143). He may have a criminal record and a history of engaging in other kinds of violent crimes. As a result, he may also be geographically transient, leaving an area quickly after he commits a crime. The *seductive molester*, which Holmes and Holmes (1996) described only briefly, "courts" (p. 141) children with gifts and attention. He may be concurrently molesting several children. The *fixated molester* seeks out affection from children, preferring young boys. He is described as having been fixated "at an early stage of psychosexual development" (Holmes & Holmes, 1996, p. 141). Because he has not completed this psychosexual development, he is still at the developmental stage "where he, as a child, found other children attractive and desirable" (Holmes & Holmes, 1996, p. 141). His interest in children develops in adolescence and remains constant. No precipitating stressor is required for him to turn to children for sexual gratification. This type of offender is typically single, immature, and socially inept. His goal is not to harm children; instead, he courts and seduces children and slowly becomes intimate with them. If sexual intercourse takes place, it is likely to occur after a significant amount of time has passed. This offender is likely to have a large number of victims. He may move from place to place to obtain victims and may be a computer bulletin board user.

Geography

"The role that geography plays in the criminal profiling process is still unclear, but it is an issue deserving of further research and study" (Holmes & Holmes, 1996, p. 148). Despite this admonition, Holmes and Holmes

(1996) recommended analyzing unidentified suspects' geographic patterns as part of the profiling process. They based their description of geographic profiling on the work of Rossmo (1995a, 1995b) and address seven factors: crime location type, arterial roads and highways, physical and psychological boundaries, land use, neighborhood demographics, routine activities of victims, and displacement.

Crime Location Type

There are five types of locations that could be connected to the commission of a murder or rape: encounter site, attack site, crime site, victim disposal site, and vehicle dump site. The presence and pattern of these sites are influenced by the modus operandi (MO) and mode of travel of the offender. The *encounter site* is the place where the offender first comes into contact with the victim. The *attack site*—often, the same location as the encounter site—is where the perpetrator first attacks the victim. If the encounter and attack sites are the same, this suggests that the offender may live close by. If the sites are different, this may mean that

> the personality of the offender may be more developed, indicating capability for growth in the range of travel in the search for victims. In other words, this type of offender is more likely to be of the organized personality type. (Holmes & Holmes, 1996, p. 159)

The *crime site* is the scene of the murder or rape—the location where the actual crime takes place. The *victim disposal site* is either where the victim is released or where the body is dumped. If the encounter, attack, crime, and disposal sites are the same, this is indicative of a disorganized offender "because this type of personality is most comfortable in familiar neighborhoods" (Holmes & Holmes, 1996, p. 159). If the sites are different, this suggests the planning of an organized offender. The *vehicle dump site*, although not defined, is presumably where the offender leaves the vehicle used during the crime.

Arterial Roads and Highways

The particular roads traveled during the commission of a crime may depend on an offender's motive and personality as well as the circumstances of the offense. Holmes and Holmes (1996) concluded this on the basis of the observation that different people select different routes to locations on the basis of such criteria as density of traffic, quickness, and visual appeal. Some streets may be more amenable to travel by car; others may be better suited for walking or other forms of transportation. Factors such as the number of intersections or traffic lights on a particular stretch of road may also influence an offender's route choices.

Physical and Psychological Boundaries

Examples of physical boundaries or barriers include walls and bodies of water. Some of these barriers can be crossed "if the traveler chooses to do so. Such choices on the part of offenders may not be initially comprehensible to investigators, but they make sense from the criminals' standpoint" (Holmes & Holmes, 1996, p. 161). *Psychological boundaries*, a term that refers to the discomfort of unfamiliar areas, are thought to influence offenders' hunting patterns.

Land Use

The way that land is used around and between crime sites, including the zoning of the areas and the presence of major attractions and transportation sites, should be noted.

Neighborhood Demographics

Information on gender ratios, racial composition, age groups, occupations, socioeconomic status, crime rates, and other variables should be collected in neighborhoods around crime sites.

Routine Activities of Victims

Investigators should collect information about the behavior, travels, and habits of victims. If a body is dumped in a place that would not be expected, given information about the victim, this indicates that the dump site is more significant to the offender than the victim. The way in which a body is dumped or displayed also has implications for offender characteristics.

Displacement

Displacement refers to changes in the patterns of crime locations during a crime series. Holmes and Holmes (1996) attributed this to such factors as offender maturation, confidence, learning, and law enforcement actions such as increased patrol in targeted neighborhoods.

Integration of Information

After considering the preceding factors, profilers "should plot the crime locations on a map and look for patterns" (Holmes & Holmes, 1996, p. 160). Further procedures for using these factors are not provided. Holmes and Holmes (1996) did briefly describe the use of computerized geographical analyses, but they asserted that "although computers play an important role, their function should be placed in the proper perspective . . . profiling . . . is only viable when the human element comes into play" (p. 164).

Victim Profiling

Holmes and Holmes (1996) emphasized the importance of collecting information on victims, and they criticized the paucity of victim information contained in most police reports provided to profilers. They advocated collecting information about physical traits, marital status, personal lifestyle, occupation, education, personal demographics, medical history, psycho-sexual history, criminal justice system history, and last activities.

Physical Traits

The category considered perhaps the most important is the victim's physical description. This includes age, gender, mode of dress, and hairstyle and hair color. These factors are thought to influence offenders' selection of particular victims.

Marital Status

Investigators not only should collect information about whether a victim is married or single but also should describe the nature of any relationships in which the victim is involved. For example, if a victim is married, is the marriage stable and happy, or fraught with conflict or abuse? Holmes and Holmes (1996) did not explicitly describe the importance of such an inquiry; however, they provided an anecdote about a victim whose conflicted marriage was the behavioral clue that led to the arrest of her husband. This implies that the relevance of ascertaining a victim's marital status and the nature of the marital relationship is to identify behavioral facts that might lead to a potential perpetrator (e.g., spouse, extramarital lover).

Personal Lifestyle

Information about the victim's friends, as well as the victim's hobbies, sports interests, drug and alcohol use, and frequented locations, should be collected. This may help the profiler ascertain where the victim may have come into contact with the offender as well as the victim's availability and vulnerability.

Occupation

Employment is thought to widen a person's network of interpersonal contact. Knowledge about a victim's occupation can provide information about people with whom he or she may have had contact, organizations to which the victim may have belonged, conferences he or she may have attended, and interests he or she may have had. This may be indicative of vulnerability or personality type because, according to Holmes and Holmes

(1996), the people who attend such group events tend to have common interests that can inform investigators about their personality traits. It is also important to evaluate past employment, with specific attention paid to prior friendships and interpersonal conflicts with other employees.

Education

Like employment, education is believed to increase a victim's network of acquaintances. The extent of a person's education should be ascertained, as well as the different schools he or she attended. A related factor, the intelligence of the victim, may also indicate the type of people with whom he or she may have been acquainted. This information is more helpful in cases involving stalking than in instances where someone is a victim of opportunity because of the greater attention to selection present in stalking.

Personal Demographics

This category includes information about the victim's neighborhood, past residences, and racial–ethnic identity.

> Most rapists and murderers tend to choose victims of their own races, so if the racial composition of the victim's neighborhood is radically different from the victim's race, several possibilities arise that may account for the victim's living in a particular area. (Holmes & Holmes, 1996, p. 185)

Unfortunately, Holmes and Holmes (1996) did not elaborate on these possibilities. Information from neighbors is also believed to assist in an appraisal of the victim's lifestyle and circle of friends.

Medical History

Information about medical history can be valuable in at least three ways. First, the presence of a communicable disease can serve to connect a victim to a perpetrator. Second, dental records may assist in identifying victims whose bodies are in advanced stages of decomposition. Third, mental health history may provide information about individuals with whom the victim may have come into contact as well as information about expected behavior and daily activities.

Psychosexual History

When examining the victim's psychosexual history, the profiler should assess the victim's fears, sexual history, and personality. This information is intended to help determine the types of people with whom the victim may have been acquainted.

Criminal Justice System History

Holmes and Holmes (1996) stated that information about prior arrests, court appearances, and pending cases are indicative of a victim's personality, although they did not specify why this is the case other than to say that involvement in the criminal justice system may indicate what kind of person the victim was. Such information presumably might indicate whether the victim engaged in illegal activities that might place him or her at risk from criminal associates or other dangerous situations.

Last Activities

This category would include routes of travel, phone calls, social activities, and meetings, with special attention to anything unusual that might have occurred. According to Holmes and Holmes (1996), such an inquiry is designed to address whether the victim did something atypical on the day of the crime that might have alerted the perpetrator to his or her "vulnerability and availability" (p. 187).

KEPPEL AND WALTER MODEL

Keppel and Walter (1999) proposed a model that attempts to compensate for some of the shortcomings they have noted in Holmes and Holmes's (1996) approach. These authors criticized Holmes and Holmes's (1996) use of typologies because they "have a wide range of function, are of limited service to investigative work, and are unsupported by empirical study" (Keppel & Walter, 1999, p. 418).

Using Hazelwood and Burgess's (1987) categories of rape, Keppel and Walter (1999) constructed a rape–murder typology intended to compensate for the kinds of failures they identified in Holmes and Holmes's (1996) approach. According to Keppel and Walter, by correctly identifying the category of a particular offense using their typology, "the perpetrator can be his own accuser" (p. 436). Each of the four categories in this typology contains information about dynamics, homicidal pattern, and suspect profile. Case examples are also provided to illustrate the integration of these various pieces of information. In an effort to provide some empirical support for their model, the authors assessed the relative frequency of the categories in the typology within a forensic population at the Michigan State Penitentiary.

Power-Assertive Rape–Murder

Dynamics

In power-assertive rape–murder, the rapes are planned, but the murder is a consequence of increased aggression designed to control the victim. The killer tries to demonstrate dominance and mastery over the victim by maintaining an assertive image and using violence. Killing the victim reinforces the offender's power by eliminating the threat the victim poses. This type of offender analyzes ways to improve on this macho image and power.

Homicidal Pattern

The hallmark of this type of offender is the assertion of power through rape and murder. The assault is often one of opportunity, with this offender bringing his own weapon, which he views as an extension of his power, to the crime scene. The male or female victim may show evidence of beating, and the clothes will often be torn off. However, there will not typically be any mutilation of the body. If the victim is killed at home, the body will be left undisturbed. If the victim has been abducted and killed, the body is likely to be dumped. In either case, the perpetrator will attempt to conceal his identity by leaving an organized crime scene, although he will not be satisfied unless he can take credit for the killing by bragging to someone.

Suspect Profile

This offender is described as being an emotionally primitive male in his early 20s. He is a macho bodybuilder and displays tattoos in an expression of his masculinity. His car is well kept, and he may use alcohol and drugs heavily. The offender's attitude is arrogant and condescending, and he is not viewed by others as a team player. His interest in athletics will be limited to individual contact sports, and he will be concerned with gaining power in these pursuits. He will have a history of burglary, theft, or robbery but will not be likely to have had contact with the mental health system unless his criminal history resulted in such a referral. He is likely to have dropped out of school and may have served in the Marines or Navy—with a poor service record or early termination of service. He may have had multiple unsuccessful relationships and demonstrates unconventional sexual interests. In addition, he may express strong anti-gay sentiment.

Power-Reassurance Rape–Murder

Dynamics

The theme of this perpetrator's offenses is that of expressing sexual competence through seduction. In this type of offense, the rape is planned, but the murder is characterized as "an unplanned overkill of the victim" (Keppel & Walter, 1999, p. 424). The perpetrator is motivated by a seduction–conquest fantasy and panics when the victim does not cooperate with this fantasy. This panic results in the unplanned assault on the noncompliant victim. After the killing, the offender may commit postmortem mutilation out of curiosity.

Homicidal Pattern

The power-reassurance offender selects a female victim with whom he may already be acquainted. She is typically 10 to 15 years older or younger than he is. He may use threats to initially gain control of the victim, and sometimes uses a weapon, after which he will attempt to act out his seduction fantasy. His first attack is unlikely to involve a weapon, but subsequent assaults might involve guns or knives. In an attempt to carry out his fantasy with the victim, the perpetrator may attempt a polite verbal dialogue in which he seeks reassurance of his sexual competence. When he is rejected, he feels threatened and kills the victim by beating and strangulation. Because his sexual assault is unlikely to be completed, there will probably be no evidence of semen at the crime scene. He may attempt to continue his relationship with the deceased victim by taking a souvenir or collecting newspaper clippings about the assault. This offender's killings are likely to be episodic and will most likely take place at night.

Suspect Profile

This type of offender is usually in his mid-20s, although this "can be variable and conditional on circumstances such as the incarceration of the offender for other crimes during his mid-20s" (Keppel & Walter, 1999, p. 425). He daydreams and fantasizes obsessively, which makes him appear emotionally scattered. Other behaviors might include window peeping and fondling clothing. He prefers to live in fantasy rather than risk rejection in real sexual relationships; thus, he is typically unmarried. He is seen by others as odd and socially isolated. This offender's educational and military history will be unremarkable. He may be seen as an underachiever and may have received a mental health referral because of this. He feels inferior and is unable to handle criticism. He is therefore likely to live at home and remain in familiar surroundings. If he works, it will be at a menial job. His mode of transportation is most likely to be walking, but if he has a car, it will be an older model that is poorly kept. His criminal history may include peeping, unlawful entry, and larceny. He leaves a disorganized crime scene with plenty of evidence.

Anger-Retaliatory Rape–Murder

Dynamics

In this type of offense, the rape is planned, and the killing is characterized by a venting of anger or revenge toward the female victim. The attack may be precipitated by a criticism of the offender by the victim or another woman who has power over him. Assaults will likely be episodic and repeated to relieve the offender's stress. "Dynamically, the rape–homicide is committed in a stylized violent burst of attack for the purposes of retaliation, getting even, and revenge on women" (Keppel & Walter, 1999, p. 427).

Homicidal Pattern

In anger-retaliatory rape–murder, the sexual assault is violent, and there is "overkill" (Keppel & Walter, 1999, p. 428) of the victim. The source of the offender's anger is a woman who criticizes or humiliates him, and the victim is typically a substitute who reminds the offender of the true object of his anger. When the actual target of his anger is someone who is younger than he, this type of offender is likely to assault her directly, rather than seeking out a substitute. The killer typically walks to the crime scene. If he drives, he will park and travel the last 200 feet to the crime scene on foot. The victim will be hit in the mouth and face, and the offender may use weapons of opportunity. The rape may not be completed, but the assault will continue until the perpetrator feels emotionally satisfied, regardless of whether the victim is still alive. Postmortem, the body is placed on its side, away from the door, face down, with the eyes covered, or in the closet with the door closed. The crime scene is typically disorganized, with the weapon left within 15 feet of the body. The offender is likely to take a souvenir before leaving the scene. Because the perpetrator blames the victim, he does not experience any feelings of guilt or responsibility. Instead, he may feel sentimental toward the victim and assist in the search for her body.

Suspect Profile

This type of offender is usually in his mid- to late 20s and targets older victims. He is viewed by others as impulsive, self-centered, and temperamental. His social relationships are superficial, and he is essentially a loner. If he is married, there is likely to be domestic violence or estrangement. The offender is also likely to engage in extramarital affairs to deal with his dissatisfaction in his primary relationship. He is sexually frustrated and may be impotent. His criminal history may include other assaults, domestic violence, and reckless driving. He is typically an underachiever, a school dropout. If he has a military history, it is likely to include a discharge reflecting his unpredictable behavior and conflicts with authority. He may have previous referrals to mental health professionals.

Anger-Excitation Rape–Murder

Dynamics

In this category, both the rape and the murder are premeditated. The victim can be either male or female, and the perpetrator derives gratification through inflicting pain and terror through prolonged torture. The assaultive acts are driven by the perpetrator's fantasies of dominance and control, as well as his primary interest in the process of killing, rather than the death itself. The offender's anger is eroticized and rehearsed through fantasy, and the ultimate intent is one of "indulgent luxury" (Keppel & Walter, 1999, p. 431).

Homicidal Pattern

The homicidal pattern of this offense reflects a planned and prolonged assault on the victim. The offender brings a "kit" (Keppel & Walter, 1999, p. 432) of weapons and tools to the crime scene. The victim may be a stranger but tends to fit some preferred type. The offender approaches him or her by using a con or ruse to lead the victim away to an isolated location. At his point, the offender will "display vacillating mood shifts that confuse the victim" (Keppel & Walter, 1999, p. 431). He may inform the victim that he is planning to kill him or her and then may become excited by the victim's terror. The assault on the victim contains elements of ritual and experimentation, characterized by bondage and domination. There may be evidence of cutting, bruises, incomplete strangulation, washing, shaving, and burning. Sexual experimentation continues postmortem, as evidenced by localized battery, skin tears, and objects inserted into the body. The condition of the body at the crime scene varies, from being left in a state of undress, to the absence of body parts that the offender has taken as souvenirs. The body may be moved to a second location or buried, and care is taken to avoid leaving evidence that could lead to the offender's detection. This type of offender is organized and commits his crimes away from home. He may attempt to involve himself in the criminal investigation.

Suspect Profile

The age of this type of offender varies. He appears socially normal and bright and has a lifestyle separate from his criminal activities. He is likely to be married and works best under minimal supervision. His employment interests might center around mechanical positions or carpentry. His educational and military history will reflect his organization, and he may have a college education. He may also have a private room in which he keeps his murder kit and souvenirs as well as a collection of pornographic material with a sadism/bondage theme. Alcohol use is not likely, but the offender may use other drugs.

Frequency of the Four Categories in an Offender Population

To determine how widespread the preceding categories are, Keppel and Walter (1999) evaluated their frequency in a group of incarcerated murderers in the Michigan state prison system. Of 2,476 inmates who were convicted of sexually related homicides, the authors found that 38% were power assertive, 34% were anger retaliatory, 21% were power reassurance, and 7% were anger excitation. These figures are offered to provide support for the use of the rape–murder typology to direct criminal investigations.

TURCO MODEL

Turco (1990) advocated the use of a psychoanalytic approach to profiling. Citing the work of Liebert (1986), Turco stated that profiling should be oriented "around the basis of Borderline and Narcissistic Personality Disorders" (p. 149). Under this framework, violent behavior is conceptualized as a process whereby offenders attempt to deal with internal frustrations related to early mother–child relationships. The female victim represents the "badness" (Turco, 1990, p. 149) of the mother. By acting out aggressions against this victim, the offender achieves a "temporary re-establishment of psychological equilibrium" (Turco, 1990, p. 149). In addition to a psychoanalytic theory of violence, Turco suggested that profiling should integrate "neurological understanding" (p. 147), because neurological dysfunctions are a significant factor in the tendency to commit homicides.

The model of profiling Turco (1990) presented consists of four dimensions. First, the profiler is to "consider the crime scene in its entirety" (p. 150). This entails viewing the scene as the manifestation of behavior and, more centrally, as a "projection of the underlying personality, lifestyle, and developmental experiences (maternal bonding) of the perpetrator" (p. 150). Turco likened this first dimension to the interpretation of a Rorschach test.

Second, Turco (1990) highlighted the importance of integrating knowledge about neurological behavior when developing a profile. Asserting that between 20% and 90% of violent offenders suffer from brain impairment or structural abnormalities, he referred to a neurological phenomenon called *dyscontrol syndrome* (p. 151) and indicated that such a syndrome is relevant to understanding the predatory behavior of killers.

Third, preparing a profile is described as requiring a psychodynamic perspective. This is defined as "an understanding of human development and . . . an appreciation of the interactions and significance of the first three years of life, the so-called separation–individuation phase" (Turco, 1990, p. 151). According to Turco, this is a skill that depends on the profiler's "level of psychiatric sophistication" (p. 151).

The fourth and final factor in Turco's (1990) model involves the study of the demographic characteristics of the crime. Crime scene evidence, as well as information about the victim and perpetrator, is to be collected to aid the profiler in composing the profile. Assessing this type of material allows clinicians an advantage, according to Turco, because "The experienced clinician has an underlying inherent understanding of psychopathology, experience with predictability, a capacity to 'get into the mind of the perpetrator' and a scientific approach without moral judgment or prejudice" (p. 151). He further specified as follows:

> The most productive circumstance likely to arise is when the profiler has both *clinical* (as opposed to academic) training and law enforcement experience. One cannot expect to obtain a graduate degree and make accurate predictions in the absence of a sound theoretical basis or clinical experience. (p. 151, italics in original)

TURVEY MODEL

In his book *Criminal Profiling: An Introduction to Behavioral Evidence Analysis*, Brent Turvey (1999) proposed a deductive model of profiling that emphasizes reliance on physical and behavioral evidence in making inferences about offender characteristics. The key elements of his approach are a conceptual distinction between *inductive* and *deductive* profiling; a description of the components of a deductive method of profiling; a behavior–motivational typology; and an analysis of potential contributions of deductive profiling to trial strategy, once an offender has been profiled and apprehended.

Inductive Versus Deductive Criminal Profiling

Turvey (1999) distinguished his approach by drawing a comparison between the "inductively rendered profiles" (p. 16) produced by most criminal profilers and his deductive method of profiling. Although the terms *inductive* and *deductive* are categories typically associated with the process of logical reasoning, Turvey applied them uniquely to his criminal profiling approach.

According to Turvey (1999), *inductive profiling* refers to "a comparative, correlational and/or statistical process reliant upon subjective expertise" (p. 14); it "involves broad generalizations or statistical reasoning, where it is possible for the premises to be true while the subsequent conclusion is false" (p. 16). In addition, "most inductive profiles involve arguments where the premises themselves have been assumed" (p. 17). The following would be an example of inductive profiling, as the method is described by Turvey:

> *Premise:* The rape victim was a White female.
> *Premise:* Most rapists commit sexual assaults against individuals within their own ethnic group.

Premise: Most rapists have not served in the military.
Conclusion: This victim was raped by a White male with no military experience.

In this example, although the first premise is likely to be confirmed by the available evidence, the second and third premises are statistical generalizations. The conclusion derived from these premises is problematic not only because the accuracy of the statistics assumed by the premises is questionable but also because of the difficulties inherent in attempting to generalize from nomothetic data to the individual offender.

In contrast, deductive profiling is a "forensic-evidence-based, process-oriented, method of investigative reasoning about the behavior patterns of a particular offender" (Turvey, 1999, p. 14). Deductive profiling "involves conclusions that flow logically from the premises stated. It is such that if the premises are true, then the subsequent conclusion must also be true" (Turvey, 1999, p. 16). Turvey (1999) provided the following example of deductive profiling:

Premise: The offender disposed of his victim's body in a remote area of the mountains.
Premise: Tire tracks were found at the disposal site.
Conclusion: If the tire tracks belong to the offender, then the offender has access to a vehicle and is able to be mobile. (p. 27)

Turvey indicated that, unlike inductive profiling, the previous example creates a "convergence of physical (tire tracks) and behavioral (remote area for disposal) evidence that suggest a specific conclusion" (p. 27). He argued that although the deductive method of profiling is not wholly scientific, it is based on scientific thinking.

Components of the Deductive Profiling Method

Turvey (1999) asserted that there are four basic components to the deductive profiling method. The first three components are those Turvey described as "for the most part based on the scientific tenets of crime scene reconstruction, and the established forensic sciences" (p. 31). They are forensic and behavioral evidence (equivocal forensic analysis), victimology, and crime scene characteristics. The first component, forensic and behavioral evidence, involves reconstructing the events of the offense, including behaviors between victim and perpetrator. Such a reconstruction requires using victim and witness statements, crime scene photographs, wound pattern analysis, blood spatter analysis, ballistics analysis, and any other relevant forensic analyses conducted on the physical evidence. Victimology, the second component, consists of analyzing victim characteristics, including physical characteristics, habits, lifestyle, relationships, and risk level. Finally, crime scene characteristics include the method of attack, the nature and sequence of sexual or violent acts, verbal behavior, precautionary acts, and other characteristics that are "determined from the forensic evidence and the victimology" (Turvey, 1999, p. 29).

The fourth component is the deduction of offender characteristics from the first three components. Turvey (1999) described this fourth component as "considerably artful, and therefore a matter of expertise and not science" (p. 31). He stated, "Deducing offender characteristics is about asking the right question of the offender's behavior" (p. 85). Accordingly, the "right" question involves defining a characteristic and determining what behaviors evidence that characteristic. If these behaviors are determined to have occurred during the commission of the offense, then the profiler can argue that the related offender characteristic is also present. For example, one offender characteristic might be *offender skill*, defined by the offender's use of precautionary measures to delay or evade capture. The behaviors that evidence this characteristic might include wearing gloves and a mask while robbing a liquor store equipped with video cameras. Therefore, according to Turvey's description, if an offender wears a mask and gloves while robbing said liquor store, the profiler has a good argument that this offender exhibits offender skill.

The Behavior–Motivational Typology

To further assist in explaining the deduction of offender characteristics, Turvey (1999) included in his text a discussion of a behavior–motivational typology. This typology is based on Groth et al.'s (1977) classification of rapists, which was later adapted by Douglas et al. for the *Crime Classification Manual* and discussed in earlier sections of this chapter on Holmes and Holmes's (1996) and Turco's (1990) models of profiling. Although these categories were originally created to describe rapists, Turvey appeared to apply them to a broader range of criminal behavior, arguing that "The needs, or motives, that impel human criminal behaviors remain essentially the same for all offenders, despite their behavioral expression that may involve kidnapping, child molestation, terrorism, sexual assault, homicide, and/or arson" (p. 170). In describing what he has added to Groth et al.'s original typology, Turvey stated that "This author takes credit largely for the fresh, extended perspective and for the shift in emphasis from classifying *offenders* to classifying *behaviors* (turning it from an inductive labeling system to a deductive tool)" (p. 170, italics in original).

Five categories of offenders are described in Turvey's (1999) adapted behavioral–motivational typology: power reassurance, power assertive, anger retaliatory, anger excitation, and profit. These categories are identical to Groth et al.'s (1977) original groups, with the exception of the profit-motivated rapist. Groth et al.'s typology does not include profit as a motivation but instead describes a category of opportunistic rapist. This opportunistic category is not present in Turvey's typology. Because of their common derivation from the original Groth et al. research, the characteristics of each type of rapist, as described by Turvey, are very similar to those described in the earlier sections of this chapter that discussed the Holmes and Holmes (1996) and Turco (1990) rapist typology. The details of these characteristics are therefore not repeated in this section.

Turvey's (1999) effort to reframe offender characteristics as behaviors is manifested in his division of each offender type into several subcategories of behaviors. These subcategories include method of approach, method of attack, verbal behavior, sexual behavior, physical behavior, MO behavior, and signature behavior. Within each subcategory, examples are provided to illustrate the behavior that would be expected from the type of offender in question. For example, under the subcategory of physical behavior for an anger-retaliatory offender, Turvey included such features as tearing the victim's clothing, using high levels of physical force, and causing significant injury to the victim (p. 176).

Turvey (1999) stated that using his proposed behavior–motivational typology can "provide a psychological snapshot of a rapist during a single instance from which some reliable inferences about motive can be made" (p. 181). However, he also cautioned that "a single offender can evidence behaviors suggestive of more than one motivation" (p. 181). Therefore, although the typology can contribute to a criminal profile, the deduction of offender characteristics is still dependent on the circumstances of the individual offenses and the expertise of the profiler.

Trial Strategy

Turvey (1999) asserted that although deductive profiling cannot be used to implicate a specific individual as having committed the offense(s) in question, it can be used to "suggest a specific type of individual, with specific psychological and emotional characteristics (i.e., motives and needs)" (p. 228). The following information can be valuable to attorneys once a suspect has been arrested: recognizing evidence; MO behavior, signature behavior, and motive; state of mind; malice aforethought; and torture.

Recognizing Evidence

Turvey (1999) argued that "the most effective criminal profilers tend to be those who have first been trained as competent forensic investigators" (p. 229). Therefore, one of the skills that a profiler can offer to a trial attorney is the ability to analyze the physical evidence to elucidate the events of the offense and the interactions between offender and victim. In addition, the profiler can evaluate the forensic evidence to inform attorneys about potential weaknesses in the collection, analysis, and interpretation of evidence as performed by law enforcement officers and medical examiners. The profiler may also potentially recognize evidence that has been overlooked.

Modus Operandi Behavior, Signature Behavior, and Motive

Turvey (1999) defined MO *behaviors* as "those committed by the offender during the commission of the crime which are necessary to complete the crime. MO behaviors are unstable across offenses and may alter as the offender gains confidence or experience" (p. 230). Signature behaviors, however, "are committed to serve the offender's fantasies, and psychological and/or emotional needs . . . are thematic in nature, are suggestive of offender intent, and can be more stable over time" (p. 230). At trial, a criminal profiler can identify MO and signature behaviors for the purpose of establishing offense linkage. The profiler can also interpret MO and signature behaviors to demonstrate that two crimes are "psychologically dissimilar" (p. 230).

State of Mind

Profilers can use offense behaviors to make suggestions about the state of mind of the offender. According to Turvey's (1999) description, offense behaviors that might provide insight into the offender's state of mind include such acts as covering the victim (remorse), slashing injuries (rage), and the general nature of the offender's behavior toward the victim prior to the attack. The only information that is to be used in analyzing offender state of mind is the offender's behavior and his or her interactions with the victim. Turvey suggested that this method of determining state of mind is superior to other, more traditional methods:

> Where forensic psychologists and other assessors may use post-apprehension interviews, polygraph examinations, or personality measures which have been duped countless times by offenders over the years, the criminal profiler carefully examines what the offender did, and has little use for what the offender has to say about what they did. (p. 230)

Malice Aforethought

Turvey (1999) defined the concept of *malice aforethought* as being related to the motivational intent and preplanning of an offense. The criminal profiler can assist at trial by identifying behaviors that suggest that an offense was premeditated. Examples of such behaviors would include bringing a weapon to the scene, wearing a disguise, wearing gloves, keeping lists of materials to bring to the crime, and conducting surveillance on the victim prior to the attack.

Torture

Turvey (1999) defined *torture* as "the infliction of severe physical pain as a means of punishment, coercion or offender gratification" (p. 232). The contribution that can be made by criminal profilers is that of establishing the presence of torture during a particular offense.

Profiling Process

In addition to the key elements described previously, Turvey (1999) offered some general sentiments about the practice of profiling. He advocated for both a scientific basis for profiling, in terms of reliance on physical and behavioral evidence, and an artful process for translating the evidence into information about an offender. In keeping with this, Turvey criticized the FBI's current profiling practices, citing the lack of peer-reviewed research as an impediment to progress. He referred to the FBI's *Crime Classification Manual* as being "a book of theories only" (Turvey, 1999, p. 10). At the same time, Turvey also was critical of the extant empirical literature on profiling, referring to the use of the polygraph, geographic profiling, and smallest space analysis (discussed in chap. 4) as "scientification . . . the bolstering of any method or theory, by a group or individual, via technological affect or professional affect, for the purposes of making the method or theory appear more credible" (p. 257). He was thus clear in his writing that some elements of profiling should not be represented as scientific and are still best considered artful and a matter of expertise.

3

PROBLEMS WITH NONSCIENTIFIC PROFILING MODELS

Despite the logic and authoritativeness of the nonscientific models of profiling, these models suffer from seven significant limitations: (a) a lack of goals and standards, (b) use of unclear terms and definitions, (c) misuse of typologies, (d) reliance on intuition and professional knowledge, (e) lack of clear procedures, (f) lack of evidence of investigative value, and (g) misrepresentation of science. These problems are present to varying degrees in each of the models reviewed in chapter 2. Because any model that is to be considered viable as a criminal profiling tool will ultimately need to remedy these limitations, each of the first six limitations is addressed in this chapter. The seventh limitation, misrepresentation of science, is addressed in chapter 5, following an evaluation of the only current scientific model of profiling.

LACK OF GOALS AND STANDARDS

The most fundamental problem plaguing the nonscientific profiling models as a whole is the failure to identify and agree on clear goals and standards for profiling. Goals are vital because they represent the aspirations of the profiling endeavor. Standards are necessary to provide the limits and guidelines to ensure that profiling moves effectively in the direction of those aspirations.

Goals

Across models, the authors state at least 10 general goals for profiling. However, as can be seen in Table 3.1, the representation of these goals across models is quite variable. In Turvey's (1999) model, a separate chapter (pp. 33–39) addresses goals and lists them clearly for the reader (i.e., to reduce the viable suspect pool in a criminal investigation, to prioritize the investigation into those suspects, to help keep the overall investigation on track and undistracted, to assist in the process of developing interview or interrogative strategy). Holmes and Holmes (1996, p. 3) also included a specific section on their major goals for profiling (i.e., social and psychological assessment of offenders, psychological evaluations of belongings found in the possession of suspected offenders, and suggestions and strategies for interviewing suspected offenders when they are apprehended). In contrast, Turco (1990) did not address goals for profiling at all in his model. Douglas, Ressler, Burgess, and Hartman (1986) and Keppel and Walter (1999) also did not include clear sections in their models that discuss goals, but they did implicitly address goals by referring to intents or uses for profiling (i.e., developing techniques and strategies for interviewing, identifying the major personality and behavioral characteristics of an individual on the basis of an analysis of the crimes, identifying the key crime scene and behavioral factors related to the killer).

To the extent that nonscientific models make reference to goals or intents for profiling, they still offer no consensus on what the appropriate goals for profiling are. For example, should profiling provide an investigative benefit of some kind? Does profiling have a role once a suspect has been apprehended? Turvey (1999), for example, advocated for the use of profiling in all phases of criminal investigation, up to and including the trial phase. At the opposite end of the spectrum, Keppel and Walter (1999) limited their discussion of profiling to the investigation phase.

The specification of goals is also lacking in the area of profiling applications. Although each model conceptualizes profiling as an applied art, there is no clear consensus among the models for discerning which types of crimes are the appropriate subject matter of profiling. Table 3.2 describes the various types of offenses for which the nonscientific models suggest applications. As can be seen in this table, there are some commonalities among models as well as a notable amount of variation. For example, with the exception of the Turco (1990) model, which does not include recommendations about specific crimes for profiling, there is support in all models for the use of profiling in cases of rape and sexual murder. At the same time, this indicates

TABLE 3.1
Nonscientific Models' Stated Goals for Profiling

Model	Analyze crime scene	Provide offender characteristics	Provide leads	Reduce suspect pool	Link crimes	Assess potential for escalation	Evaluate suspect belongings	Interview strategy	Testify at trial
Douglas et al. (1986)	X	X	X					X	X
Holmes and Holmes (1996)		X					X	X	
Keppel and Walter (1999)	X		X					X	
Turco (1990)	No goals stated								
Turvey (1999)	X	X	X	X	X	X		X	X

TABLE 3.2
Types of Offenses Suitable for Profiling

Model	Rape	Child molestation	Nonsexual murder	Serial murder	Sexual murder	Arson	Threats	Hostage taking	Internet crime
Douglas et al. (1986)	X		X	X	X	X	X	X	
Holmes and Holmes (1996)	X	X		X	X	X			
Keppel and Walter (1999)	X				X				
Turco (1990)	No offenses specified								
Turvey (1999)	X		X	X	X	X			X

that there are only two of nine categories of crime for which there is unanimous agreement among models. Part of the difficulty in interpreting this variation is that the models do not provide any explanation or justification for why their choice of applications is appropriate, whether the crimes they suggest are the only crimes that are appropriate for profiling, or why other crimes are not appropriate. For example, Keppel and Walter (1999) limited their suggestions for profiling to rape and rape–murder; however, they did not discuss whether profiling can and should be used for other types of crime as well. The techniques offered by Douglas et al.'s (1986) model also appear to be specific to profiling sexually violent crimes, yet these authors suggested that profiling also has a wide range of other applications, including investigating individuals who write threatening letters. No further explanation is provided to justify such a broad approach. Similarly, Turvey (1999), in his behavior–motivational typology, broadened Groth, Burgess, and Holmstrom's (1977) typology of rapists to include other types of offense on the basis of his assertion that all criminal motives are "essentially the same" (Turvey, 1999, p. 170). Unfortunately, he did not offer any support for such an assertion.

Although the nonscientific models are vague about how narrow or broad the goals for applying profiling should be, they do stop short of explicitly claiming that their profiling processes can be applied to all types of crime. It seems, then, that there must be limitations, but these limitations are not adequately explained to the reader.

Standards for Profiling

There are no standards for evaluating whether profiling accomplishes any of the various goals that are proposed within the models. For example, how would one determine whether profiling is helpful to an investigation? One could ask law enforcement agents about their subjective experiences of profiling, or one could look at multiple cases in which profiling was used and determine how many of those cases were solved. One also could look at cases that did and did not use profiling and determine which group of cases were more likely to have been solved. Because these models are nonscientific, they do not include a formal consideration of reliability, validity, and utility.

However, even within this nonscientific framework there should be some attempt to specify the indicators of success relative to various stages of the criminal justice process. For example, the use of profiling techniques to brainstorm leads early in an investigation could be relatively liberal. It would not seem necessary to place severe constraints on profiling during a stage in which investigators are merely trying to generate ideas. However, one would expect more rigorous standards for the use of profiling during the trial stage of an offense. Here, there should be a specification of limits to the kind of profiling work that could potentially affect a suspect's life or liberty.

The lack of clear goals and standards evidenced by these models sets the stage for conceptual inconsistencies and a general lack of coherence. Without clear aspirations provided by goals, and a road map for the profiling endeavor provided by standards, it is not surprising that these models are unable to be conceptually precise.

USE OF UNCLEAR TERMS AND DEFINITIONS

A second basic element that is problematic in the nonscientific models is vocabulary. Although easily taken for granted, terms are the starting point from which procedures and concepts are built. Unfortunately, there are problems with terminology both within and among the nonscientific profiling models.

First, the terminology used to describe profiling techniques and various elements of crimes is not consistent among models. For example, the Douglas et al. (1986) model describes serial killers as individuals who have three or more victims, with an emotional cooling-off period between each victim. Holmes and Holmes (1996) also described serial killers as having three or more victims, but they did not include an emotional cooling-off period component in their definition. Turvey (1999) used the term *serial homicide* (p. 287), rather than *serial killer* or *serial murder*, and defined this as "two or more related cases involving homicide behavior" (p. 287). Another example is the definition of *modus operandi* (MO). Turco (1990), Douglas et al. (1986), and Turvey (1999) all described MO as an element of criminal behavior that changes over time. In contrast, Holmes and Holmes (1996) described MO as remaining similar and being repeated many times during a series of crimes. In discussing the aspect of signature, Turvey (1999) and Douglas et al. (1986) both highlighted that signature behaviors are those that fulfill psychological needs for the offender. Holmes and Holmes (1996) simply defined *signature* as "the unique manner in which [the offender] commits crimes" (p. 42). Turco did not include signature in his discussion of MO. Although this lack of consistent terminology among models is disappointing, it is not surprising. It reflects the reality that there is still considerable disagreement within this field about what the important terms are and how best to define them.

Second, although disagreement about terminology among models is somewhat palatable as long as the field is still evolving and moving toward a consolidation of vocabulary, within models authors must define terms clearly if their models are to be valid and reliable. This basic requirement is unfortunately lacking in the nonscientific models. Some, such as the Turco (1990) model, simply introduce terms such as "dyscontrol syndrome" (p. 151) or "pre-Oedipal matrix" (p. 151) and leave them with no further definition or explanation. Other models present novel terms (often coined by the authors) with vague definitions. Examples of this include Turvey's (1999) "scientification" (p. 257) and Douglas et al.'s (1986) "organized/ disorganized offenders" (p. 412). Such catchphrases seem to serve the purpose of allowing the authors to claim that they have invented something new in the realm of profiling. However, without clear definitions it is impossible to evaluate the meaning of these words, to differentiate them from ideas that have been considered before, and to evaluate whether they incrementally add value to the profiling process.

Third, in some models there is a failure to distinguish between the terms presented. For example, in Douglas et al.'s (1986) model, the distinction between *spree murders* and *serial murders* is left unclear. Similarly, in Holmes and Holmes's (1996) model the authors use the terms *pedophile* and *child molester* interchangeably, even though they initially discuss them as separate concepts.

Because of this failure to define terms, explain their meanings clearly, and distinguish them from similar terms, assessing the validity of each model is impossible. The problems with profiling vocabulary also indicate that these models will likely be used inconsistently by different profilers. Finally, the reviewed models establish a weak foundation for their profiling concepts.

MISUSE OF TYPOLOGIES

With the exception of Turco's (1990) model, each of the nonscientific models of profiling uses at least one typology. Unfortunately, these models are limited by their failure to adequately address the appropriate use of typologies, present consistent typological categories, and present sufficiently distinct typological categories. The failure to address these issues compromises the conceptual clarity of the models.

Appropriate Use of Typologies

By clustering crimes or offenders according to general similarities among them, typologies can provide profilers with a general picture of an offender. As would be expected, typological categories are often somewhat general, and an individual may not match every element of a category, or may match elements of more than one category. Unfortunately, some of the authors, such as Holmes and Holmes (1996) and Keppel and Walter (1999), misuse typologies by advocating that offenders be matched to typological categories as if they were working with taxonomies. This is conceptually confusing because it creates the expectation of certainty in the assignment of an offender to a specific category, even though there is only a limited amount of behavioral information available. In addition, these authors provided no supportive arguments for using typologies in such a manner.

Inconsistent Presentation Within Typologies

The typologies discussed in the reviewed models are themselves problematic. The Holmes and Holmes model (1996) contains numerous examples of inconsistencies within typologies because of its exclusive reliance on typology matching (i.e., trying to match offenders to typologies). First, in their serial killer typology, the authors began with an "initial distinction" (Holmes & Holmes, 1996, p. 63) whereby they divided serial killers into those who are geographically stable and those who are geographically transient. They then leave this distinction and proceed to separate serial killers into various categories according to motive, with no further mention of their geographic stability or transience and no explanation as to how these geographic categories are related to motivational type. Second, in the arson typology, the authors presented three ways to approach the categorization of arsonists: Two of these approaches are based on motive, and the third is based on the organized–disorganized offender dichotomy. No information is provided on the relationship of these three typologies to each other, or whether they are to be used separately or in combination. Third, in the child molester typology, Holmes and Holmes (1996) used the terms *pedophile* and *child molester* interchangeably. In addition to being problematic for definitional reasons, once the authors combined these terms into one concept they then separated them again under the headings of *situational* and *preferential* child molesters—with preferential child molesters being pedophiles. This is problematic because Holmes and Holmes (1996) did not consistently present pedophiles and child molesters as either a singular entity or a combined concept. The reader is left without a clear understanding of whether these two terms represent one or two concepts. Fourth, in the rapist typology, the authors defined the motive of the power-assertive rapist as an "impulsive act of predation" (Holmes & Holmes, 1996, p. 125). However, they then report that this type of rapist commits his offenses in "a 20–25 day cycle, a time span strangely similar to the length of a menstrual cycle" (Holmes & Holmes, 1996, p. 127). Not only is the rationale for comparing the rapist's MO to a menstrual cycle unclear but, more important, the implication that this type of rapist offends cyclically belies the earlier statement that he is impulsive. Fifth, in discussing geographic profiling, Holmes and Holmes (1996) asserted that crime scenes, dumping sites, and other crime locations represent "choices on the part of the offender [and] should not be considered to be mere accident" (p. 154). This typology is incongruent with their assertion that many criminals are disorganized offenders. If certain individuals are disorganized, it would seem difficult to apply a geographic profile that shows organization—at least in the location of the crimes. This lack of coherence also applies to other categories of individuals who assault victims impulsively or out of opportunity (e.g., various types of situational child molesters, and the "visionary" serial killers, who are described as being "truly out of touch with reality"; Holmes & Holmes, 1996, p. 64). Because impulsivity implies a lack of preplanning, a location or geographic profile would also seem difficult to establish for these offenders.

Other models also evidence similar problems. Turvey (1999), for example, claimed that his adapted behavior–motivational typology applies to many types of criminal motives, yet each typological category specifically addresses sexual behavior. Keppel and Walter (1999) provided information about the kinds of statements each category of offender in their rape–murder typology would make to their victims during the assault. Unfortunately, these statements are unlikely to be a source of assessment, because the victim will be deceased and therefore unable to report what was said to her.

In order for these typologies to be useful, they must be constructed in a manner that is conceptually coherent. It is unfortunate that in the nonscientific profiling models there is very little cohesion among concepts within individual typologies, making them theoretically problematic and difficult to use.

Overlap Among Typological Categories

When there is significant overlap among categories in a typology, the same crime information could be consistent with more than one type of offender. This is a problem inherent to all typologies. In the area of profiling, this makes it difficult not only to identify the correct category for a particular offender but also to justify the existence of distinct categories of offenders when large numbers of characteristics are present across the various types. Although this does not render typologies completely useless, it does necessitate that models using typologies consider the implications of this problem and make every attempt to clarify categories to the extent possible.

The nonscientific models of criminal profiling do not address this problem. For example, in the Douglas et al. (1986) model, whose relevant typology is the *Crime Classification Manual* (Douglas, Burgess, Burgess, & Ressler, 1992), there is potential overlap between the categories of spree murder and serial murder. With regard to the definitions of these terms, there appear to be two primary differences between these two types of killings. The first is described as an emotional "cooling-off period" (Douglas et al., 1986, p. 410) that is present only between serial murders. What is the difference between the serial and spree murders if there is a long-duration spree murder that continues from one evening until the following afternoon, with breaks between each victim? How long must a pause in killing last to constitute emotional cooling off? If the difference lies in the thought processes of the offender rather than the length of time, how is a profiler to ascertain this difference on the basis of crime scene evidence? The second difference between serial and spree murderers is a deliberate selection of victims characterized only by serial murderers. Although the general picture of the spree murderer provided by the authors is of a person who typically kills random people who cross his path, the possibility remains that a spree murderer might target certain individuals more than others. For example, a disgruntled employee might go to various locations of a chain restaurant and kill employees at each location. In this case, victims would be deliberately selected, even though the general picture would otherwise be that of a spree murder rather than a serial murder. Douglas et al. (1986) did not make these finer distinctions or address situations in which a killing overlaps two different categories.

Similar problems can be found in Holmes and Holmes's (1986) model. Their child molester typology contains considerable overlap in terms of behavioral and personality characteristics. For example, both sadistic and fixated child molesters prefer child victims, use computer bulletin boards, and victimize in large numbers. Immature, regressed, and fixated child molesters are all likely to molest children they know, have a nonaggressive personality, refrain from abducting or harming the child victim, and tend not to be antisocial. There is also conceptual overlap between categories in the arsonist typology. For example, both the crime-concealment arsonist and the profit-motivated arsonist are likely to be single adults with arrest records, commit their crimes in the evening without accomplices, use alcohol or drugs, live more than 1 mile from the crime scene, and flee the scene after the fire is set. The vandalism and excitement types of arsonists are both likely to be unemployed, middle-class juveniles with arrest histories, who set their fires in the afternoon, live less than 1 mile from the crime scene, remain at the crime scene after the fire is set, and do not use alcohol or drugs.

Keppel and Walter's (1999) typology also contains considerable overlap among categories. For example, at least two different types of offenders are likely to leave a disorganized crime scene; three types of offenders are likely to take souvenirs, have a previous criminal history, and have had previous contact with the mental health system; and all four types of offenders may have served in the military and are likely to plan their assaults, use a weapon, leave bruises on the victim's body, view pornography, and have emotional and relational problems.

In Turvey's (1999) behavior–motivational typology, four of the five categories include using surprise as a likely method of approach, all five categories include attack with a weapon, and three of the five categories are described as containing an attack of short duration. In addition, it is difficult to fully evaluate the extent to which Turvey's categories overlap, because the types of information he included in his typology are not consistent across categories. For example, he did not address signature behaviors in the power-assertive category, he did not address the duration of the attack in every category, and he did not address the use of foreplay with victims in every category. It may be that these elements are not present in the categories for which they are not addressed, but this is not made clear to the reader.

Value of a Typology

Even if an unidentified offender could be correctly matched to a typological category, it is unclear how that classification would be useful to investigators in terms of identifying and apprehending that offender. For example, how would it be helpful for a law enforcement agency to be told, even with certainty, that the unidentified suspect is an anger-exploitive rapist—that he is a macho sociopath who picks victims up in bars and drives a flashy car? This same information could be obtained from a surviving victim, eliminating any incremental investigative value of consulting a profiler. If there is no surviving victim, should detectives conduct sweeps of bars and interview all men therein who drive "flashy" cars? What constitutes "macho" or "flashy"? It does not seem that the classification of an unidentified offender into a typological category, which essentially resembles the generalities of a horoscope, provides any useful information that could not also be provided by a lay observer. Providing such information is therefore unlikely to advance a criminal investigation.

RELIANCE ON INTUITION AND PROFESSIONAL KNOWLEDGE

Whether the authors condemn it or embrace it, each of the nonscientific models entails some use of intuition. Holmes and Holmes (1996) advocated maximizing the use of intuition, stating that profilers are "aided by an intuitive sense, that is . . . a 'feel' for certain kinds of crime" (p. 7). At the other end of the spectrum, Turvey (1999) stated that intuitive judgments "should be left out of investigative strategy, suggestions, or final profiles unless reasonable articulable arguments for their inclusion exist" (p. 38).

Although one could say that all psychological evaluations and assessments use some degree of intuition, or at least judgment, the use of intuition in profiling is limiting for two reasons. First, using intuition reduces the profile's reliability. It seems unlikely that multiple profilers would have the same subjective experience, given the same set of information. It also seems unlikely that judgments based on intuition could be repeated consistently, given the same set of information. If profiling outcomes cannot be accomplished reliably because of the use of intuition, the result is that investigative decisions will be made haphazardly. But for the intuition of a particular profiler, an innocent suspect might not be made the target of an investigation, whereas another profiler could lead the investigation in a different direction with a focus on a different suspect.

Second, none of the nonscientific models attempt to validate their recommendations. If different profilers have different intuitions about the same case, only one can be correct. In addition, because there is no way to determine in advance which intuitive judgments are correct and which ones are wrong, the potential consequences become more dire, the longer it takes an investigative agency to verify the accuracy of profiler intuition in a particular case. At the very least, an investigation could momentarily be steered in the wrong direction if the profiler speculates incorrectly that an offender is of a certain age or physical type. A moderate consequence might be that a serial offender, for example, is able to kill more victims while an investigation focuses away from him and toward the wrong type of perpetrator, on the basis of a profiler's intuitive recommendation. Perhaps the most severe outcome might be that a law enforcement agency never realizes that the profiler's intuitive judgments were incorrect and pursues, apprehends, and brings to trial an innocent suspect while the real perpetrator remains free. Therefore, although these models characterize intuition in various ways, ranging from an ideal method to a necessary evil, the risk of making mistakes is increased with intuition, and the consequences are significant.

LACK OF CLEAR PROCEDURES

For numerous reasons, all of the models fall short of providing the reader with clear procedures to create an offender profile. First, if one of the basic goals of profiling is to identify an unknown offender from crime information, it would seem appropriate to focus the most attention in a model on explaining exactly how offender characteristics are to be determined from the crime scene evidence. Unfortunately, none of the reviewed models provides this information. For example, the Douglas et al. (1986) model advises the reader to include the offender's physical characteristics (height, weight, eye color, etc.), hobbies, and interests in the finished profile, yet there is no mention of how these characteristics are to be ascertained. Holmes and Holmes (1996) advised the reader that "The profiler must take into account the total crime scene in order to form a mental image of the personality of the offender" (p. 39), but this instruction is hardly sufficient for determining how this mental image is to be derived, what parts of the offender's personality are being imagined, and how this translates into accurate offender characteristics. Turvey (1999) explained that offender characteristics are to be "deduced" from crime scene evidence, but his deductive method is an ill-defined process that is never adequately operationalized in his book. Turco (1990) limited his procedural instructions for determining offender characteristics to suggesting that the reader "consider the crime scene" (p. 150) and use "understanding . . . and . . . appreciation" of psychodynamic principles (p. 151). He discussed four key dimensions of profiling (i.e., a projective consideration of the crime scene in its entirety, integrating knowledge about neurological behavior, taking a psychodynamic perspective, and studying the demographic characteristics of the crime) that seem to bear no clear relationship to each other, except for the first and third, which are sufficiently vague that they appear to represent the same concept (see chap. 2), and Turco provided no procedures for transforming these dimensions into a profile of offender characteristics. Keppel and Walter (1999) made reference to the kinds of offender characteristics that typify the different categories of their typology, but they provided no information on how to arrive at such characteristics.

This failure on the part of all the reviewed models to clearly explain how to derive offender characteristics from crime scene evidence is problematic because in most cases these characteristics are required as part of the output of a profile. Furthermore, it is this absence of procedures that opens the door for the use of intuition in profiling practice. Indeed, some authors (Holmes & Holmes, 1996; Turvey, 1999) consider the determination of offender characteristics to be an artful skill. As discussed in the previous section, the use of such intuition in criminal profiling is problematic.

Second, given that four of the five nonscientific profiling models reviewed advocate for the use of typologies, it is troubling that none of these models explains how to use one. How does one select a typological category for a particular offender? This is a basic procedural issue, which none of the models using typologies explicitly addresses. It would seem that there are at least three possibilities for selecting a typological category for a particular unidentified offender. First, one could look at the descriptions of each category separately and, on the basis of some threshold of fit, determine whether the unidentified offender matches that category. This process would be repeated for each subsequent category in the typology, which could result in the offender fitting into all of the categories, some of the categories, or none of the categories. Alternatively, one could look at the four categories collectively and determine which category is most similar to the hypothesized characteristics of the unidentified offender. If none of the categories seemed appropriate, then the offender would not be matched. In this process, either no category or only one category would be selected, on the basis of the closest fit with the offender. Finally, one could force the assignment of the offender into a typological category; that is, similar to the second method, the categories would be evaluated together to determine which category is the closest match for the unidentified offender. However, rather than having the option of leaving the offender unmatched to a category, the profiler would be required to select the best of the available options. A potential consequence of this process is that two different offenders, one of whom matched very closely the description of a category and one of whom was a poor match but who was an even poorer match to the other categories, could be placed into the same category.

Despite these various options, none of the models advises the reader as to which of these three methods, if any, should be used in selecting a typological category. Keppel and Walter (1999), in their model and accompanying study, seemed to endorse the method of forcing an offender into a typological category, because they used this method themselves. Unfortunately, because they did not explicitly address the issue of procedures, it is not possible to infer that they would necessarily recommend this method for the practice of profiling. Likewise, Douglas et al. (1986), by providing choice points in their model, seemed to indicate that only one category should be selected at a given time (crime classification, motive/intent, etc.), but again, because no explicit directions are provided, this inference may not reflect the authors' true recommendations. Turvey (1999) wrote that one should not use his behavior-motivational typology as a diagnostic tool for offenders and should not force an individual into a particular category, but he did not clearly explain what one should do in order to use this typology. Finally, Holmes and Holmes (1996) provided no procedural instructions for any of their numerous typologies.

Third, part of the difficulty in attempting to match an unidentified offender to a category is that in cases in which the typological categories contain some conceptual overlap, no procedures are provided to aid the profiler in choosing one category over the other. Where there are conceptual weaknesses in the distinctions among categories, clear procedures could serve as a moderator explaining how to make investigative decisions in the face of ambiguous data. For example, procedures could be introduced to create a hierarchy of the elements within typological categories. If a category contained information about sexual interests, employment history, and personality, then procedures could be implemented to prioritize these pieces of information according to importance. In such an organization, sexual interests might be the most important element, followed by employment history, followed by personality. Thus, if an unidentified offender matched the sexual interests pattern of one category, but the personality pattern of another category, the procedures could require that he be assigned to the category that most closely matched his sexual interest pattern, because sexual interests would have been designated as the most important element. Likewise, procedures could be implemented to aid the profiler in the case that the unidentified offender matched the sexual interests pattern of one category and both the employment history and personality elements of another category. Here, a model could dictate that the number of matched elements should override the priorities of those elements in the hierarchy. Thus, the offender would be matched to the category that most closely matched these multiple elements. None of the models that use typologies specifies methods to use in making distinctions between typological categories. Perhaps these models' authors rely on intuition or professional judgment in deciding which category is appropriate for a particular offender. However, if this is the case, there are still no instructions to the reader directing him or her to apply intuition at this stage of the profiling process or explaining how one should develop appropriate intuitive strategies for profiling.

Fourth, clear procedures are also lacking in the area of assessing offender motive, MO, and signature. Douglas et al.'s (1986) model and Keppel and Walter's (1999) model explicitly discuss the importance of inferring offender motive. Turco (1990), Holmes and Holmes (1996), and Turvey (1999) did not explicitly discuss motive; however, these models do embed the consideration of motive in the assessment of an offender's MO and signature. Turvey further implied the importance of assessing motive by including the behavior–motivational typology in his model.

Despite the seeming importance of offender motive, or intent, to the profiling process, procedures for this assessment are lacking. Douglas et al. (1986) and Keppel and Walter (1999), while directly instructing the reader to consider offender motive, did not actually provide any information about how to accomplish this. For example, Douglas et al. (1986) recommended that profilers determine whether a crime scene has been staged. Recall that in staging, the crime scene is altered in an attempt to mislead the police, making it an issue of offender intent. The profiler must distinguish between a crime scene that might have been altered for other reasons, or out of disorganization, and a crime scene in which the intent of the offender was to mislead. No guidelines are provided to aid in making this decision. Keppel and Walter (1999) discussed many types of offender motive (e.g., expressing dominance, acting out sexual fantasies, expressing revenge) in their typological categories, but they provided no procedures for determining the motive of a given offender or translating behaviors and crime scene features into motives. Turvey first organized motives into a typology and then asserted that an offender's behaviors can actually be "suggestive of more than one motivation" (p. 181). He did not provide procedures to assist in determining the correct motive from a set of behaviors and instead referred the reader to the artful component of profiling and encouraged a reliance on professional expertise. In the absence of clear procedures linking evidence to offender motive or intent, a profiler would essentially need to know or have access to the offender to establish his intent. If this were possible, it would render the profiling process useless; investigators could instead apprehend the offender and commence without the assistance of a profiler.

Fifth, a related problem is that all of the nonscientific profiling models that discuss both MO and signature include them together, as related concepts. As mentioned previously, part of the difficulty with understanding how to assess MO and signature is that the authors of the nonscientific profiling models are not in agreement as to the definitions of these terms. Nonetheless, it would still be possible for the authors to provide clear procedures for the determination of these concepts, as defined by their particular model. Unfortunately, this has not been done.

Part of the problem is that there is insufficient information to allow the reader to determine which pieces of evidence or behavior should be attended to as reflecting MO or signature and which kinds of information are not indicators of these concepts. For example, if an offender snatches a child from a playground in broad daylight, is this indicative of the offender's MO, or is it indicative of an impulse-control disorder that is unrelated to the successful commission of a child abduction? How does one determine the difference? Similarly, how does one determine whether a body discovered in an awkward position was posed in a manner symbolic to the offender (signature) or whether it simply fell into that position upon death?

In addition, there are no procedures provided to assist in the differentiation of these two concepts in practice. Even if the authors could agree on definitional criteria that distinguished between MO and signature, how is the reader to use these criteria to ascertain which concept is represented by a particular act or piece of evidence? For example, if a victim reports that her assailant wore a mask, is this reflective of that offender's MO? What if the victim reports that the offender wore a Halloween mask? Is this still an indicator of MO, or is this now an element of signature? If the difference is the reasoning behind the offender's choice of mask (e.g., convenience vs. a desire to masquerade as a Halloween monster), how is the reader to determine this from the victim's report? Likewise, how does one determine from the presence of elaborate bindings on a victim whether the purpose was to prevent escape (MO) or whether the offender had a fantasy-related reason for binding the victim in this manner (signature)? Without clear procedures, the task of determining elements of MO and signature from crime scene evidence becomes quite confusing.

Sixth, more generally, the authors provide varying degrees of detail concerning what kinds of information to collect and what to do with that information. For example, Douglas et al. (1986) and Turvey (1999) provided detailed information about what pieces of evidence to collect, but they did not provide precise information on how to weight the various pieces of information or combine them to reach a correct profile. In contrast, Keppel and Walter (1999) provided no basic guidelines about what evidence to collect and what to do with that evidence once it has been collected.

Seventh, there is insufficient guidance in these models to arrive at the output characteristics of a profile. Table 3.3 outlines the determinations that each author suggests should be made in a finished profile. As can be seen from the items marked by footnotes, in very few cases are sufficient procedures provided to allow the determination of these characteristics (also see the examples provided in the preceding paragraph).

Eighth, as demonstrated in Table 3.4, in only two cases are there sufficient procedures provided to achieve at least one of the stated goals for the models. For example, the Douglas et al. (1986) model provides sufficient procedures for analyzing a crime scene but not for providing offender characteristics and leads, conducting interviews, or testifying at trial. Likewise, the Turvey (1999) model also provides sufficient procedures to analyze a crime scene but does not provide enough information to allow the reader to provide leads, reduce a suspect pool, link crimes together, assess an offender's potential for escalation, conduct interviews, or testify at trial.

Ninth, the data in Table 3.5 make evident not only that there are few procedures offered but also that these procedures come at the beginning of a crime analysis, with no additional procedures provided as determinations become more difficult. For example, both the Douglas et al. (1986) model and the Turvey (1999) model offer procedures for collecting evidence and analyzing crime scenes but do not offer procedures for reconstructing a crime, linking evidence to offender characteristics, linking offenses, using typologies, or determining MO and signature.

LACK OF EVIDENCE OF INVESTIGATIVE VALUE

One remaining possibility for redeeming the nonscientific profiling models is that despite the criticisms discussed in this chapter, the practice of profiling through one or more of these models somehow works. It is certainly not unreasonable to think that one might first identify a useful phenomenon, such as profiling, and then struggle to build a model that adequately explains it. Unfortunately, this is not the case with the nonscientific models of criminal profiling. None of the models has provided any evidence that profiling, as currently practiced, has any substantial investigative value.

TABLE 3.3
Nonscientific Profiling Models: Output Characteristics

Model	Output characteristics	
Douglas et al. (1986)	Demographic characteristics Physical characteristics Habits Beliefs/values Preoffense behavior	Postoffense behavior Motivation Staging Investigative recommendations
Holmes and Holmes (1996)	Social/psychological core variables of personality Race Age Employment status/type Religion Education Interview suggestions/strategies	Intelligence Family Residence Vehicle Psychosexual development Psychological evaluation of suspect belongings
Keppel and Walter (1999)	Crime dynamics Homicidal pattern Suspect profile	
Turco (1990)	Neurological behavior Psychodynamic characteristics Demographic features	

Turvey (1999)	Crime reconstruction
	Wound pattern analysis
	Profile of victim:
	  Timeline[a]
	  Psychological autopsy
	  Risk assessment
	Offender risk
	Method of approach[a] (if living victim)
	Method of attack[a] (if living victim)
	Method of control[a] (if living victim)
	Victim resistance[a] (if living victim)
		Nature/sequence of sexual acts[a] (if living victim)
		Precautionary acts
		Modus operandi
		Signature
		Trial strategy
		Psychopathy
		Sadism
		Case linkage
		Offender state of mind
		Malice aforethought (premeditation)

Note. [a]Sufficient procedures are provided to achieve this goal.

TABLE 3.4
Stated Profiling Goals

Model	Analyze crime scene	Provide offender characteristics	Provide leads	Reduce suspect pool	Link crimes	Assess potential for escalation	Evaluate suspect belongings	Interview strategy	Testify at trial
Douglas et al. (1986)	X[a]	X	X					X	X
Holmes and Holmes (1996)		X					X	X	
Keppel and Walter (1999)	X		X					X	
Turco (1990)	No goals stated								
Turvey (1999)	X[a]	X	X	X	X	X		X	X

Note. [a]Sufficient procedures are provided to achieve this goal.

TABLE 3.5
General Categories of Procedures Provided by Nonscientific Profiling Models

Models	What types of evidence/information to collect	How to analyze crime scenes	How to reconstruct a crime	Linking evidence to offender characteristics	Linking offenses	Using typologies	Determining modus operandi and signature
Douglas et al. (1986)	X	X					
Holmes and Holmes (1996)							
Keppel and Walter (1999)							
Turco (1990)							
Turvey (1999)	X	X					

According to Holmes and Holmes's own discussion of a study conducted by the FBI (Holmes & Holmes, 1996, p. 44, who did not cite the original study), of 192 cases in which profiling was used, only 88 were solved. Of those 88 cases, profiles resulted in identifying the offender in 17% of cases. If these figures are accurate, this actually indicates that profiling was successful in approximately 8% of cases in which it was used. Copson (1995, as cited in Canter, 2000) found that the use of profiling was successful in only 3% of cases in which it was used. Although it may be the case that profilers are typically consulted in cases in which traditional law enforcement techniques have already failed, 3% to 8% is still a rather modest success rate.

This failure to provide convincing evidence for the investigative value of nonscientific profiling does not prevent some authors from claiming that profiling is effective. Douglas and Olshaker have written a series of books in the popular media (Douglas & Olshaker, 1995, 1997, 1998, 1999, 2000) describing Douglas' profiling success stories, without spending equal time discussing the limitations to his endeavors. Holmes and Holmes (1996), while conceding that profiles should not be the sole tools used in investigations, nonetheless provided personal opinions and anecdotal examples to suggest that profiles are incrementally useful to, and accurate for, law enforcement. Rather than providing evidence to corroborate these claims, they simply argued that on the basis of the (unspecified) education and training of profilers, it is "reasonable to expect that [they] will be of value to law enforcement" (Holmes & Holmes, 1996, p. 6).

CONCLUSION

The nonscientific models of profiling suffer from several problems that render their concepts unclear and their procedures mysterious. As described in this chapter, these difficulties stem from a basic lack of goals and standards and manifest themselves in imprecise terminology, confusing approaches to categorizing information, a reliance on intuition, and a lack of procedures. Because of these problems, it is not surprising that these models have neither the scientific evidence to support the investigative value of profiling nor the tools to even explore the question of whether profiling is valuable.

It is interesting that each model makes some reference to being scientific, even though none of these models contains sufficient science to support any such reference. What is promising is that these references imply an awareness that there is a contribution to be made by using science. Certain questions about profiling—such as whether profiling helps law enforcement solve cases and, if it does, how profiling actually works—simply cannot be answered without stepping into a scientific framework. The nonscientific models of profiling may contain important insights about profiling, but if any useful information is to be gleaned from them, there must be some systematic attempt to verify their claims. Without scientific inquiry, models of profiling provide only speculation. Science is needed to help the profiling field move from the realm of conjecture to the possibility of truths.

4

THE CURRENT MODEL OF SCIENTIFIC PROFILING

Although the authors of the nonscientific profiling models described in chapter 2 use scientific terminology or make reference to scientific tenets to varying degrees, none of those models claims to represent a completely scientific approach to profiling. Each author either directly emphasizes the importance of an artful component to criminal profiling or implies as much by encouraging the use of intuition, investigative experience, and professional judgment. As an alternative, a model could use science as its foundation. Currently, the Canter model, discussed in this chapter, is the only one that arguably fits this description.

THE CANTER MODEL

The impetus for much of Canter's work has been his criticisms of artful profiling, as conducted by the FBI, independent psychologists, and other law enforcement agents. In the *Offender Profiling Series*, Alison and Canter (1999b) stated that profiling processes, "whilst presented with great conviction are, at best, subjective opinion, common sense or ignorance or at worst, deliberate deception" (p. 6). They faulted the media and American culture in general for being unable to discard the myth of the expert profiler, who succeeds in finding the perpetrator when the police fail. They further argued that current accounts of profiling lack systematic procedures and are devoid of any references to psychological principles. In their view, this constitutes a misrepresentation of psychology that raises ethical concerns.

Having spent some time visiting the FBI, Canter had additional specific criticisms about their profiling approach. "Neither the *Silence of the Lambs* nor the publications and lectures of FBI behavioral science agents indicated how to produce an 'offender profile'" (Canter, 1994, p. 35). Instead, FBI profilers claim to rely heavily on intuition, and "any approach that deviates from this 'gut feeling' is perceived as inferior and unlikely to bear fruit" (Alison & Canter, 1999b, p. 7). Although critical of the intuitive approach, Canter was also critical of the irony that this approach is actually inconsistent with the FBI's own practice. According to Canter, much of the information presented in profiles by Douglas, for example, contains general characteristics typical of known perpetrators of violent crime (e.g., previous criminal convictions, poor relationships with women). Therefore, Douglas's profiles appear to actually use data and probabilistic information rather than to rely exclusively on intuitive judgment. Canter also argued that FBI profiles contain assertions about characteristics that the profiler deems unlikely to be present in the unidentified offender. These are also based on probabilistic data because typically these characteristics have low base rates in the population to begin with (e.g., no military experience). Thus, an FBI profiler would not need intuitive expertise to make these observations.

Canter (1994) criticized the lack of research in the FBI's approach to profiling: "For them, research is collecting interview material, but little systematic use is made of it . . . Bob Ressler said he had a bunch of statistics somewhere but he clearly did not give it much credence or significance" (pp. 82–83). This lack of science is significant, Canter asserted, because of the legal implications of profiling. It could be argued on ethical principles that any licensed psychologist who engages in profiling should not ignore the scientific framework of psychology when creating profiles. More important, however, acting outside the parameters of science has serious implications even for profilers who are not psychologists when such "judgments are likely to influence serious decisions across an investigation and within a court of law" (Alison & Canter, 1999b, p. 9).

To address these criticisms, Canter presented a scientifically based model of profiling, in which he argued that the profiling inferences important to police investigators, including those that the FBI claims to invoke through intuitive methods, are actually empirical questions that can be answered by psychological research. Canter identified the following categories from which these profiling inferences and empirical questions are derived:

- *behavioral salience*, which refers to the important behavioral features of a crime that may help identify the perpetrator;

- *distinguishing between offenders*, which refers to the question of how to indicate differences between offenders, including differences between crimes;
- *inferring characteristics*, which refers to inferences that can be made about offender characteristics that may help to identify him or her; and
- *linking offenses*, which refers to the question of attributing multiple offenses to the same offender.

According to Canter (2000), the tasks of profiling research are to develop scientific ways to assess these categories within a psychological framework and to use that information to infer and provide offender characteristics that will be useful to law enforcement agents.

The concept of linking behaviors, personalities, and other human characteristics is not a new endeavor in the field of psychology. Similar questions about behavioral consistency across situations, and differences between and within individuals, make up most psychological inquiries. Canter pointed out, however, that the application of these types of inference to investigative situations is unique for two reasons. First, the material available to profilers is limited. The information provided by a crime scene is typically limited to the identity of the victim, the location where and time when the crime took place, and an account of what happened. Profilers are unable to directly observe the crime or have direct contact with the offender when the crime is taking place. Even in cases in which a victim gives an account of the crime, that person is not able to provide reliable information about the perpetrator's thoughts, personality characteristics, or other internal processes—the variables with which psychologists typically work. Thus, predictor variables in profiling research are limited to those that are external to the offender. Second, the kind of information that a profiler is asked to provide in an offender profile is also likely to be limited in that it must be information that will be of use to law enforcement investigators. So, for example, information about an unidentified offender's living situation or physical characteristics would be useful to an investigation, whereas information about the offender's unconscious psychodynamic conflicts would be difficult for investigators to uncover and might not be as useful.

With these limitations in mind, Canter represented the concept of linking offense actions and offender characteristics with the following canonical equation:

$$F_1A_1 + \ldots F_nA_n = K_1C_1 + \ldots K_mC_m,$$

where $A_{1 \ldots n}$ represents n actions of the offender and $C_{1 \ldots m}$ represents m characteristics of the offender. The left side of the equation contains the kinds of information about a crime that would be available to law enforcement. The right side represents the offender characteristics that would be useful to the investigation of the crime.

The possibility of empirically based profiling relies on the presence of reliable relationships between actions (A) and characteristics (C). That is, it must be the case that "there are some psychologically important variations *between* crimes that relate to differences in the people who commit them" (Canter, 2000, p. 29, italics in original). To apply profiling to the categories of empirical questions described previously, one must be able to use information from a particular crime to correctly make inferences about the perpetrator. Unfortunately, according to Canter, there is no clear and simple relationship between these variables. First, there are no uniquely strong relationships between a given action and a given characteristic. A variety of combinations of actions can give rise to a variety of combinations of characteristics; thus, there are many possible relationships within a data set of crimes that link actions to characteristics. For example, an offender who wears latex gloves to commit a burglary may do so because he has had the experience of being apprehended after fingerprints were found at the scene of a previous burglary. In this situation, wearing latex gloves (A) would indicate previous criminal experience (C). Another offender who wears latex gloves to commit a burglary may do so because he is an avid watcher of crime shows on television. From watching these shows, the offender has seen fictional burglars apprehended because they left their fingerprints at the scenes of their crimes. In this case, wearing latex gloves (A) would be linked with avid crime show watching (C). As can be seen from these two scenarios, there is no unique relationship between wearing latex gloves and a single offender characteristic. Instead, there are at least two possible characteristics that could be derived from this single action. A second problem with establishing clear relationships between actions and characteristics is that variations in the inclusion of variables in the action set (A) may change the weightings ($F_{1 \ldots n}$ and $K_{1 \ldots m}$) in the characteristics set (C). So, for example, if a victim fails to report a particular action, analyses would generate different offender characteristics than if that action were reported. The task at hand is therefore to develop methods to accurately establish the values of the weightings ($F_{1 \ldots n}$ and $K_{1 \ldots m}$) in the equation.

According to Canter, theory is the key to establishing the weightings in the preceding canonical equation. Other nonscientific profiling approaches essentially use common sense, sometimes labeled *intuition*, to infer offender characteristics. Canter (1994) instead advocated for using scientific study to build "psychological theories that will show how and why variations in criminal behavior occur" (p. 344). "What are required scientifically are explanatory frameworks that can lead to hypotheses about the sorts of offender characteristics that are likely to relate to particular offence behaviour" (Canter, 2000, p. 27).

Before addressing specific theories, there are two hypotheses that Canter discussed as a basis for considering scientific explanatory frameworks for profiling: (a) offender consistency and (b) offense specificity. The *offender consistency hypothesis* posits that there are consistencies between the manner in which an offender carries out a crime on one occasion and the way he or she carries out crimes on other occasions. These similarities are attributable to characteristics of the offender rather than to features of the situation in which the crime was committed. Crime is thus an extreme form of noncriminal activity and therefore also likely to reflect variations that occur in an offender's ordinary, day-to-day interpersonal activities. In addition, this hypothesis requires considering both the degree of variation within a single offender's actions and the variation across multiple offenders. Canter (1994) stated, "The actions that may be characteristic of a person across a series of offenses may be quite different from those actions that help to discriminate him or her from other possible offenders in a large pool" (p. 348). This means that there are certain consistencies that will allow the linking of a series of offenses to a single offender and other consistencies that will set that offender apart from a larger pool of suspects. An example of how offender consistency can be applied to profiling is the determination of an offender's spatial criminal range. According to Canter, offender consistency should extend to the locations of a single offender's crimes, such that these locations will evidence some degree of structure or consistency.

Offense specificity addresses the degree to which offenders are specialized in the types of crimes they commit. According to Canter, three possible arguments can be made about degrees of offense specificity. One possibility is that offenders do not specialize; accordingly, the commission of any particular crime depends on two things: the social processes that determine the preparedness of an individual to be criminal and the appropriate opportunity or circumstance for an individual criminal act. If this argument is correct, criminals could be difficult to distinguish from each other because under the right circumstances, an individual with criminal tendencies would be just as likely to commit one type of crime as another. A second argument is that violent or emotional crimes are committed impulsively. According to this approach, criminal acts are so unstructured that no offender characteristics, other than impulsivity, are likely to be revealed in crimes. This argument would render the profiling endeavor useless, because it would mean that no useful information is likely to be gleaned from examining a criminal's actions during the commission of a violent crime. A third argument, which Canter called the *modus operandi* (MO) *argument*, views an offender's actions as unique to that individual. Under this argument, offenders are highly specialized, and their criminal acts necessarily reveal idiosyncratic personality characteristics.

Although Canter's view of offender consistency indicates that there are likely to be consistent patterns within the actions of a single offender, offenders are often eclectic in their crimes; that is, individuals who commit one type of crime are likely to have also committed other types of crimes. Given that offenders show consistency in their criminal actions, the first two theories of offender specificity, involving either circumstance or impulsivity, will not adequately explain criminal behavior. However, given that offenders are not completely consistent in their actions, the MO argument of offender specificity is also unlikely to be successful.

To illustrate this interplay between offender consistency and offender specificity, Canter framed criminal actions as a hierarchy. At the lowest level, there is the most general difference between people who commit crimes and those who do not. At the next level, criminal actions can be divided into classes of crime (e.g., property crimes vs. violent crimes). At the third level are more specific types of crimes (e.g., homicide, theft). Next are patterns of criminal behavior, addressing the differences between individuals who commit the same type of crime in different ways. At the fifth level is MO, and at the sixth and most specific level one would examine specific criminal signatures (e.g., a particular type of weapon or binding technique). Because, as previously indicated, offenders do not necessarily specialize, Canter (2000) stated that the hierarchy should be considered as "an inter-related set of dimensions for describing crimes" (p. 30).

Theories Linking Actions to Characteristics

Although offender consistency and offense specificity establish a basic rationale for linking offender characteristics to offender actions, theoretical approaches are still necessary for attempting to explain these links. Canter (1995) discussed five theoretical approaches: psychodynamic typologies, personality differences, career routes, socioeconomic subgroups, and interpersonal narratives. Each of these approaches takes at least one of three general theoretical perspectives: attempting to explain how offender characteristics (C) cause offender actions (A), attempting to look for intervening variables that are produced by C to cause A, or attempting to find a third variable or set of variables that causes both A and C.

Psychodynamic Typologies

The focus of this approach, the "internal emotional dynamics of the criminal" (Canter, 1995, p. 350) rather than criminal acts themselves, is exemplified by the rapist and serial killer typologies used by Holmes and

Holmes (1996) and the FBI (see chap. 2). By presenting only a few broad types of offenders in a typology, these typologies provide a small number of simple hypotheses about the link between A and C. Canter referred to these hypotheses as simple equations involving themes such as power and anger. Criminal activity is described as an avenue for compensating for perceived inadequacies related to these themes. It is not surprising that psychodynamic typologies tend to be used specifically for violent crimes; as Canter pointed out, there do not appear to be any examples of such typologies for fraud or burglary.

Personality Differences

This approach holds that A and C variables are linked through underlying personality characteristics. According to Canter, psychological research has used this approach, comparing convicted offenders who have been separated into groups according to their crimes. For example, such studies would compare rapists with child molesters, or murderers with wife-batterers. Canter asserted that the goal of such research is typically to establish personality differences between criminals who commit different types of crime. Although Canter criticized this approach because of the heterogeneity of offenses committed by many offenders, he did acknowledge that an individual's personality is likely to be reflected in the way he or she commits offenses. He stated that the task is "identifying those 'real world' A and C variables that do have direct links to personality characteristics" (Canter, 1995, p. 351).

Career Routes

Canter (1995), describing this approach as deriving from general criminological theory, posited that a criminal career unfolds as an individual gains experience, success, or interest in particular types of crime. The individual begins as a general offender but specializes as his or her career continues. Canter described two possibilities for relating this approach to his canonical equation. The first is that a matrix of equations is necessary—one equation for each stage in a criminal career. The second, simpler possibility is a single equation that deals with C variables as aspects of an individual's criminal stage.

Socioeconomic Subgroups

A social theory of offender differences would hypothesize that A and C variables both reflect socioeconomic processes. This theory depends on the existence of distinct social characteristics for subgroups of offenders (e.g., robbers are from a distinctly impoverished sector of society). Canter (1995) pointed out that such links between social characteristics and offender subgroups would be difficult to establish because it is likely that most criminals are drawn from similar socioeconomic groups. Discriminating between them on the basis of social characteristics is therefore unlikely to be fruitful.

Interpersonal Narratives

Canter's own theoretical perspective is based on *interpersonal narratives*, an approach that he asserted "attempts to build links between the strengths of all the approaches outlined above" (Canter, 1995, p. 353). According to Canter, any crime is an interpersonal transaction that involves characteristic ways of dealing with other people. Although there will, of course, be commonalities across a range of offenders who have committed similar crimes, there will nonetheless be a more limited set of criminal activities within which an individual offender will tend to operate. This includes both the types of crimes committed and the actions within a particular type of crime; Canter did not specify whether his discussion of interpersonal transactions applies to nonviolent or property crimes as well as violent crimes. From the previously stated premise, Canter derived two related hypotheses: that individual offenders will have overlapping sets of repertoires that will have characteristic themes associated with them, and that predictions can be made about the correlation between themes of an offender and his other characteristics.

Recall Canter's hierarchy of criminal actions. According to this heuristic, criminal actions vary from those that are very general to those that are specific to individual offenders. Canter (2000) applied his interpersonal-narratives theory to the task of "describ[ing]" (p. 32) these criminal behaviors by identifying dominant interpersonal themes. Canter conceptualized these themes as being distinct from the independent categories typical of typologies. Because Canter argued that there are no truly pure types of crimes or criminals, the practice of dividing crime information into a set of independent categories is problematic. Instead, Canter (2000) proposed that criminal behaviors be arranged in a "radex" (p. 31) structure—a series of concentric circles that move from the general at the center to the specific at the periphery, with the dominant interpersonal theme distinguishing between different offense qualities conceptually radiating around the center.

Canter provided an example of the interpersonal themes he believes to be involved in violent crime. He stated that

> the crucial distinctions between the dramas that violent men write for themselves are the variations in the roles that they give their victims . . . variations in the emphases of the vicious interpersonal contact are therefore the first major themes to consider when interpreting any violent crime. (Canter, 1994, p. 339)

The following themes illustrate interpersonal narratives as manifested in the various roles in which offenders cast their victims. Within each role theme is a dimension that refers to the level of desire for control involved in the offender–victim interaction, which Canter (1994) described as "the degree of power or aggression" that the offender shows, which "reflects his deformed approach to the control of other people" (p. 340). This dimension interacts with the role of the victim to produce variations in the interpersonal narrative. As Canter (1994) stated, "The destructive mixture of a callous search for intimacy and an unsympathetic desire for control is at the heart of the hidden narratives that shape violent assaults" (p. 340). The three victim roles discussed are victim as object, victim as vehicle, and victim as person. The desire-for-control dimension is divided into either high desire for control or low desire for control. Note that although these themes relate to victim roles, the characteristics described by Canter are predominantly those of the offender.

Victim as Object

Some offenders completely lack any feeling for their victims. They make no attempt to see the world from the victim's view; neither is the victim expected to play an active part in the assault. In this role, the victim is likely to be one of opportunity and may be encountered by the offender in a nondescript public place.

In cases of high desire for control, the victim's body may be mutilated, with parts being cannibalized or taken away as souvenirs. The offender is described by Canter as similar to the FBI's concept of the disorganized offender. He is likely to be of low intellect and may lack contact with reality. This perpetrator will likely live alone, or be in transition, moving in and out of institutions. His community will probably know him as an eccentric. The offender's background will have been somewhat dysfunctional, with frequent changes of parenting during childhood and adolescence, and possible poverty. The offender will be aware of the criminality of his actions but may not try to evade capture, other than by changing his crime venue when suspicions are aroused. His crimes are likely to come to notice accidentally and, once captured, the offender is likely to confess.

If the offender has a low desire for control, victims are more likely to be selected because of some feature that is attractive to the offender. Thus, the sexual component of the crime will be more prominent than acts of mutilation or dismemberment. Typically, murder is not the goal of the assault but is instead a consequence of the offender's other violent acts toward the victim (e.g., hitting the victim to keep her under control). Rather than being bizarre or disorganized, an offender with low desire for control is obsessed with obtaining more victims. He may find a secluded area where victims can be kept over a longer period of time in privacy. Rather than impulsively snatching victims off the street, this offender is likely to commute to look for victims in areas where vulnerable individuals who are attractive to him are likely to be found. The offender will then target any person who comes along in that group. (Note that in the initial description of victim as object, the offender is described as being likely to encounter victims of opportunity. It is possible that a difference in level of desire for control accounts for the discrepancy presented here. Canter did not specifically address this discrepancy in his writings.) The offender will not have much verbal interaction with victims and may come prepared with weapons and binding materials to overpower them quickly. Socially, this type of offender is likely to be quiet and isolated. He will be employed in a "non-demanding job" (Canter, 1994, p. 349) that requires little contact with other people. When asked questions about his crime, this type of offender is likely to respond nonchalantly, or with disinterest, as if he does not understand the seriousness of his actions.

Victim as Vehicle

The central theme of this role is the offender's "anger with himself and the fates" (Canter, 1994, p. 350). This offender casts himself in the role of the tragic hero and feels denied his rightful place. Committing assaults allows the offender to steal back his lost power.

At a high desire for control, this offender is similar to the FBI's concept of spree murderers. He may act in one episode to kill many people in an expression of anger and frustration and may also evidence what Canter (1994) called the "Samson syndrome" (p. 351), intensifying the experience by committing suicide after destroying his victims.

At a low desire for control, the offender is aware of having a destructive mission, and the killings become more deliberate and serial, rather than consisting of a single intense event. Desiring recognition, this offender will talk at length with law enforcement and want his story told through the media. He is intelligent and appears socially facile, using superficial charm to manipulate victims and gain their trust. The offender

> will have much more apparently social contact with his victims than our first group, but this will be an interaction in which the victim has to be harnessed to the offender's will. It is not sufficient for them just to be used; they must be exploited. (Canter, 1994, p. 353)

Although this offender is more "sane" than offenders who cast victims as objects, he still lacks remorse and empathy. Central to the "inner despair that drives these men" (Canter, 1994, p. 353) will be some relationship problem—a significant breakup or death of someone close to the offender. Canter conceptualized the offender's assaults as attempts to rebuild these relationships in his inner narratives. In general, however, this offender's background will be more stable than that of the offenders in the victims-as-objects category. "There will be obvious episodes in their lives that trigger the emergence of their violent inner narratives" (Canter, 1994, p. 354); thus, his offenses will not be entirely unpredictable or spontaneous. Canter described this offender as similar to the FBI's organized offenders. He is older and likely to have children and a history of failed relationships. He travels to commit crimes and is very dangerous because his assaults are not limited by any sense of compassion or empathy for the victim. He may kill in response to the victim's reactions or simply to avoid leaving a witness. If there is a preexisting relationship between offender and victim, the assault is likely to be particularly violent.

Victim as Person

In this theme, offenders "recognize the existence of their victims as particular people" and "try to understand the experience of their victims" in what Canter (1994) described as a "parody of empathy" (p. 357). The inner narratives of this offender cast him as a hero in a dramatic adventure. The offender views violence as normal, and although he appears to be capable of normal social interaction, there is a lack of true empathy for his victims. This offender may believe that he understands the viewpoints of others, but often he misinterprets victims' reactions. For example, this type of rapist may assault a woman and then ask her for a date later that week. Victims are selected largely by circumstance. Situations that might normally induce anger or annoyance escalate for this offender into violent confrontations that range from bar fights to murder. This individual typically offends indoors, and the physical assaults are sometimes an unplanned extension of a robbery or home invasion. A second manifestation of the victim-as-person role can be found in offenders who attack elderly women in their homes. These offenders are typically teenage boys from the neighborhood who commit nonsexual attacks against their victims during burglaries or thefts. The victim is typically known to the offender and may even be a family member. In this type of offense, the victim is selected to provide some sort of gain for the perpetrator—he is therefore unlikely to commit similar subsequent assaults. A third manifestation of this victim role is in the rapist who believes that he is forging some personal relationship with the victim through the assault. This victim is likely to be stalked, and the offender is likely to assault her in her home. During the rape, he may seek out personal information about her to gain a feeling of intimacy. This may become his preferred form of sexual fulfillment. This type of offender begins his assaults in his home range and may initially target women he knows. He may also be married to a younger, subservient woman who is easily manipulated. Canter did not specifically address the control dimension in his discussion of the victim-as-person role.

Testing of Hypotheses

Canter used a multidimensional scaling technique called *smallest space analysis* (SSA) to test his interpersonal-narratives theory and his more basic hypotheses of offender consistency and offense specificity. This method accomplishes two tasks. First, the statistical procedure calculates the correlations between a set of variables and then represents the correlations as proximities in a spatial field. The more correlated two variables are, the closer together their points will be in this space (for a detailed introduction to SSA, see Schiffman, Reynolds, & Young, 1981). Second, Canter used his theories to identify dominant themes among these variables. Thus, the space in which the correlations are plotted is divided into sections that represent distinct interpersonal themes. In some cases, the variables that are hypothesized to cluster into distinct offender themes are specified in advance. The analysis is therefore conducted to confirm the existence of these clusters. In other cases, the themes are identified by a visual examination of the clustering of variables in the SSA scatter plot. Canter asserted that, in this way, his approach can be used "in both [a] hypothesis testing and hypothesis generation mode" (personal communication, December 4, 2002). Using data from SSA and the incorporation of his interpersonal-narratives theory, Canter addressed the categories of empirical profiling questions introduced at the beginning of this chapter.

Behavioral Salience

Canter described the assessment of behavioral salience as an empirical endeavor, in that to understand which behavioral features of a crime are important, one must have some basic understanding of the base rates of various criminal behaviors. Unfortunately, he did not further describe the manner in which base rates should be informally or formally considered in an assessment of behavioral salience. Once behavioral features of a crime are determined, Canter used SSA analyses to demonstrate that his hierarchy of criminal actions empirically corresponds to his radex heuristic. That is, when one examines an SSA scatter plot of criminal actions, one finds that the most frequent aspects of a crime are indeed at the center of the scatter plot, whereas less frequent actions, such as those that make up criminal signatures, are found around the periphery. Canter conceptualized behavioral salience as the location of an action at different distances from the center of this pattern of actions. According to Canter, this model of behavioral salience is refutable because it is possible that distinct subgroups of actions could occur in any class of crime which, whilst frequent, were typically associated with distinct sets of rarer actions. In such a case, the concentric circles that make up the radex would not be found. (Canter, 2000, p. 35)

Rather than relying exclusively on the SSA scatter plot findings of various criminal actions to elucidate salient acts as previously described, Canter (2000) suggested that a consideration of theory be used to elaborate on "central criminal acts" (p. 36). For example, if the central criminal act is a violent one, then theory can be used to consider whether that violent act was instrumental or expressive. Canter and Fritzon (1998) considered a series of arsons by evaluating them according to whether they were directed at certain types of targets. By doing so, they sought to distinguish between "person-oriented" and "object-oriented" arsons (Canter & Fritzon, 1998, p. 73). They hypothesized that there would be a thematic distinction between arsons that were committed as an expression of emotion (expressive) and those that were set for some secondary gain (instrumental). In Canter's view, such an elaboration of the central criminal acts helps to give criminal acts their investigative salience. He asserted that "the elaboration is clearest when the acts can be seen in the general context of other actions committed during similar crimes" (Canter, 2000, p. 36).

Distinguishing Between Offenders

A central reason for Canter's argument that the behavioral salience of an act should be considered in the context of other behaviors that may co-occur with it is that "any single action may be so common across offenses or so ambiguous in its significance that its use as a basis for investigative inferences may suggest distinctions between offenders that are unimportant" (Canter, 2000, p. 36). Accordingly, to effectively distinguish between offenders, one must consider the patterns of their criminal actions, with an understanding of the interpersonal psychological themes that these acts reveal. Canter proposed that these thematic foci of acts—for example, the victim role themes that drive certain violent offender behaviors—are what differentiate crimes and, ultimately, offenders.

Inferring Characteristics

Canter argued that an understanding of the distinctions that can be made between offenders, via interpersonal themes, provides a basis for hypotheses linking offender actions (A) to characteristics (C) as represented in his canonical equation. Rather than approaching criminal behavior as a reflection of psychological dysfunction, Canter advocated for moving toward studying and understanding the structure of criminality and how that structure relates to characteristics of an offender that will be of use in an investigation. (Canter did not elaborate on his meaning in discussing a *structure* of criminality.) According to Canter, even though single criminal actions may be unreliable, a group of actions that represent dominant interpersonal themes in the offender's criminal style can be strongly related to important offender characteristics. It should therefore be possible to infer offender characteristics on the basis of these thematic elements.

Canter acknowledged that the inference of offender characteristics has not typically included consideration of an offender's social context. He stated that other approaches "suffer from dealing with the criminal as an individual independently of the social or organizational context in which he or she operates" (Canter, 2000, p. 42). According to Canter, social context is important because "the social processes that underlie groups, teams and networks of criminals can reveal much about the consistencies in criminal behavior and the themes that provide their foundation" (Canter, 2000, p. 42). Thus, he asserted that social factors are necessary to understanding the important themes involved in offender behavior.

Linking Offenses

The prospect of linking offenses is based on the hypotheses of offender consistency and offense specificity. To the extent that offender acts show consistent patterns, and to the extent that the acts of one offender can be distinguished from those of other offenders, the linking of offenses and the attribution of those offenses to an individual offender should be feasible.

Canter discussed two examples of offender consistency that potentially allow the attribution of a series of crimes to a single offender: behavioral consistency and spatial consistency. According to Canter, *behavioral consistency* is evidenced when there are elements that are consistent across a series of crimes committed by a single offender. These consistencies are hypothesized to be reflective of the perpetrator's interpersonal narratives. Canter provided some support for behavioral consistency, citing an unpublished study conducted at his research center that used SSA to evaluate rapists' actions (Mokros, 1999, cited in Canter, 2000). According to Canter, this study revealed that behaviors present in different crimes committed by the same person were indeed closer to each other on an SSA scatter plot than the actions of different offenders. Replications demonstrating the veracity of this finding would imply that evaluating criminal actions using SSA might allow profilers to identify which crimes or criminal acts were committed by a particular offender and which acts are likely to be the work of a different offender.

Spatial consistency extends the idea of behavioral consistency beyond the conceptual space in which an offender operates to include patterns in the offender's physical space. According to this concept, offenders who engage in spatially consistent crime behaviors have a *home range* and a *criminal range* (Canter & Gregory, 1994, p. 170). The home range is an area, familiar to the offender, that surrounds his or her place of residence. The criminal range is "a finite region which encompasses all offense locations for any particular offender" (Canter & Gregory, 1994, p. 170). Using this distinction between home range and criminal range, Canter and Gregory (1994) divided offenders into *commuters* and *marauders* (p. 171). Marauders are those offenders who use their home or some other fixed base as a focus for their activities; that is, the locations of their homes and the locations of their crimes show little or no distance (e.g., a child molester who offends against children in his neighborhood). Because they operate in their home areas, geographic profiling models that analyze the patterns of offense locations can therefore be used to determine the likely location of these offenders' homes. In contrast, offenders who are commuters travel away from their homes to other areas to commit their crimes (e.g., a sex offender who travels to red light districts to abduct prostitutes). Because there is no necessary relationship between their home and offense locations, it is therefore more difficult to use geographic profiling techniques to model the home locations of these offenders.

Implications for Criminal Investigations

Canter (2000) suggested that an empirical approach to the categories of profiling inferences previously described, using interpersonal themes as a framework for understanding offenses and offenders, implies that "the days of the 'heroic' expert are numbered" (p. 43). Through the continued development of these theories, the field of what Canter (2000) called "investigative psychology" (p. 25) could provide police with the means to conduct scientific profiling, either through computerized processes or police training, without having to consult outside "experts."

5

PROBLEMS WITH THE SCIENTIFIC MODEL OF PROFILING

As a scientifically based model, the Canter model should distinguish itself from the nonscientific models of profiling according to the following scientific criteria: development of a theory about criminal profiling; hypotheses generation; operationalization of methods used in profiling; and empirical validation, including a consideration of both disconfirming evidence and the limitations of the supporting research. Although the Canter model improves on the nonscientific models by adhering to many of these criteria, there are still several fundamental limitations to Canter's approach. This chapter describes the criteria that distinguish between scientific and nonscientific profiling models and evaluates the degree to which the Canter model is successful at achieving the criteria for a scientific model. The chapter concludes by critically considering the attempted use of science by the nonscientific models of profiling.

A THEORY ABOUT CRIMINAL PROFILING

The first characteristic of a scientific model of profiling is a guiding theory (i.e., an integrated set of principles offered to explain phenomena), the purpose of which is to generate hypotheses about an unidentified offender. For example, one might begin with a guiding theory that crime scene evidence reflects offender personality characteristics. One prediction that might result from such a theory is that a sadistic offender personality will be evidenced in the crime scene by multiple superficial wounds on a living victim. This manifestation will occur through behavior in which an offender repeatedly injures a conscious victim for the purpose of enjoying the victim's suffering. The variables that would be of interest to an investigator using this theoretical framework would include wound patterns, weapon information, offender actions and statements, and offender personality. The methods for considering such variables could include interviews with the victim and (if available) the offender, physical evidence analyses and reports from forensic scientists, offender personality assessment measures, and a statistical analysis that would relate information about offender personality to offender behavior to patterns of evidence left at the crime scene. The application of these methods to the variables of interest would yield information that could be used to evaluate the accuracy of the predictions made. One result might be that high scores on a measure of offender sadistic personality are found to be predicted by crime scene evidence of multiple superficial wounds inflicted on a living, conscious victim. Each of the steps in this example are consistent with the general theory that offender personality is manifested in crime scene evidence via offender behavior. The results therefore inform the investigator about the veracity of the original theory, in this case by fitting in with and supporting the theoretical framework.

Consider what would happen if the previously outlined steps did not follow the guiding theory. For example, what if an investigator considered the same crime scene variables and used offender DNA analysis to evaluate the crime scene variables? One could still argue that this process is scientific, and one could demonstrate that the offender was present at the crime scene and committed certain acts on the victim. However, such an analysis would reveal nothing about offender personality, which is the theory being examined.

AN ANALYSIS OF CANTER'S MODEL

Theoretical Framework for Canter's Model

The first step in evaluating Canter's theory is to ascertain its goal. Alison and Canter (1999a) claimed that they were interested in building a theory of "investigative psychology that is far broader than 'criminal profiling'"; they asserted that, in their program, "the focus on profiling is minimal and is seen as a small part of a much broader perspective on understanding, exploring, explaining and aiding police enquiries" (p. 29) and, furthermore, that "'profiling' is seen as a somewhat redundant area of activity that is more of a media promoted anachronism than a developing field" (p. 29). However, these statements are taken from Canter's book series entitled *Offender Profiling* (e.g., Alison & Canter, 1999b), and he has written numerous other articles and books devoted specifically to the profiling endeavor. His full-length book, *Criminal Shadows* (Canter, 1994), is a collection of his profiling success stories, punctuated by descriptions of the theoretical framework in which he places these profiles. Given the problems with nonscientific profiling models described in chapter 3, Canter may indeed have good reason to attempt to differentiate his scientifically based model from the nonscientific models. However, his assertion that investigative psychology is qualitatively different from profiling is simply contradicted by his own work. Canter's model is therefore addressed in this book under the rubric of profiling.

Canter's model (2000) uses a somewhat complex theoretical framework that includes considerations of general criminality and his own concepts of offender consistency and offender specificity and ultimately attempts to identify unknown offenders by applying techniques to the known physical and behavioral evidence. By setting up this framework, Canter established a rationale for profiling that leads to the possibility of inferring an offender's characteristics on the basis of his or her actions. The actions with which Canter is concerned are both criminal and noncriminal, and his theory holds, in essence, that criminal behavior is an extension of noncriminal behavior. Any interaction between an offender and victim is therefore likely to reflect themes (i.e., his interpersonal narratives) in the way that the offender interacts in noncriminal aspects of his life.

On the one hand, Canter's theoretical framework appears to be a step in the right direction. The idea that an offender's criminal behavior could hold some similarities to his or her noncriminal behavior is certainly facially valid. Canter's overall theory and model are still evolving and have not yet developed to the point where empirical testing has clearly spoken to their validity. On the other hand, a closer examination of the components of Canter's interpersonal-narratives theory raises several questions and concerns that weaken his overall approach.

Analysis of Interpersonal Narratives

The interpersonal-narratives theory is based on five components. First, individuals who commit crimes show consistency in their behaviors across both criminal and noncriminal domains. Second, criminals are neither exclusive generalists nor exclusive specialists. Although a criminal's actions may overlap with the actions of other criminals, individual criminals are sufficiently unique that their crimes should be distinguishable from the crimes of another criminal. Third, the interpersonal-narratives theory holds that violent interactions between offender and victim contain various themes that address two issues: the role the victim plays in the offender's search for intimacy and the degree of power or aggression that the offender displays in attempting to achieve intimacy. Fourth, there are three basic themes, or roles, for offenders and victims: victim as object, victim as vehicle, and victim as person. Fifth, there are two basic levels of desire for control related to these themes or roles: high and low (Canter, 1994).

Criminal Consistency Across Criminal and Noncriminal Domains

The question of whether criminals show consistency in their criminal and noncriminal behaviors has been contended for more than 100 years. In fictional literature, the possibility that criminals might evidence disparate personality characteristics across criminal and noncriminal domains was popularized by Robert Louis Stevenson's (1886/2000) *Dr. Jekyll and Mr. Hyde*. In this work, the docile personality of Dr. Jekyll is described as carrying "every mark of capacity and kindness" (Stevenson, 1886/2000, p. 5). In stark contrast, his alter ego, Mr. Hyde, terrorizes London by trampling a small girl and clubbing an esteemed London citizen to death with a walking stick. When Stevenson was writing about Jekyll and Hyde, Jack the Ripper was active in the gaslit Whitechapel area of London. Whereas in *Dr. Jekyll and Mr. Hyde* the characters were unaware that the kindness of Dr. Jekyll and the violence of Mr. Hyde were actually accounted for by a single individual, the Ripper murders incited widespread fear precisely because the public realized that whoever was committing these violent attacks at night was, by day, walking largely unnoticed among the general population.

However, if the lore of *Dr. Jekyll and Mr. Hyde* and the hysteria surrounding Jack the Ripper were accurate and criminals did not evidence consistency, then any study of criminal behavior would be a fruitless endeavor, as criminal actions would, in essence, be random, unpredictable, and arguably unstoppable. Thus, Canter (1994) made a valid point by noting that criminals must evidence some degree of consistency across criminal and noncriminal domains. This is indeed an essential component to any profiling theory. Unfortunately, Canter's model is not the first to identify the issue of offender consistency and apply it to criminal investigation. In fact, Canter (1994) himself credited the FBI with having distinguished "the probability of continuity or consistency in a criminal's behavior from noncriminal situations to criminal ones" (p. 85) in the context of profiling. As Canter (1994) pointed out, "It is a simple idea, once you spot it" (p. 85).

As such, this element of Canter's model is not a novel addition to the field of profiling.

Criminals as Generalists or Specialists

The second component of Canter's interpersonal-narratives theory addresses one of the most fundamental arguments in the field of criminology. Since the publication of Gottfredson and Hirschi's (1990) seminal discussion of a theory of crime that posits offenders to be mostly generalists, the field of criminology has devoted considerable effort to debating the issue of whether offenders generalize or specialize, with two camps of scholars emerging on opposite sides of the argument.

The essential tenets of Gottfredson and Hirschi's (1990) model are as follows. Individuals who exhibit low self-control are more likely to take advantage of opportunities to engage in criminal behavior when they are presented. Furthermore, those people who are lowest in self-control are more likely to start engaging in norm-violating or criminal behavior earlier in life, to commit more offenses, to engage in a variety of types of crime, and to eventually desist with advancing age (Dean, Brame, & Piquero, 1996; Gottfredson & Hirschi, 1990). What follows from these basic tenets is that because individuals who exhibit low self-control are unlikely to specialize and instead commit a variety of crimes, the causes for one type of crime (e.g., stealing) are the same as the causes for another type (e.g., assault). Furthermore, if one controls for frequency of offenses, correlates of offending do not predict differences between individuals who commit violent offenses and those who do not (Piquero, 2000).

There are at least two arguments against the theory that offenders are generalists. The first argument is that different crimes serve different needs (Cornish & Clarke, 1986), and it is therefore important to focus on crime-specific characteristics. Literature consistent with this position suggests that the importance of situational context varies across different types of offenses (Nagin & Paternoster, 1993; Paternoster, 1989). The second argument asserts that distinct developmental pathways are associated with different types of offending, with pathways to violent offending being different from those that lead to nonviolent offending. Rather than being fixed, these trajectories are attributable to varying causes that can change over the course of an offender's life (Loeber & LeBlanc, 1990).

Canter's essential position is that offenders are sufficiently specialized to allow the profiling of their crimes. It is true that if all offenders were generalists, the only distinction that might be made with a science of profiling would be that between offenders and nonoffenders. The extent to which offenders specialize, however, and the extent to which distinctions between types of offender specialization can be identified through profiling techniques, remains to be seen. By noting that offenders must specialize to some degree, Canter identified a necessary premise of profiling. Again, however, this is not a novel point in the larger context of criminology.

Violence as a Reflection of the Offender's Search for Intimacy and Power

If one breaks down the interpersonal-narratives theory to its basic assertion, one finds that Canter's core statement about the roles of offenders and victims is that violence reflects an offender's search for intimacy and power (Canter, 1994). Offenders may conceptualize intimacy in different ways, and may require different degrees of power, but, in essence, intimacy and power are the basic components of Canter's model of violence, as evidenced by his use of role themes reflecting these two dimensions.

This element of Canter's theory is perhaps the weakest because of its similarity to the artful profiling approaches described in previous chapters. The identification of power and intimacy as central components of violent offending is a feature that is consistent across all models of profiling discussed in this book. As discussed in previous chapters, the nonscientific models of profiling are replete with examples of typologies, theories, and arguments that discuss offenders' search for dominance over their victims and their general lifelong intimacy deficits. The way in which Canter places the themes of power and intimacy into a framework of victim role themes is discussed next, but it is important to first note that regardless of whether he is able to construct a new typology or set of dimensions to describe power and intimacy, this construction will merely be new packaging for an established, albeit unproven, set of ideas. It is ironic that, as discussed in chapter 4, Canter dismisses the use of psychoanalytic typologies as a theoretical link between offender actions and characteristics, without apparently noting the similarity of his emphasis on intimacy and power to those same typologies.

Victim–Offender Role Themes

Canter (1994) identified three roles that victims play in the minds of offenders: victim as object, victim as vehicle, and victim as person. In terms of theory-building, it is difficult from the outset to treat Canter's role themes as part of a novel scientific approach because, as just discussed, they derive from a fairly commonsensical and nonscientific premise. A further examination of the descriptions Canter provides of his role themes ultimately reveals the same imprecise and unsubstantiated distinctions attempted in weaker, nonscientific profiling models.

Canter uses the term *themes* to signify his departure from nonscientific models' use of types. He argues that there are no discrete dimensions in criminal behavior and that it is therefore misleading and problematic to construct typologies that contain distinct types or categories. Other than this preemptive acknowledgment that his role themes will contain just as much overlap as nonscientific offender typologies, Canter does not provide anything new or incrementally useful in his victim role themes. Canter's victim role themes are not substantially different from the categories of any other typology, and his caveat about overlapping dimensions effectively concedes this point. The result is that Canter's themes are flawed in the same manner as the nonscientific typologies discussed in chapters 2 and 3. The reader is referred to chapter 3 for a discussion of the particular criticisms of nonscientific typologies. In addition to the flaws that are inherent in using a typological framework, Canter's role themes are themselves problematic for two overarching reasons: lack of conceptual clarity and inclusion of untestable assertions.

Lack of Conceptual Clarity

Although conceptual clarity is an issue that has been discussed in the context of nonscientific models and their use of typologies, examining the conceptual clarity of Canter's themes is a worthy endeavor, for two reasons. First, as a scientific model of profiling, the Canter model should have its basic conceptual foundation clear and prepared for empirical study. To the extent that concepts within the model are imprecise, it will be difficult to later obtain valid results through empirical testing. Second, given that Canter's role themes are an integral part of his interpersonal-narratives theory, it is important to evaluate the themes as an indicator of the strength of his overall theory. If there are weaknesses in his themes, then the interpersonal-narratives theory also necessarily suffers.

Two aspects of conceptual clarity that have been previously addressed with regard to the nonscientific models are category overlap and a lack of clarity in specifying offender characteristics, which makes category placement difficult. Canter preemptively addresses these issues by arguing that boundaries between categories or dimensions in a typology are always bound to be fuzzy. It is therefore not surprising to find conceptual overlap between Canter's role themes. For example, for the victim-as-person role, Canter used the example of domestic killings. He described these as situations in which a tense relationship between two people escalates into a violent episode. In many instances, Canter (1994) asserted, it is an "accident of circumstance" (p. 358) that determines who becomes the victim and who becomes the offender. Although this example fits the victim-as-person role in the sense that the conflict is between two individuals, as opposed to between the offender and society in general, it would seem difficult to argue that there is a clearly defined role between victim and offender in a situation where an individual becomes a victim by "accident." Why could the victim not be viewed by the offender as an object or a vehicle in such a situation? Within the same role theme, Canter (1994) also described victim-as-person offenders as being driven in part by wrongs they believe to have been inflicted on them by women. Although the target of the resulting violent attack may be a specific woman, this description also appears to be consistent with a situation in which a victim is a representative of other women in the offender's life. Such a description would then fit with the victim-as-vehicle or the victim-as-object roles. Canter did not address how to determine which role theme fits best. Merely acknowledging that the lines between roles are not clear is not sufficient for a scientific approach to profiling. Developing a clear theory of profiling requires either that this problem be remedied or that one consider alternative approaches to examining offender characteristics and their relationship to interpersonal narratives. Canter's model does not accomplish this.

In addition to flaws in the conceptual clarity between Canter's role themes, there are conceptual problems within each theme. For example, when discussing the victim-as-object theme, Canter (1994) at one point stated that offenders may be of low intellectual ability but later claimed they may be more intelligent and manipulative. If such offenders can either be of low or high intelligence, it would not seem that intelligence is a characteristic that is useful to include for the purposes of defining a role theme and distinguishing it from other themes. In the same role theme, victim-as-object offenders are described as lacking contact with "most of normal human reality" (Canter, 1994, p. 345). They are unable to "distinguish thoughts from secret voices or fantasy from reality" (Canter, 1994, p. 345). However, Canter then distinguished these individuals from those who are psychotic, and he expressed reluctance in comparing them with individuals with schizophrenia or other psychoses. This is problematic because, according to the *Diagnostic and Statistical Manual of Mental Disorders* (American Psychiatric Association, 1994), the characteristics described by Canter are some of the hallmarks of a psychotic episode: "The term 'psychotic' refers to . . . a gross impairment in reality testing . . . delusions . . . hallucinations . . . disorganized or catatonic behavior" (American Psychiatric Association, 1994, p. 273). It seems that Canter is attempting to distinguish his offender themes from conventional descriptors of mentally disordered behavior, but as a result the constructs to which he is referring are unclear.

In discussing the victim-as-vehicle theme, Canter (1994) stated that some of these offenders are similar to psychopaths and claimed that they "know what the story of human relationships ought to be but this always appears to be a part they play, not a role with which they are at one" (p. 352). Later, however, he stated that key episodes, such as the loss of a relationship or death of a loved one, will fuel these offenders' "inner despair"

(p. 353) and trigger a violent episode. It would seem that in order for the loss of a relationship to have such an impact on an individual, that individual would need to have made some level of investment in the relationship that does not appear to be consistent with Canter's initial description of these offenders. How would an individual who only plays a part in relationships have a loved one in the first place, much less experience inner despair on the loved one's death?

In discussing the victim-as-person theme, Canter (1994) described some offenders as committing physical assaults in the course of a robbery or fraud, deciding that the victim can "easily provide them with some gain" (p. 359). In another example, Canter (1994) described the offender as stalking a victim in an effort to forge some personal relationship with her through an eventual sexual assault. These two examples seem to describe disparate types of relationships between offender and victim. In the first example, it is unclear how such a situation exemplifies the victim's significance to the offender as a person rather than a vehicle. The second example appears to be more consistent with the victim-as-person theme. Inconsistencies such as these limit the cohesiveness of Canter's role themes and detract from the clarity of his overall interpersonal-narratives theory.

Finally, the rationale for dividing each theme into high and low levels of desire for control is unclear. First, Canter addresses high and low levels of desire for control specifically only for the victim-as-object and victim-as-vehicle themes. He does not address level of desire for control in the victim-as-person theme. Because Canter also does not address the absence of the desire for control dimension in the victim-as-person theme, it is unclear whether the dimension is not applicable or whether he simply left it out for other reasons. Second, the use of the terms *high* and *low* is misleading. It is not the case that offenders who exhibit the high dimension are somehow more controlling then those in the low dimension. Instead, it appears that Canter uses the high-desire-for-control dimension to refer to physical control or aggression and the low-desire-for-control dimension to describe controlling a victim through manipulation or coercion. As a result, even examples of low desire for control contain descriptors that appear to the reader to be reflective of highly controlling behavior: "The victim has to be harnessed to the offender's will . . . they must be exploited" (Canter, 1994, p. 353). Third, Canter does not conceptually establish whether offenders have preferences for either physical or mental control over their victims or whether it is simply the case that offenders who are not socially and intellectually sophisticated enough to manipulate their victims must resort to using physical aggression to gain control over them. If the mechanism is offender preference, then it would seem that certain role themes might lend themselves to one type of desire for control or another. For example, there might be a relationship between perceiving a victim as an object and preferring the use of physical force as a method of control. In contrast, perceiving a victim as a person might incline someone to use social skills, manipulation, or coercion. If the mechanism is instead related to intellectual or social sophistication, then the role themes might actually be a redundant construct. Intelligent offenders could simply be expected to assess and interact with their victims as persons and manipulate them into vulnerable situations, whereas less intelligent offenders might simply grab a victim of opportunity and use physical force to subdue her.

Inclusion of Unverifiable Assertions

The second conceptual issue in Canter's role themes is that he includes assertions that are arguably unverifiable. For example, in regard to the victim-as-object theme, he stated that "Sexuality and . . . bizarre sexual acts dominate the personal narratives" of these offenders (Canter, 1994, p. 344). Even if personal narratives could be demonstrated to exist, how would one know what proportion of them is devoted to sexuality and bizarre sexual acts? Similarly, in discussing the victim-as-vehicle theme, Canter (1994) asserted that offenders use assaults to live out the sense of power and freedom that is absent in "the other stories they are forced to live" (p. 351). Statements such as these are not refutable, in the sense that investigators do not have access to the full array of inner thoughts of offenders. Even if offenders could be questioned after apprehension as to why they committed violent acts, it is not clear that scientists could even begin to ascertain the information necessary to prove or disprove such assertions. For example, could an offender speak insightfully about his own personal narrative? If an offender were in fact forced to live a story, would he be aware of it, and could he describe that story to social scientists?

Summary of Analysis of Canter's Theory

Canter incorporated several established principles and novel themes into his interpersonal-narratives theory that give the reader the initial impression of complexity and originality in the Canter model. On closer examination, however, two main flaws emerge. First, the portions of Canter's theory that are complex are not original. His discussion of concepts such as offender consistency, criminal generalization versus specialization, and the role of power and intimacy in violence already has a history in the psychology and criminology literature. Second, the portions of Canter's theory that are original lack complexity. As discussed, an evaluation of Canter's role themes and dimensions for level of desire for control lack rigor in their comprehensiveness and conceptual clarity. Even before considering Canter's testing of these theoretical elements, it is clear that building a science of profiling using such concepts will be difficult. Distinctions among themes are unclear, as Canter (1994) readily acknowledges, and even within themes there are insufficient distinctions made for the role themes to be of real utility.

HYPOTHESES GENERATION

A scientific model of profiling breaks its theoretical framework down into testable parts. As described previously, theories generate predictions that are tested with scientific methods. The testing of such hypotheses either lends support to the theory or provides disconfirming evidence. Whereas theories are generated somewhat freely and creatively, hypotheses are constrained in two ways. First, the kinds of hypotheses generated in a scientific model of profiling should be concrete and testable. For example, the prediction that offenders who commit murders are inherently evil is unlikely to be a testable hypothesis. Although this certainly depends on one's definition of *evil*, taken as it is, this prediction is neither sufficiently concrete to allow an investigator to precisely determine what is being predicted nor capable of being subjected to empirical testing, because it is too vague to allow the selection of methods and statistical tests. Second, a hypothesis must follow logically from the investigator's theoretical framework. Recall the profiling example discussed in the first section of this chapter. In this example, the guiding theory was that an offender's personality will manifest itself in the evidence left at a crime scene by means of his behaviors during the commission of the crime. According to such a theoretical framework, one would expect hypotheses to address such relationships as those among criminal behavior, evidence, and offender characteristics. One would not expect an investigator to generate hypotheses about offenders' unconscious conflicts or significant archetypes from this theoretical framework.

Hypotheses in the Canter Model

Within the Canter model, the generation of hypotheses is constrained by the lack of clarity in Canter's discussion of his theory of interpersonal narratives. Although Canter's hypotheses follow from his theoretical framework in a very basic sense, their utility is limited from the outset because they will necessarily reflect the ambiguity inherent in the theory they are designed to address. For example, consistent with his interpersonal-narratives theory, Canter advanced hypotheses to address offender consistency and offense specificity. In general, hypotheses related to offender consistency and offense specificity ask whether offenders act along consistent themes and whether these themes can be distinguished from those of other offenders.

To examine this empirically, Salfati and Canter (1999) proposed two specific hypotheses that address offender consistency and offense specificity. In their study of stranger murders, they proposed that (a) offenders will evidence themes in their homicide actions similar to those in their previous actions (offender consistency), and (b) there will be evidence of stylistic distinctions centered on thematic distinctions (offense specificity). Even without examining the results of this study, one can see the difficulty in obtaining clear and useful information. Both hypotheses incorporate Canter's interpersonal-narratives themes as part of the empirical question. On the basis of the previous discussion of these themes, it is therefore apparent from the outset that any information obtained from the posing of such hypotheses will only be as clear as the role themes themselves. The lack of conceptual clarity in the original theory therefore adversely affects the generation of hypotheses.

Likewise, Canter's hypothesized hierarchy of criminal behaviors addresses whether salient behaviors can be identified and later organized according to his offender themes. Once again, the inclusion of the offender themes introduces an element of ambiguity into the proposed analysis. For example, in their study of child sexual abuse, Canter, Hughes, and Kirby (1998) hypothesized that offense actions common across the set of child molestation cases will have a high frequency, whereas salient behaviors that distinguish among different types of child molestation offenses will have a lower frequency. Hypotheses related to examining offense actions and their frequency across child molestation cases are not necessarily problematic. However, the use of Canter's themes as a framework for organizing these more explicit hypotheses hinders the results by putting them into a context that lacks sufficient conceptual clarity.

Canter follows the methods of science in hypothesis generation to the extent that hypotheses should derive directly from one's theoretical framework. It is clear that Canter's research is a direct effort to test the concepts in his interpersonal-narratives theory. Unfortunately, because there is in fact a strong link between theory-building and hypothesis generation, Canter's hypotheses suffer from the flaws in his theory. In particular, the incorporation of the interpersonal-narratives role themes into hypothesis generation can only weaken subsequent empirical analyses because of the ambiguity and lack of conceptual cohesion in the themes themselves.

OPERATIONALIZATION AND SELECTION OF METHODS AND STATISTICS

A scientific model of profiling must operationalize its methods; that is, scientific models of profiling must clearly define and explain methods and put them into concrete terms that can be understood and replicated by other scientists. Furthermore, the selection of methods must follow logically from the theoretical framework and be appropriate for addressing the model's theories and hypotheses. There are three basic areas in which this type of operationalization is essential: use of terms, research methods for profiling, and methods for profiling practice.

Terms

As has been previously discussed, there is a lack of agreement in the profiling field about what the important terms are and how to define them. In nonscientific profiling models this has been an obstacle to conceptual clarity. For the purpose of constructing a scientific model, terms must be clearly identified and defined so that they will be understood by the reader and distinguishable from other concepts important to profiling. For example, an investigator may hypothesize that offenders who use a "con" approach to obtain victims are more intellectually sophisticated than offenders who surprise victims and physically overpower them. To operationalize this hypothesis, the investigator must define and explain the two types of offender approaches being considered (the con and the surprise) and distinguish them from each other. The investigator also must operationalize *intellectually sophisticated*. This term could refer to a high level of general intelligence, as measured by an IQ test; it could refer to verbal facility, as measured by IQ or other tests of verbal ability; or it could refer to sophistication gleaned from previous criminal experience, as measured by criminal record and improvement at evading capture over time.

With some exceptions, which are noted in the next paragraph, Canter is fairly clear in his use of terms. Although he often uses novel terminology, such as *behavioral salience* and *interpersonal narratives*, he provides definitions for these terms that are sufficient to allow the reader to understand them. For example, *behavioral salience* is defined as the important behavioral features of a crime that may help identify the perpetrator (Canter, 2000). In terms of research, behavioral salience is further operationalized as the location of an action at different distances from the center of the pattern of actions on a smallest space analysis (SSA) scatter plot.

However, there are two difficulties with Canter's terms. The first problem is that Canter does not draw a sufficient connection between his terms and the practical manifestations of these terms that would be useful to law enforcement investigators. For example, Canter's description of behavioral salience is clear enough to allow the reader to understand it conceptually and to navigate through the results of Canter's research. Indeed, the audience for his published works may largely consist of scientists and students of science, for whom Canter's definitions are likely to be sufficient. What is needed, however, is an additional step that relates terms such as *behavioral salience* to the pragmatics of crime investigation. What does it mean if a particular behavior is identified as salient? Does it make this behavior unique to an individual? Does it make the behavior a more important investigative focus than other elements of the crime? What is it about the behavior that makes it salient, and how will that be of use to investigators? An important part of Canter's profiling approach is his position that scientific profiling inquiries must provide information that is of use to law enforcement. Canter's model unfortunately fails to achieve this goal.

Second, although some of Canter's terms seem to represent concepts that are present in the nonscientific models of profiling, he makes no attempt to reference the other models' concepts or compare his terms with theirs. For example, what is the difference between the "thematic facets" described by Canter (2000) and the typological categories included in the nonscientific models? Likewise, is an interpersonal narrative fundamentally different from an offender motivation? In addition, Canter uses terms such as *modus operandi* and *signature*, but he does not discuss whether he agrees with other authors' definitions of these words (which are not uniform) or whether he has his own definitions. Without a clear explanation of terms that relates them to other terms being used in the field, it is difficult to determine to what extent Canter adds anything new to the study of profiling and to what extent he simply reworks existing concepts.

Research Methods for Profiling

Methods used in the scientific study of profiling must be clearly described, explained, and justified. Methods for data collection and analysis must be reported in such a manner as to allow studies to be replicated by other investigators. For example, investigators should describe in detail any questionnaires used; any instructions given to participants; and methods for data entry and analysis, including the kinds of statistical tests that were used and why they were chosen. Methods must also be justified in the sense that they must follow logically from the investigator's theoretical framework and must be usable in a manner that will address the hypotheses posed by the investigator. For example, one's theoretical framework of profiling might suggest that various cognitive aspects of offenders can be extrapolated from crime scene evidence. A resulting hypothesis might be that offenders who premeditate their offenses come prepared with weapons and other necessary materials and do not opportunistically use items that are native to the crime location. To address such a hypothesis, one might conduct offender interviews, review police reports and inventories of items found at the scene, and consider forensic analyses of weapon ownership and manner of use. One would not expect that an investigator would use such methods as projective personality tests, personality inventories, or other methods irrelevant to the theoretical framework.

It is in the area of research methods that the weaknesses in the theory and hypotheses of the Canter model are exemplified and the model begins to fundamentally lose coherence. Consistent with Canter's theoretical framework, the main focus of his empirical research centers around attempting to establish links between various offender actions and offender characteristics. To accomplish this, Canter and his colleagues (Canter & Fritzon, 1998; Canter & Heritage, 1990; Canter et al., 1998; Salfati & Canter, 1999) have conducted studies using SSA to evaluate data from cases of serial murder, arson, child sexual abuse, and rape. The goal of these studies has been to examine the spatial representation of crime actions or elements and evaluate them through the interpersonal-narratives perspective. Note that Canter and his colleagues have conducted other research in the profiling field. However, the four studies that are reviewed in this section are currently the only ones that pertain directly to testing the interpersonal-narratives theory. Some of Canter's other research on profiling is included in the next section of this book.

There are four main areas in which methodological problems with Canter's model are apparent: data sources, data coding, selection of SSA as an analytic tool, and evaluation of results.

Data Sources

First, the data sources used in these studies are problematic. Each of the aforementioned studies used archival data obtained from police agencies. In the cases involving serial murder and arson (Canter & Fritzon, 1998; Salfati & Canter, 1999), the data comprise information from solved cases. From these cases, the authors have selected variables relating to both the crime and the offender. Canter et al. (1998) used data from child sexual abuse incidents that were reported to police but not necessarily solved. Canter and Heritage's (1990) study does not specify whether the cases used were solved or unsolved; however, the data were collected exclusively from victim statements. The variables derived from these two cases (Canter et al., 1998; Canter & Heritage, 1990) therefore relate only to characteristics of the offenses and not to those of the offender. In all four studies, the use of police archives as a source of data is limited by four factors. First, the information in police records is not collected or stored for research purposes. It is therefore not possible to ensure that the information contained in these records has been collected according the standards that would be expected in a scientific study or that the data were collected according to any protocol prescribed by the studies' authors. When data are collected for research purposes, steps must be taken to minimize the influence of random variation and error in each case. These steps are not likely to have been taken by the police in their documentation of reported crimes.

Second, there is no way to ensure that the information collected is uniform across cases. Although variables such as demographic information about victims and offenders (if available) might be collected in every police report, other information is likely to vary across reports. Factors such as police experience, interview questions, victim memory of events, and witness availability could influence the comprehensiveness of individual reports. Consider the following example:

> A female victim is approached by a male purse snatcher on a busy metropolitan street late at night. This neighborhood is known for its heavy gang activity. She has just left her job at a convenience store, where she works the graveyard shift. It is the end of the month, and she has just received her paycheck. The offender approaches the victim, grabs her by the arm, and demands her purse. She struggles with him, has her purse ripped from her arm, and dislocates her shoulder.

In one scenario, the victim is interviewed by a veteran officer with several years of experience investigating similar types of crimes in the precinct where the robbery took place. In an alternative scenario, the victim reports the crime to an inexperienced officer who has just been transferred to the precinct from a rural area and happens to be on duty the night of the robbery. As one can imagine, the first officer's familiarity with the type of crime and environment in which the crime took place might lead him to ask very different questions of this victim. This officer might be concerned with such information as a physical description of the offender, whether he wore any items of clothing that signified membership in a particular gang, what the offender said when he approached the victim, and what property was taken. The second officer, with less experience with this type of crime and environment, might be more inclined to ask different questions— perhaps asking the victim about her injury, whether she recognized the offender, why she was walking down that street late at night, and why she did not comply with the attacker's demand to surrender her purse. The two police reports generated by these officers would therefore likely show qualitative differences in the accounts of the two crimes. They would differ in the amount, type, and comprehensiveness of information collected. This type of variation is problematic, because in the four reviewed studies the data were, in essence, collected by the police. As can be seen in this example, without appropriate controls and guidelines for data collection the potential for incomplete or inconsistent inclusion of crime actions is high.

Third, even if law enforcement agencies collected information reliably and consistently, this would still not solve the problem of the information's validity. In these four studies, there is no verification of the truth or accuracy of information contained in the police reports. This is particularly the case in the child sexual abuse study (Canter et al., 1998), because it used unsolved cases in which the crime events were not confirmed through the legal process. Accuracy of events may indeed be difficult for police and researchers to establish in violent crimes. Victims and witnesses may not remember every element of a traumatic incident, they might remember events incorrectly (Cutler & Penrod, 1995; Loftus, 1996), or their memories may be distorted by police interrogation (Bruck & Ceci, 1995). Even in solved cases, in which information about the offender is also available, there is still the risk that any information obtained from offenders (e.g., confessions, allocutions) will still be influenced by the offender's desire to avoid or minimize punishment. Dishonesty has historically been one of the hallmarks of criminality, and empirical research has demonstrated that particular types of offenders—namely, sexual offenders and psychopaths—are likely to deny, minimize, and otherwise lie about their offenses (Hare, Forth, & Hart, 1989; Laflen & Sturm, 1994; Rogers & Dickey, 1991). Although legal records may be the best available documentation of crime resolution, it is still difficult to rely on them for their accuracy in chronicling crime details.

The fourth issue pertains to the two studies that used solved cases: Canter and Fritzon (1998) and Salfati and Canter (1999). These solved cases involve offenders who have been apprehended using traditional law enforcement methods. These offenders may not share the same characteristics as those who are able to evade capture and whose cases might thus become the subject of profiling. Conclusions drawn about apprehended offenders are therefore difficult to generalize to the at-large criminal population. Solved cases admittedly may be the only ones in which both crime information and offender characteristics are available for simultaneous study. If a major goal of profiling research is to examine the relationship between crime characteristics and offender characteristics, the use of solved cases may currently be the only option. Nonetheless, this is a limitation that should be clearly stated in any research study that uses this type of data for the purposes of profiling.

Coding of Data

The second methodological problem in the Canter model is the coding of case evidence for research use. The variables selected for the reviewed studies are not a comprehensive reflection of the information contained in the police files. In each of the four studies, Canter and his colleagues have selected the variables thought to best reflect differences between the offender themes or types under investigation. So, for example, in Canter et al.'s (1998) study of child molesters, the variables selected were those that the authors believed would best reflect the intimate, aggressive, and criminal–opportunist types of child molesters. Variables unrelated to these types were not included in the analysis. Although this method of selecting variables does not necessarily detract from an effort to demonstrate that certain variables of interest cluster together into offender themes, it does result in a loss of what might be critical information. If these omitted variables were included in the analyses, other, more powerful relationships between criminal behaviors and offender types may have been revealed. Unfortunately, because none of the studies provides information about the proportion of case information comprising the variables of interest, it is unclear from the research how much information was lost.

Second, the selected variables were coded dichotomously according to their presence or absence in a given case. For example, in Canter et al.'s (1998) study of child molesters, one variable examined was "the offence was committed outdoors" (p. 555). For each of the 97 cases analyzed, this variable was coded as either present or absent. For some variables, this dichotomous coding system appears to be appropriate. For example, "the offender kissed the victim on the lips" and "the child was alone at the time of the offense" (Canter et al., 1998, p. 555) are variables that one could code with the appropriate case information as either "yes" or "no." However, the coding of other variables requires much more judgment. For example, the variable "desensitization (a.k.a. minimization) occurred" is described as

> the lowering of a child's threshold to sexual behaviour and can include the following: allowing the child to observe sexual behaviour taking place physically (e.g. between the offender and the child's mother, or between the offender and other younger children), or through pictures (i.e., pornographic magazines or video-cassettes), or by physically touching the child—making any indecent action appear as a legitimate mistake. (Canter et al., 1998, p. 554)

How is a coder to determine the simple presence or absence of this variable? How does the coder know whether the offender made an indecent action appear to be a mistake? Are there other forms of desensitization, such as discussing inappropriate sexual topics with young children, or telling sexually explicit stories, that are not included in the previous description? No guidelines for coding are included in Canter's studies, and no interrater reliability information is presented, making it difficult to determine whether these variables were indeed coded uniformly by individuals who might have had different interpretations of the case information. Finally, as is the case with Canter's selection of which variables to analyze, the dichotomous coding of these variables, even if it could be done reliably, necessarily results in a loss of information in situations in which there is no simple yes or no answer. Thus, with variables that are present in degrees, rather than in an all-or-nothing fashion, forcing information into the categories of "present" or "absent" means that potentially important information could be excluded or that trivial information could be included.

Selection of Smallest Space Analysis as an Analytic Tool

The third methodological issue is whether the selection of SSA is appropriate for addressing Canter's theory and hypotheses. Smallest space analysis is a statistical tool with which each variable of interest is correlated with every other variable of interest to produce a correlation matrix. Because Canter's variables are coded as dichotomous, he uses Jaccard's coefficient as a measure of association. These correlations are then rank-ordered and represented as points in a visual space (scatter plot), such that the higher the correlation between two variables, the closer they will appear on the SSA scatter plot.

There are three limitations to the selection of SSA. First, Canter uses SSA in both an exploratory and confirmatory manner. In three of the studies—Canter and Fritzon (1998), Canter and Heritage (1990), and Salfati and Canter (1999)—Canter conducted the SSA analysis on variables with no a priori prediction, to explore the themes that may emerge. This use of SSA appears to be quite limited. The technique itself does not partition the scatter plot into themes; this is instead accomplished by the researcher's visual examination of the data, which involves a significant amount of interpretation. In at least one study (Canter et al., 1998), Canter did have an a priori prediction of the clusters that are expected to emerge from the data, which is confirmed by his visual examination of the SSA scatter plot. In this case, the use of SSA to confirm the existence of themes could provide evidence in support of Canter's interpersonal-narratives theory, assuming that the variables and data are free from error. For example, if Canter can predict three clusters of child molester variables (Canter et al., 1998), and can specify in advance which variables will emerge together in clusters (e.g., a cluster containing "intimate" variables, such as affection, promises of gifts, and kissing), then this provides empirical support for the idea that there are three distinct clusters, or themes, of child-molesting behavior. Unfortunately, discerning why such themes emerge is beyond the scope of SSA. The importance of Canter's themes as providing a link between offender actions and offender characteristics is therefore not adequately addressed by this statistic.

Second, because SSA is a nonmetric statistical tool, it does not provide any information about the strength of the associations between variables in a given cluster. By examining an SSA scatter plot it is possible to make the general determination that some variables are more associated than others; however, it is not possible to determine how associated two variables are. It is unclear why Canter and his colleagues have not incorporated the use of factor analysis to remedy this problem. By computing factor loadings for each variable in each of the offender themes, the authors could not only determine which variables are central to the theme of interest but could also compute the degree to which other variables in the cluster are associated with that theme. The selection of factor analysis over SSA would seem to provide more meaningful analyses in this regard.

Third, SSA is inadequate for determining how well crime variables predict offender characteristics—which is the crux of Canter's profiling equation. Even in cases in which offender characteristics are considered along with offense actions (Canter & Fritzon, 1998; Salfati & Canter, 1999), the use of SSA does not address the predictive power of the offender themes. Canter and Fritzon (1998) strived to compensate for this problem by using Spearman's ρ to calculate the correlations between themes of offense actions (A) and themes of offender characteristics (C). There are two difficulties with using such an approach. First, the attempt to correlate these various themes presupposes that there are legitimate theme groups to compare. The authors' calculations of Cronbach's α for each group, ranging from .38 to .83, already hint that the success of such an endeavor will be limited. Second, the selection of a correlational method to evaluate these data does not speak to the predictive power of the model. Even if the correlations were to emerge as expected (which was not entirely the case in Canter & Fritzon's [1998] study), this provides only a limited amount of information about the tendency of certain offense variables to co-occur with certain offender characteristics. It does not allow one to infer that offense actions were the result of certain aspects of the offender's background. The selection of a correlational measure may contribute to outlining a basic framework of offender themes, but it is not adequate for assessing the role of interpersonal-narratives as a link between A and C variables.

Interpretation of Results

The fourth methodological problem is the Canter model's interpretation of results provided by the application of SSA to the data. There are three main ways in which this interpretation is problematic. The first problem is the interpretation of SSA data from a two-dimensional perspective. The visual space of an SSA scatter plot is not always best represented in two dimensions. To determine the best representation of the data, one calculates a Guttman–Lingoes' coefficient of alienation. The smaller the coefficient of alienation, the better the fit of the scatter plot to the original matrix of correlations. Although the coefficients of alienation in Canter's research range from .13 (Canter & Fritzon, 1998) to .30 (Canter & Heritage, 1990), Canter always represents his data in a two-dimensional space. In a separate study, in which a coefficient of alienation of .30 was obtained (Godwin & Canter, 1997), the authors characterized this number as "a little high, indicating that the original matrix . . . may require more than two dimensions to represent all their nuances" (Godwin & Canter, 1997, p. 31). Nonetheless, the authors display and interpret the data in two dimensions, citing "simplicity and clarity" (Godwin & Canter, 1997, p. 31). In Canter and Heritage's (1990) study of rapes, the two-dimensional space is also chosen for the sake of "simplicity" (p. 195), despite its higher coefficient of alienation (.30 vs. .22 for three dimensions). It is not clear how much the visual scatter plot is altered by forcing the data into two dimensions, but using two dimensions in cases in which such a representation is not the best fit weakens the foundation for any subsequent interpretation of results.

Second, in the studies that contain no a priori hypotheses about variables that should cluster together, there is insufficient evidence to support Canter's assertion that offender actions correspond to the hypothesized offender themes. Although SSA presents a spatial representation of characteristics that are likely to co-occur, Canter's imposition of offender themes on the SSA scatter plot is not always supported by this analysis.

For example, consider the SSA scatter plot depicted in Figure 5.1. This figure is an example of the type of spatial representation that would result from an SSA analysis; it is taken from Salfati and Canter (1999). This figure has been altered such that the lines inserted by the authors to distinguish between offender themes have been removed. As can be seen, the data points are labeled according to their corresponding crime features. Certain clusters in the data arguably are apparent in a visual examination. Consider the various options for where lines might be drawn to distinguish among these clusters.

Figure 5.2 is the same SSA scatter plot, with lines drawn by the original authors to distinguish among the Instrumental Opportunistic, Expressive Impulsive, and Instrumental Cognitive offender themes (Salfati & Canter, 1999). As can be seen from the positions of the variables, an Instrumental Cognitive offender might be likely to commit the acts within the boundaries of that offender theme—such as striking the victim in the head, transporting her, hiding the body, and placing the body face up. However, a closer examination of the SSA scatter plot leads to several questions: Why are "property not id," "face up," and "outside" included in the Instrumental Cognitive category rather than the Expressive Impulsive category? What is the justification for including "sexual" and "part undr." in the Instrumental Opportunistic category rather than a separate, fourth category? It appears that the decision to distinguish among these three themes is based not solely on the data but on differences that the authors perceive to be valid. Indeed, the authors wrote that "any variables that fell in between two regions were allocated to the region whose theme is best reflected" (Salfati & Canter,

Figure 5.1. Homicide crime scene scatterplot. From "Differentiating Stranger Murders: Profiling Offender Characteristics From Behavioral Styles," by C. G. Salfati and D. Canter, 1999, *Journal of Behavioral Sciences and the Law, 17*, p. 400. Copyright 1999 by John Wiley and Sons, Ltd. Adapted with permission.

1999, p. 401). Therefore, it might easily be the case that a victim who was attacked outside was victimized by an Expressive Impulsive offender rather than the Instrumental Cognitive offender to whom this variable is attributed. Salfati and Canter (1999) did not provide sufficient evidence that their interpretation is the correct one.

Third, as discussed earlier, the use of SSA is not adequate for establishing an explanatory relationship between offender actions and their corresponding clusters, or between offender actions and offender characteristics. Recall that in the Canter model the interpersonal-narratives theory is posited as providing an explanatory link between the two halves of the canonical profiling equation. Unfortunately, an SSA analysis does not provide such a link. Canter's model interprets the clustering of data points as being

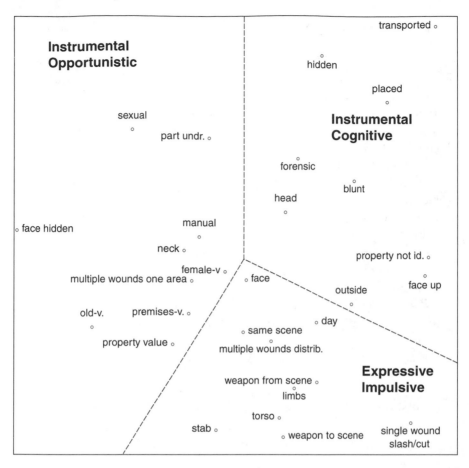

Figure 5.2. Homicide crime scene themes. From "Differentiating Stranger Murders: Profiling Offender Characteristics From Behavioral Styles," by C. G. Salfati and D. Canter, 1999, *Journal of Behavioral Sciences and the Law, 17*, p. 400. Copyright 1999 by John Wiley and Sons, Ltd. Reprinted with permission.

explained by their correspondence to offender themes; that is, Canter posits that particular data points cluster together because they represent the hypothesized thematic facet. For example, re-dressing a victim and releasing a victim would be thought to cluster together because they both represent the offender's concern for the victim as a person. At best, it could be said that these variables correspond to some underlying factor. Unfortunately, as previously discussed, there is insufficient evidence not only to unequivocally establish that these two data points belong to the same offender theme but also to establish that these data points co-occur as the result of the offender role theme specified by the model. The use of SSA to support the explanatory role of interpersonal narratives as a link between offender actions and characteristics is therefore flawed.

Methods for Profilers in Practice

In discussing profiling, it is vital that scientific models explain exactly what profilers are doing in the conduct of their work. One of the limitations discussed in the nonscientific models of profiling is that none of the models explains how to profile. This must be remedied in any scientific model of profiling, for two reasons. First, without a clear description of profiling procedures there is no way to ensure that profiling is being conducted and measured reliably across profilers. On a related note, without clear procedures there is no way to ensure that an individual profiler will produce similar profiles from the same data on separate occasions. Second, a description of profiling procedures makes it possible to examine what is being done in profiling. Without such a description, the process by which investigators go from evidence to conclusions about offender characteristics remains a mystery. The clear description of procedures ensures that a valid phenomenon is being measured.

To accomplish this, each step in the profiling process must be described. In this description, the following points must be addressed.

- *Evidence and information.* What are the important pieces of evidence and information that should be collected for profiling? How does an investigator decide which data are important to consider? How is this information gathered? By whom is the evidence gathered? For example, if the victim is deceased, a victim history may be one of the pieces of information that should be collected. How does an investigator decide whether a victim history is necessary? How is this history ascertained (e.g., through interviews, documents, etc.)? Who gathers this evidence—does the investigator rely on the information provided by law enforcement, or should he or she actually go and procure this information independent of law enforcement agents?

- *Interpretation of evidence.* How does an investigator interpret evidence to determine such things as the sequence of events at a crime scene, the nature of violent or sexual acts committed, the presence of staging, the theft of souvenirs or trophies, or premeditation? Is this interpretation assisted by evaluations conducted by forensic scientists? If so, how does an investigator use this information to interpret evidence? For example, a given crime scene might contain a deceased victim with a bullet wound, no weapon present, and jewelry and electronics missing (per the neighbor's report of items missing). At face value, this appears to be a burglary that resulted in the shooting of the homeowner, but how does an investigator officially arrive at such a conclusion? How does the evidence inform the investigator about what happened at the crime scene? Does the investigator consult a coroner's report? Will such information determine for the investigator whether the shooting was premeditated or impulsive? How does the investigator determine whether the missing items were stolen for their value or whether they were taken to make the shooting look like part of a burglary?

- *Determining offender characteristics*. Once an investigator has collected and interpreted the evidence, how does he or she determine various offender characteristics? Are there certain relationships between evidence and characteristics that can be relied on in practice, such that the presence of a certain kind of evidence indicates a particular offender characteristic? How does one determine which offender characteristics are important to the investigation of the crime?

Generally speaking, the Canter model does not devote any significant time to describing profiling practice. Given Canter's focus on empirical research rather than investigative experience as a tool for crime-solving, it is not surprising that his model prescribes neither methods for evidence collection nor methods for the interpretation of that evidence. The starting point of the Canter model therefore assumes that the relevant facts, including the interpretation of evidence that would yield such information as cause of death, order of events, and weapons used, are accurate and available. Although this choice may represent a legitimate philosophical difference between a professionally based nonscientific approach and a scientific one, it would nonetheless be worthwhile to the reader and, ultimately, to investigators, if Canter's model were to provide a basic discussion of the kinds of evidence used in profiling practice; the quality, accuracy, and source of any interpretations that may be made about the evidence; and the importance of complete and accurate evidence for hypothesis testing. As discussed in the previous section, the quality of the data, hampered by potential inconsistencies in the collection of evidence and information across cases, is one obstacle to Canter's empirical study of profiling. It would therefore be worthwhile to discuss ways to address this limitation in the context of profiling practice.

The more conspicuous absence in methods of profiling practice is Canter's failure to clearly explain methods or procedures for transforming the findings of his empirical studies into offender characteristics that will be of use to investigators. The canonical equation that Canter uses to demonstrate his fundamental profiling question requires that offender characteristics be discernable from offender actions. In building his model of profiling, Canter comprehensively addresses the first half of this equation.

His hypotheses of behavior salience, offender consistency, and offense specificity and his hierarchy of criminal actions are all examples of his willingness to thoroughly evaluate offender actions from a variety of perspectives. However, Canter does not adequately address the second half of his canonical equation: producing offender characteristics that law enforcement agents can use in identifying perpetrators. In considering the link between offender actions and characteristics, what Canter does offer is his theory of interpersonal narratives. To illustrate, he includes a description of the victim role themes that are derived from this theory. This discussion of victim role themes includes the various offender characteristics that are thought to be associated with each theme. Unfortunately, Canter derives these offender characteristics on the basis of a theory and has yet to provide sufficient information as to how to arrive at these offender characteristics from a real set of criminal actions. This presumably is achieved through some unspecified application of the interpersonal-narratives theory, but Canter provides no procedures to explain how this operates in practice. Therefore, despite Canter's framing of the profiling question as an equation linking offender actions to offender characteristics, Canter does not provide sufficient procedures for the completion of such an equation in practice.

It may be that Canter provides no procedures for deriving offender characteristics from actions in practice because these procedures have not yet been adequately developed and verified. Canter certainly cannot be faulted for not having all of the answers in a model that is relatively new. However, if there are as yet no reliable ways to reason from actions to characteristics in an investigation, this must be clearly expressed in the model. Otherwise, Canter's description of offender characteristics through the victim role themes makes it appear that Canter has conceptually leapt to the end of the profiling equation without explaining to the reader how he arrived there.

EMPIRICAL VALIDATION

In a scientific model, once hypotheses are specified, and terms and methods of testing and practice are operationalized, researchers can proceed to the actual testing of hypotheses generated by the model's theory. The goal of this process is to demonstrate that the overall model and theoretical framework can truly accomplish what it claims (e.g., prediction of offender characteristics).

There are two main ways in which scientific profiling models must be empirically validated. The first is with regard to outcome. The essential question of outcome is, Does profiling work? The manner in which this question is addressed may vary according to different models. For example, one way to address outcome would be to ask whether profiling techniques are helpful in generating leads and ideas in a cold investigation. Another way to address outcome would be to determine whether predictable relationships can be demonstrated between certain types of crime scene evidence and certain offender characteristics. Still another way to address outcome would be to ask whether the overall process of profiling (as defined by an individual model) is more likely to produce an offender arrest than traditional law enforcement methods.

The second manner in which scientific profiling models must be empirically validated is with regard to process. The essential question of process is, How does profiling work? Here, a scientific model must evaluate whether profiling operates according to the processes that one would expect. For example, one fundamental question to consider is, What do profilers actually do? Researchers could examine whether investigators trained in profiling techniques attend to and process crime scene information differently than do untrained investigators or laypersons. Researchers could also examine the reasoning and decision-making processes that profilers apply when analyzing a case.

The process of empirical validation, by addressing outcome and process, will yield information that can be used to evaluate the model's theoretical framework. This represents a significant departure from the nonscientific models of profiling in that it presents an opportunity for critically evaluating one's profiling model.

The Canter model is still evolving, and it is therefore too early to judge whether it will ultimately survive the empirical validation process. However, general evaluative observations are possible.

For the Canter model, the question of outcome is addressed by the canonical profiling equation. Thus, the question, Does profiling work? is operationalized by asking whether offender characteristics (C) can reliably and validly be determined from offense actions (A). The studies that have been reviewed in this section have provided some early, albeit limited, evidence that patterns can indeed be found in the actions and characteristics of offenders across different cases of a crime type. This represents a significant improvement over the efforts of nonscientific profiling models, which have not evaluated this assumption in a systematic fashion. However, what Canter's model has not yet demonstrated is that offender characteristics can be reliably and validly deduced by considering these offense actions either singularly or in their patterns. This is the fundamental issue that must be resolved before the Canter model can claim empirical validation with regard to outcome. Furthermore, none of the research reviewed has addressed whether any of Canter and colleagues' findings can successfully be applied to real, unsolved cases. The question of outcome is therefore unanswered for profiling effectiveness as well as efficacy.

The issue of process validation is also addressed by the canonical profiling equation. As stated earlier, the question for the profiling process is, How can offender characteristics be derived from offender actions? In this regard, the issue is whether Canter's interpersonal-narratives theory provides the link that allows C variables to be predicted from A variables. Canter's hypothesized process is that a consideration of the roles that victims and other individuals play in the offender's interactions should allow the determination of C variables from A variables. What the Canter model has accomplished in this regard is to provide some evidence for the existence of offender themes, based on crime actions. It is not yet clear that the groups that have emerged from studies using SSA are best defined as themes of interpersonal narratives, but establishing the existence of themes is a first step to providing the explanatory link between A and C. Unfortunately, there is as yet insufficient support to assert that this process is empirically valid. More research is needed to establish the mechanisms involved in the canonical profiling equation and whether those mechanisms can produce successful predictions about offenders.

CONSIDERATION OF DISCONFIRMING EVIDENCE

Through the process of hypothesis-testing, scientific models may have elements of their underlying theories contradicted. For example, offenders who inflict multiple superficial wounds on living, conscious victims might be found to have sadistic personalities in only one fourth of the cases in a particular study. Although disappointing for the investigator whose theory has just been challenged, this information is still important and can be used to reconsider hypotheses about the relationship between sadistic personalities and crime scene variables.

This opportunity is one of the most important distinctions between scientific and nonscientific profiling models. In nonscientific models there is no hypothesis testing or systematic evaluation of assumptions. Because of this, nonscientific profiling models are insulated from being contradicted. Where nonscientific profiling practice fails to confirm an expected relationship or phenomenon, nonscientific profilers might be inclined to treat the result as a simple anomaly, because no information would be available to indicate otherwise. However, although the failure to identify and consider disconfirming evidence can protect fragile theories, it also prevents the field from learning anything new. The scientific search for knowledge requires that one will occasionally be wrong. Where science departs from nonscience is in the fundamental belief that the possibility of being wrong cannot prevent one from asking the questions important to the field. Without the consideration of disconfirming evidence, it is not possible to evaluate a model's veracity and move toward improving it.

A concern that arises as Canter and colleagues continue to test the various elements of the Canter model is their treatment of data that do not fit with expectations. There are several instances in which the authors note disconfirming or ambiguous evidence but, rather than evaluating the impact of this evidence on the model, treat the evidence as anomalous and create an explanation to make it consistent with the model. For example, in discussing correlations between scales of actions and characteristics of arsonists, Canter and Fritzon (1998) noted a "bias in the relationships found in the current data set" (p. 89). Despite this mention, however, the authors go on to assert that "this system of correlations . . . provides strong support" for their hypotheses (p. 90). A second example is the Canter model's treatment of variables that appear on the SSA scatter plot in unexpected regions. In Salfati and Canter's (1999) study, variables with ambiguous placement are simply moved into categories in a way that the authors believe to make sense. In Canter and Heritage's (1990) study of rape, explanations are created for the appearance of variables in unexpected places. The appearance of a variable indicating that the offender implies knowing the victim in the "impersonal interaction" category is handled as follows: "This is difficult to interpret at this stage, but possibly implies that the offender had prior knowledge of the victim, having identified her as a desirable object" (Canter & Heritage, 1990, p. 200). Likewise, high coefficients of alienation for the SSA scatter plots do not deter the authors from representing the data in a two-dimensional space (Canter & Heritage, 1990; Godwin & Canter, 1997), and analyses are carried out on data that are characterized as "potentially unreliable" (Canter & Fritzon, 1998, p. 77). Taken together, these examples are indicative of a practice whereby information that does not fit with the goals or conclusions of the Canter model is either disregarded or made to fit—a practice reminiscent of the tactics used by nonscientific profiling models. Although Canter notes that the information with which profiling researchers have to work is constrained, it is still necessary to conduct a scientific study of profiling as rigorously as possible. It is not expected that every hypothesis will be confirmed or that every criminal phenomenon can be explained with the tools scientists currently have at their disposal. What is required, however, is an appropriate consideration of all evidence in an empirical study, even in the early exploratory stages of a model such as this.

DISCUSSION OF LIMITATIONS

The final element of a scientific model of profiling is the discussion of limitations. Through the process of empirical validation, investigators become aware of their models' limitations. This is because, as previously discussed, even though the scientific testing of hypotheses may yield data that support a model, this process is also likely to provide an investigator with information that requires modification of the original theoretical framework. From a conceptual standpoint, limitations should be discussed to give direction to future research. If one part of a theory does not find support in an empirical study, perhaps researchers can move in a more fruitful direction. If certain conditions of a study limit the generalizability of the results, this information can be used to improve the conditions of future studies. Moreover, discussing limitations is a way to address the results of an individual study in a broader context. By doing so, authors can address whether a theory has found support, discuss why the results may have turned out as they did, and think creatively about how to improve the theory and test it in the future. From a more practical standpoint, limitations should be discussed so that the scope of a model's explanatory power is made clear for use in the field. Scientific investigators must not go beyond this scope in applying profiling methods to real-world cases. For example, a series of studies might demonstrate that in cases of female sexual assault–homicide victims, the covering of the victim's face by a male offender indicates offender remorse. Even if such a study could be replicated numerous times and determined to be wholly valid, this application of this finding would be limited to cases involving female victims and male offenders in the type of scenario described. It would not be appropriate for one to draw similar conclusions about male victims, female perpetrators, or other types of crimes.

Some nonscientific models discuss limitations to their approaches. Turvey (1999), for example, cautioned readers that the categories in his behavior–motivational typology contain some overlap, limiting the degree to which an offender can be clearly assigned to only one category. Likewise, Holmes and Holmes (1996) cited limitations to the computer models of profiling discussed in their book. However, the difference between nonscientific and scientific models of profiling is that nonscientific models, rather than using these limitations to draw boundaries around the applications of these methods, promote the use of intuition or professional knowledge to compensate for what cannot be scientifically demonstrated. Thus, where the behavior–motivational typology cannot accurately be relied on to classify an individual, a profiler, according to Turvey, should use his or her professional expertise to make such a determination. Holmes and Holmes (1996) similarly retreated into the use of intuition when their logical or science-related explanations were insufficient. In a scientific model of profiling, the application of profiling methods should be constrained by the limits of those methods.

Canter is one of the only profiling authors to have discussed the limitations of the profiling endeavor as a whole. The disparity between the current limits of profiling techniques and the claims that are made by profilers about their effectiveness are discussed in the *Offender Profiling* series (Alison & Canter, 1999a). Alison and Canter (1999a) argued therein that psychologists should refrain from purporting to provide expertise in an area that is not yet empirically supported. Although Alison and Canter's (1999a) cautions are laudable, theirs is an ironic position to take because Canter has used his model for aiding in police investigations, knowing that it is not yet empirically validated.

To their credit, Canter et al. (1998) characterized their research as a "first step" (p. 550) and encouraged future research to clarify gaps in Canter's studies. In the individual studies conducted by Canter and his colleagues, however, significant time is not devoted to a discussion of limitations (Canter & Fritzon, 1998; Canter & Heritage, 1990; Canter et al., 1998; Salfati & Canter, 1999). Given the instances of potentially disconfirming evidence previously discussed, it would be preferable for the authors to more formally address limitations to data sources, analytic tools, conclusions, and practical applications.

DISCUSSION OF THE CANTER MODEL AS A SCIENTIFIC MODEL OF PROFILING

There are two main strengths evident in Canter's approach to profiling. First, it is to his credit that he has advocated for a science of profiling, having identified several problems with the current art of profiling as conducted by the FBI and other independent profilers. In many ways, Canter's criticisms are consistent with the evaluation of nonscientific profiling models presented in this book. Profiling without science amounts to guesswork, and attempts to create structure within nonscientific profiling models have resulted only in vague categories and procedures that lack coherence, comprehensiveness, and utility. Canter has recognized that science is needed both to anchor and to evaluate profiling. He has identified novel methods to empirically test investigative inferences, and he has considered scientific bases for organizing crime actions and offender characteristics.

Second, Canter has attempted to place profiling within a theoretical framework of criminal behavior, which provides a rationale for profiling and creates the possibility of inferring an offender's characteristics from his actions. This rationale is not present in the nonscientific models, which instead take for granted that offender behavior reflects personality without considering a foundation for why this might be the case. The result is that nonscientific models rely on either vague pieces of psychoanalytic theory or completely atheoretical conjecture.

Despite these strengths, there are also several limitations to Canter's model, which are described in this chapter. These include conceptual weaknesses in his theory, resulting limits to hypothesis generation, problematic data selection, coding, application of methods, interpretation of results, and an absence of procedures to transform the model into a practical investigative tool. There is one other conceptual problem with the Canter model that emerges when one compares his model with the nonscientific models of profiling. Although Canter criticizes the use of typologies, he actually does not solve the problems inherent in typologies with his offender themes. Canter attempts to draw some distinctions between offender themes and the typologies of other profiling models by describing the themes as flexible and overlapping. As discussed, however, the reality of behavioral typologies is that they always contain general categories that overlap in practice. Thus, similar to the other reviewed models, the Canter model presents descriptions of various kinds of offenders, dividing them according to the roles that they assign their victims. Although Canter includes the caveat of category flexibility, his themes ultimately amount to yet another kind of offender typology, fraught with the same problem of category overlap.

Canter's attempt to bring science to profiling is laudable, but it is clear from the review in this chapter that there is still considerable room for improving his model. Despite Canter's stated commitment to science, he periodically steps outside the bounds of science by failing to critically consider the impact of each of his empirical findings on his theory and by proposing offender themes that parallel the nonscientific typologies of weaker profiling models. The basic profiling problem, as described by Canter, is that of linking offender actions during the commission of a crime to behavioral characteristics that will help to identify the offender. Unfortunately, Canter has not yet provided such a link through his research.

USE OF SCIENCE BY NONSCIENTIFIC PROFILING MODELS

Now that the tenets of science have been examined, and Canter's scientific model of profiling has been analyzed in the context of these tenets, it is worthwhile to revisit the use of science in the nonscientific profiling models, discussed in chapters 2 and 3. In chapter 3, these nonscientific models were critically evaluated from outside a scientific framework, given that their authors largely portray them as artful models of profiling. Nonetheless, because there are instances in which all of the models invoke science in support of their various claims, it is still important to briefly examine the models' relationship with science to determine whether any of the criteria have been satisfied that distinguish scientific from nonscientific models of profiling. Such an examination shows that two of the models contain no science whatsoever, and the other three models contain fragments of science insufficient to support their claims.

Models With No Science

The Turco (1990) and Holmes and Holmes (1996) models are completely devoid of science. Turco, in advocating for a psychoanalytic approach to profiling, likens part of his profiling process to a Rorschach test. Projective tests have historically been controversial, and a recent meta-analytic review of projective techniques published in *Psychological Science in the Public Interest* (Lilienfeld, Wood, & Garb, 2000) led the authors to conclude that experts "should not be allowed to state or imply that projective techniques are widely accepted by the scientific community" (Lilienfeld et al., 2000, p. 57). As described by Turco, the first dimension of his model is essentially a projective technique—and is thus not accepted as scientific by the scientific community. In addition, the fourth dimension of Turco's model incorporates the term *science* in a conceptually confusing manner. Turco (1990) characterized the psychoanalytic profiler as using a scientific approach but then emphasized the importance of clinical training over academic training. His conception of science seems to be limited to procedures that have some theoretical basis, regardless of the validity of that theoretical basis. He further implied that accurate predictions cannot be made in the absence of clinical training, but he provided no evidence to support this assertion. Turco did not demonstrate that accurate predictions can be made at all, much less that clinical intuition is the cornerstone to accuracy.

It is interesting to note that the fact that the Turco (1990) model is bereft of science does not prevent the author from criticizing Douglas, Ressler, Burgess, and Hartman's (1986) model as lacking a scientific basis:

> The . . . shortcoming is that there is *no real theoretical basis* for these descriptions, therefore no scientific basis for building future information, integrating theories from various disciplines consistent with observable data in the scientific approach and allowing a higher degree of predictive value. Lacking hypotheses, testing and theory development, science is difficult to take root. A random application of factual information has little place in the scientific approach. (Turco, 1990, p. 149, italics in original)

As is discussed shortly, the Douglas et al. (1986) model actually does incorporate some pieces of basic scientific principles. Turco, despite his scientific language, does not use a scientific approach in his model.

From the outset, Holmes and Holmes (1996) described profiling as an art rather than a science. In keeping with this position, the authors ultimately discarded the idea of practicing profiling on the basis of science even though they periodically refer to science to support some of their assertions. In referring to science, the authors stated that "As certainly as a psychometric test reflects psychopathology, the crime scene reflects a personality with a pathology" (Holmes & Holmes, 1996, p. 40). They also cited research findings on rape and rapists and relied on statistics in their discussion of arsonists, pausing to criticize what they believe to be flaws in the U.S. Department of Justice's data collection methods. Unfortunately, none of these references serves to add any science to the model itself.

For the most part, Holmes and Holmes (1996) recommended using psychodynamic theories—a practice that maximizes the use of intuitive judgment. One of the basic tenets of the psychodynamic approach is the interpretation of information presented by the subject or client. This interpretation is necessary because individuals are believed to be motivated by unconscious conflicts. Because these individuals are unaware of their own unconscious motivations, the role of the psychoanalyst is to bring these conflicts or motives to the surface through interpretation of that person's thoughts and actions. However, because the nature of unconscious processes renders them unavailable for direct or objective observation, any use of psychodynamic theory thus requires a certain degree of subjective judgment. Not only does this limit the value of this approach as per the earlier discussion on the use of intuition, it also results in a lack of scientific rigor. Therefore, although Holmes and Holmes (1996) may liken their profiling approach to a science, or refer to the scientific work of others, their model also contains no science.

Models With Insufficient Science

Three of the nonscientific models reviewed (Douglas et al., 1986; Keppel & Walter, 1999; Turvey, 1999) do in fact contain various scientific elements. It is unfortunate that, despite the steps that these authors take toward science, profiling, as described by these models, is not scientific.

The Douglas et al. (1986) model evidences certain strengths in terms of the comprehensiveness of the authors' recommendations for data collection and the attempt to carve out trends in analyzing evidence through a behavioral lens (e.g., analyzing the positions of bodies and discarded weapons to evaluate the sequence of offender actions and degree of offender organization). By attempting to add structure to the art of profiling, the authors take a first step toward science. Unfortunately, as discussed in chapter 3, the classification categories and procedures are poorly defined, and the resulting profile is therefore imbued with guesses. Furthermore, because FBI profilers are explicitly trained not to put profiles in writing (Hazelwood & Burgess, 2001), the extent to which profiles can be systematically or scientifically reviewed is also limited.

Douglas and his colleagues have attempted to add a scientific component to their investigative practice primarily by collecting and interpreting evidence through interviews conducted as part of the Criminal Personality Research Project, discussed in chapter 1. In subsequent publications (Burgess, Douglas, & Burgess, 1997; Burgess, Hartman, Ressler, Douglas, & McCormack, 1986; Ressler, Burgess, Douglas, Hartman, & D'Agostino, 1986; Ressler, Burgess, Hartman, Douglas, & McCormack, 1986), the authors conducted descriptive studies of the data collected in these interviews. For example, they evaluated background characteristics of 36 sexual murderers to propose a motivational model of sexual homicide (Burgess et al., 1986). The authors also evaluated these same 36 sexual murderers to assess differences between those who had a history of sexual abuse and those who did not (Ressler, Burgess, Hartman, et al., 1986), and they evaluated differences between organized and disorganized offenders in the same sample (Ressler, Burgess, Douglas, et al., 1986). The culmination of their research was an attempt to bring science to the art of profiling in the form of a taxonomy modeled after the *Diagnostic and Statistical Manual of Mental Disorders* (4th ed., text rev.; American Psychiatric Association, 2000), the *Crime Classification Manual* (Douglas, Burgess, Burgess, & Ressler, 1992), and a motivational model described in *Sexual Homicide: Patterns and Motives* (Ressler, Burgess, & Douglas, 1988).

Conducting structured interviews is, unfortunately, not science per se. Organizing descriptive information into a taxonomy is not, in itself, scientific. Likewise, making untested and arguably untestable propositions about the internal motivations of sexual murderers from a sample of 36 individuals is not scientific. Certainly, there are opportunities for science in the Douglas et al. (1986) model. For example, with adequate data, researchers could study the accuracy of profiles produced using the Douglas et al. (1986) model and could systematically evaluate the components of both the *Crime Classification Manual* (Douglas et al., 1992) and the authors' motivational model of sexual homicide. However, as discussed in this chapter, such an endeavor would require adherence to the various components of scientific inquiry. The influence of science in Douglas et al.'s (1986) model is limited to the authors' primitive attempts to impose organization on an artful practice, and the authors do not adhere to even one of these scientific components.

A similar problem is presented by the Turvey (1999) model. Like Douglas et al. (1986), Turvey very comprehensively described the kinds of evidence to be collected. He went even further, to explicitly advocate for reliance on physical evidence over intuition. However, as discussed in chapter 3, the most important conclusions regarding offender characteristics and the relationship between evidence and offender personality ultimately are left to nonscientific professional expertise. These conclusions are therefore not scientific, and Turvey's advocacy for a reliance on scientific evidence (e.g., blood spatters, medical reports) becomes meaningless, because intuition is ultimately used in the synthesis of that evidence.

Keppel and Walter (1999) took a portion of the Douglas et al. (1986) model and unsuccessfully attempted to bring science to a rape–murder typology by improving the clarity of the typological categories. Within the typology, the authors made an effort to operationalize profile characteristics by including physical characteristics of offenders and fairly detailed behavior patterns. Their criticism of other typologies is that although

> typologies of murderers have descriptive value, they have failed to provide investigators with the elements necessary for crime scene assessment . . . Although general indicators may apply to a myriad of circumstances, the static descriptors of these types of classification systems only address the obvious. (Keppel & Walter, 1999, p. 419)

It is unfortunate that, despite their effort to bring an element of reliability to their typology by providing greater detail and specificity, it is not clear how Keppel and Walter remedy such criticisms with their own work. As discussed previously, no procedures are provided for how to assess a crime scene or identify relevant information. In addition, the lack of conceptual clarity in their typology, as discussed in previous sections, results in their categories also being a collection of general indicators that could apply to myriad circumstances and people.

In a further attempt to add science to their model, Keppel and Walter (1999) conducted a study of incarcerated men, asserting that the results would "assist law enforcement officers in knowing how common each type of rape–murderer is" (p. 434). Unfortunately, the results of this study are not sufficient to support such an assertion. First, because the study was conducted with a sample of individuals who had been apprehended and convicted using traditional law enforcement methods, there are limits to the degree to which the findings are relevant to profiling, which is typically reserved for cases that are not solved through these methods. Although profiling methods are typically used by law enforcement when traditional methods have failed, the models that have incorporated some kind of data collection have used as their reference groups offenders who have been apprehended. This is a problem because it is likely that offenders who have been caught using traditional law enforcement methods are very different from offenders who are able to evade capture. It is ostensibly this second group of offenders to which profiling techniques are to be applied, making it likely that techniques that are developed on the basis of information from apprehended offenders will be less successful than expected when used in the field. Second, Keppel and Walter's method of categorizing inmates using their own typology to verify the presence of those categories in the offender population is problematic. There was no control group to allow for offenders to be excluded from one of the four typological categories. No criteria were presented for how raters determined that an offender fit into one group rather than another, and no information was provided about how offenders would be classified if they matched criteria for more than one category. Finally, although Keppel and Walter did not describe their classificatory methods in detail, the percentages demonstrate that every inmate they reviewed was forced into one of the four categories. This procedure not only provides no indication of how well inmates actually matched the category criteria but also does not allow inferences about how representative these categories are of the nonincarcerated offender population. Therefore, the claim that these results are informative with regard to the prevalence of these types within the criminal population is not supported.

Conclusion

An examination of the nonscientific profiling models from a scientific framework reveals that two of the models—Holmes and Holmes's (1996) and Turco's (1990)—contain no science. The other three models—Douglas et al.'s (1986), Keppel and Walter's (1999), and Turvey's (1999)—bring the appearance of science by attempting to organize their concepts, propose untested models, or apply simple statistics to small, nonrandomized data sets. On closer inspection, however, these efforts do not constitute science, and the models do not evidence even one of the components that distinguishes scientific models from nonscientific models. The five nonscientific models of profiling are therefore most appropriately considered from the perspective of art, rather than science.

II

THE FUTURE OF PROFILING

6

FROM GOALS TO THEORY

The analysis of the nonscientific and scientific models of profiling presented in the first section of this book reveals that there is currently no single model of profiling that can be considered to be comprehensive or accurate. Although these models have components that might be used to supplement a science of profiling, no single model is adequate for use as a template. In addition, despite assertions made by the existing profiling models, there is currently little reliable and valid evidence to demonstrate that any piece or combination of pieces of crime scene evidence predicts any offender characteristic or provides any other important insight about the crime in question. Rather, current nonscientific profilers have built a practice around anecdotal evidence, based on the supposition that their subjective investigative experiences reflect reality.

By building and testing a scientific model of profiling, the profiling field will eventually have the information required to lend credence to whatever current profiling inferences and practices find support in empirical testing; eliminate inferences and practices that are not supported by testing and provide no benefit to investigators; and be able to seek out new, fruitful directions for improving profiling science and practice. Part II of this book is therefore devoted to discussing the development of a science of profiling from its most basic elements and describing how this science can enhance profiling practice.

GOALS OF CRIMINAL PROFILING

A model of profiling should be designed to achieve clear goals. Regrettably, as discussed in Part I, the identification of clear goals for profiling has, thus far, been impeded by the lack of consensus among existing models as to what the appropriate goals for profiling are. This difficulty is due in part to the fact that some profiling models have not explicitly stated goals for profiling and in part to the fact that where profiling goals have been stated, they differ from model to model. Nonetheless, if one examines the history of profiling and considers each of the current profiling models from the perspective of ascertaining what, in its most general sense, each model is designed to accomplish, several goals for profiling are identifiable. These goals involve the use of profiling techniques throughout various stages of the criminal justice process, including narrowing down the suspect pool (Douglas, Ressler, Burgess, & Hartman, 1986) and helping to shape strategies to provoke offenders to come forward to facilitate interrogation (Douglas & Olshaker, 1995) and prosecution (Turvey, 1999).

There is one overarching goal, however, derived from the current profiling literature, that should guide research and practice: gathering and analyzing crime scene information to assist law enforcement in identifying unknown perpetrators. From the early fictional detective tales (e.g., Doyle, 1892–1927/1992; Poe, 1814/1982), the professional and popular works of John Douglas (e.g., Douglas & Olshaker, 1995; Douglas et al., 1986), and the scientifically based Canter model (Canter, 2000), profiling is consistently described as a process whereby information is gathered from the scene of a crime and inferences are made in an effort to apprehend the unknown perpetrator. For example, Doyle's (1892–1927/1992) Sherlock Holmes is described as having said that "it is difficult for a man to have any object in daily use without leaving the impress of his individuality upon it in such a way that the trained observer might read it" (p. 92). This sentiment is echoed in Douglas et al.'s (1986) corollary assertion that "Investigative profilers analyze information gathered from the crime scene for what it may reveal about the type of person who committed the crime" (p. 404). Canter (2000) put it in a more scientific framework, discussing the creation of "measures of those aspects of criminal activity available to police investigators and of those characteristics of the offender that are useful to help identify and prosecute those offenders" (p. 26). These descriptions reveal that although individual approaches to the practice of profiling may vary, each of the extant profiling models aspires to a similar goal: using crime information to assist in identifying an unknown offender. This is the common point of agreement from which a science of profiling can begin to be built.

IDENTIFYING A *TYPE* OF OFFENDER, OR *THE* OFFENDER?

Given this primary goal, the next question is how specific the iden-tification must be. Some of the nonscientific profiling models assert that profiling should be used to identify the type of individual responsible for perpetrating a given crime, rather than a specific individual. For example, Douglas et al. (1986) stated, "Profiling does *not* provide the specific identity of the offender. Rather, it indicates the kind of person most likely to have committed a crime" (p. 402, italics in original). Likewise, Turvey (1999) wrote that profiling does not uniquely identify one perpetrator. Instead, according to descriptions in the previously reviewed models, crime scene evidence is to be analyzed through some unspecified process, and the profiler is to generate a set of offender characteristics that range from interpersonal narratives (Canter, 1994); to offender habits (Douglas et al., 1986); to grooming, employment history, and self-esteem (Turvey, 1999). These char-acteristics are purported to describe the type of offender who would be responsible for the crime in question, rather than implicating a particular individual.

However, the belief that profiling should be used only to describe types of offenders is contradicted in published accounts of profiling success stories by these same authors in two ways (e.g., Canter, 1988; Douglas & Olshaker, 1995; Holmes & Holmes, 1996). First, in published accounts by Canter (1994), Douglas and Olshaker (1995), Ressler and Shachtman (1992), and Holmes and Holmes (1996), the set of offender characteristics that is pro-duced by the profiler is consistently portrayed as narrowing the suspect pool sufficiently that only one individual, the true perpetrator, remains. This individual is then apprehended and compared with the law enforcement profile to demonstrate the accuracy of the profile's predictions and to assert that the individual charged is in fact the guilty party by virtue of his similarity to the profile. For example, in describing his work on the John Duffy case, also known as the Railway Rapist case, Canter (1988) wrote as follows:

> Using a combination of psychological theories and procedures we were able to create a description of the offender that turned out to resemble John Duffy remarkably closely . . . the whole profile was found to fit only one of the suspects and helped to focus police attention on that man to the extent that they were eventually able to charge him. (Canter, 1988, p. 14)

Following Duffy's conviction, Canter (1988) wrote, "A year and a half is a long time for a psychologist to wait to see if he has described the right person" (p. 15). Likewise, Douglas and Olshaker (1995) described a suspect as fitting "the profile to a T," even though they noted that this individual was "a suspect in another crime" rather than the crime at hand (p. 189). Holmes and Holmes (1996) discussed a profile produced by Ronald Holmes, writing that "This profile proved to be remarkably accurate" (p. 24). (Unfortunately, the authors later noted that the profile did not actually lead to the apprehension of the offender; instead, one of the victims recognized him at a shopping center and called the police.)

Second, profiling is discussed by at least two models (Douglas et al., 1986; Turvey, 1999) in the context of strategies for interrogation. According to Douglas et al. (1986) and Turvey (1999), a profile of offender characteristics can inform investigators as to how the true perpetrator might react to certain interrogation tactics. For example, Douglas and Olshaker (1995) discussed a case in which a bloodstained rock, believed to be the murder weapon, was recovered from a crime scene. The police had a suspect in mind and were preparing to question him. Douglas and Olshaker (1995) offered a suggestion for how the officers should interrogate their suspect:

> Without saying anything about it, place the bloody rock on a low table at a forty-five-degree angle to his line of sight so that he'll have to turn his head to look at it. Closely observe all his nonverbal cues—his behavior, respiration, perspiration, carotid pulse. If he is the killer, he will not be able to ignore that rock, even though you haven't mentioned it or explained its significance. (p. 190)

Again, these strategies are presumed to be effective only with the true perpetrator of a crime, extending beyond the scope of describing types of offenders. It appears, then, that despite the disclaimer that profiling is used only to describe types of offenders, the authors of the reviewed profiling models also apply the profiling process to single alleged offenders in their own practices.

The ambivalence evident in the differing descriptions previously listed most likely occurs because the validity of criminal profiling has not yet been established. It seems that the identification of a single individual is perhaps the ideal goal of profiling. It certainly would provide an immense benefit to law enforcement if the profiling field could develop behavioral techniques that consistently identified unknown offenders and led to the solution of difficult cases. However, as shown in Part I, the science of profiling has not yet sufficiently developed to be able to identify individual offenders. How such a science should develop is considered in the next section.

OPERATIONALIZING THE GOAL OF PROFILING

Adapting this general goal of profiling to a scientific model is a somewhat different process from that which has been attempted in nonscientific profiling. In the latter, the effort to identify the specific offender responsible for a particular offense or series of offenses has historically involved viewing criminal profilers as uniquely talented individuals who examine crime scene evidence and produce uncannily accurate descriptions of the unidentified offender.

Rather than relying on some unspecified inherited or learned skill set, a scientific approach to profiling would involve three major steps, which are discussed in the following sections.

Step 1: Evaluating Crime Scene Evidence

Considering that the goal of profiling is to identify an unknown offender, and given that the only information available in a profiling scenario is likely to be the crime scene evidence, a scientific approach to profiling must begin with a discussion of crime scene evidence and a plan for relating it to characteristics of the unknown offender. Chapter 7 addresses this in the following manner: First, the concept of crime scene evidence will be defined. This definition will encompass not only physical evidence, such as blood, fibers, and weapons, but also witness descriptions (when available), victim information, and other pieces of information that can be derived from the crime events themselves. Second, the types of crime scene evidence that are likely to be available for use in generating predictions about offender characteristics will be identified, and their potential utility will be described. For example, the description of firearms in chapter 7 includes a list of firearm components that can be tested by forensic scientists, the types of analyses that can be conducted, and the information that can be gleaned from those analyses. Third, crime reconstruction will be discussed as a strategy for relating crime scene evidence to offender behaviors. This procedure involves using logic and findings from forensic science to identify the timeline and sequence of crime events and offender actions. The process of extracting offender behaviors from pieces and patterns of crime scene evidence through crime reconstruction is an element that is essential to making predictions about unknown offenders. Although pieces of crime scene evidence alone (e.g., glass fragments on the outside windowsill of a burglarized home) may not be directly valuable to understanding an offender, translating that crime scene evidence into information about the unknown offender's behavior (e.g., the window was broken from the inside) is the first step toward making predictions that may lead to his apprehension (e.g., the burglar was someone who was already inside the house rather than someone who gained entry through force). The strategy of crime reconstruction will be evaluated with regard to its ability to generate reliable and valid predictions about behaviors on the basis of crime scene evidence.

Step 2: Relating Information From Crime Reconstruction to the Motives, Personality Characteristics, and Behaviors of Known Offenders

To attempt to identify *unknown* offenders on the basis of crime scene evidence, one must first describe the relationships that link crime scene evidence to characteristics of *known* offenders. Aside from using the direct links that can be found between certain types of crime scene evidence (e.g., DNA) and offenders, scientists must begin to empirically examine potential relationships between the types of crime scene evidence and offender actions derived from crime reconstruction and other offender characteristics that may assist in identifying an unknown perpetrator. Chapters 8, 9, and 10 discuss this process in the following manner. First, in chapter 8, the three main groups of offender characteristics believed to be valuable to law enforcement investigations are identified and defined. These three groups of offender characteristics are motives, personality, and behavior. As discussed in the following sections, motives and personality are latent, unobservable constructs that demonstrate their value to investigation through their expression as behaviors. In turn, behavior encompasses both the crime-related behaviors derived from crime reconstruction and the more general life behaviors of an offender that may be predicted from motive, personality, and crime-related behaviors. Second, chapters 9 and 10 discuss in greater detail the offender characteristics of motive and personality, respectively, and their relationship to the offender characteristic of behavior. Studies from the offender literature will be reviewed for each offender characteristic, to provide information about the nature of that characteristic and its potential utility in a criminal investigation. This literature is also selectively reviewed to exemplify the few links that have already been demonstrated between offender behavior and motive and personality.

Step 3: Testing Profiling Predictions

To advance the profiling field, it is essential that the proposed relationships between the components of a model be validated. To accomplish this, chapter 11 presents a model of the structure of relationships between crime scene evidence and offender characteristics, based on the offender literature and the evaluation of chapters 8, 9, and 10. Next, chapter 12 discusses the steps involved in testing the predictive power of relationships among crime scene evidence, motive, personality, and offender behaviors. First, the types of data sets to be used for testing predictions are suggested, and potential variables to be extracted from those data sets for testing are discussed. Second, hypothesis testing is discussed to establish links between crime scene evidence and important offender characteristics. This discussion will address the differences in testing both direct and indirect relationships between variables in the model. Although there may certainly be direct relationships between crime scene evidence and offender characteristics, there are also likely to be more complex interrelationships between these two sets of variables. For example, in a relatively direct relationship between crime scene evidence and offender characteristics, a witness might describe to an investigator that she defended herself from an attacker by dousing him in the face with boiling water. In this example, the crime scene evidence might lead to the prediction that the perpetrator will seek medical treatment for burns on his face. In a more complex example, a timid offender might be inclined to flee if his victim begins to approach him with a pot of boiling water, whereas an offender more inclined to be a risk-taker might not flee. In this example, the timidity or boldness evidenced in an offender's personality might moderate his response to the unexpected event of being approached with a pot of boiling water, such that one might predict that only the bold offender would sustain burns on his face. In turn, other personality characteristics, such as the offender's ability to cope with pain, might lead to further differential predictions about whether he would seek medical attention. Hypotheses designed to address the links between crime scene evidence and offender characteristics must take both of these processes into account to comprehensively explain the profiling process.

Taken together, the processes described in chapters 7 through 12 will arm investigators with the science to test predictions that have long been adhered to in profiling practice as well as novel predictions that are sure to develop as the field matures. Although building this science of profiling involves a great deal of starting over, the overarching goals of a science of profiling are actually quite consistent with the aspirations of the extant profiling models and with the tradition that began with profiling's early beginnings in literature and the work of John Douglas and Robert Ressler. The hope of a profiling science is that it will become a tool for law enforcement investigators to use when traditional investigative methods fail to identify an offender from the available information. However, the lesson learned from the existing approaches to profiling is that, without science, the field will be unable to determine whether profiling works and, if it does work, how. Professionals in the field of profiling must not only begin to answer questions about its efficacy and effectiveness to be respected as a science but also ensure that the practice of profiling provides an incremental benefit beyond traditional investigative methods and contributes to increasing the accuracy of criminal investigations.

As noted earlier, at this stage in the development of profiling techniques the goal of a science of profiling should not be to replace the law enforcement officer. Any application of science to individual crimes will necessarily involve the discretion of law enforcement investigators, and although a science of profiling may not be able to supplant the role of the law enforcement officer, by using scientific principles, and by relying on the scientific psychological literature, it may be possible to increase investigative accuracy and efficiency. Therefore, chapter 13 discusses heuristics for current profiling practice, given the state of the science and the importance of law enforcement investigative practice.

7

CRIME SCENE EVIDENCE

In any crime perpetrated by an unknown offender, the primary source of information available to investigators will be the crime scene. Although portrayals of modern-day crime scene investigation focus on the physical evidence related to the commission of a crime, the crime scene is also a source of witnesses, victim information, and other potential investigative leads. Discussion of crime scene evidence in this chapter therefore reflects the view of a crime scene as a comprehensive source of investigative information that includes physical evidence, witness statements, and victim information and statements. To begin to identify relationships between crime scene evidence and characteristics of unknown offenders, this chapter discusses the concept of a crime scene, proposes the pieces of crime scene evidence believed to be important to an understanding of crimes and offenders, and discusses the potential uses of and roles for these pieces of evidence either singly or in combination with other pieces of evidence.

CRIME SCENES

The first step in any criminal investigation, whether it will become the subject of profiling or not, is to identify the crime scene. Turvey's (1999) model, which is currently the only extant profiling model to incorporate a glossary of terms, defines a *crime scene* as "a location where a criminal act has taken place" (p. 436). Turvey elaborated on this definition by discussing three types of crime scenes: primary scenes, secondary scenes, and disposal sites. A *primary scene* is "the location where the offender engaged in the majority of their [*sic*] attack or assault upon their [*sic*] victim or victims" (Turvey, 1999, p. 445). A *secondary scene* is defined as "any location where there may be evidence of criminal activity outside the primary scene" (Turvey, 1999, p. 447). A *disposal site* is described as follows: "This term is used to refer to the place where a body is found. A primary scene may be used as a disposal site, or the offender may move the body to another location" (Turvey, 1999, p. 438). Although these definitions communicate some of the basic ideas involved in understanding the parameters of crime scenes, some additional explanation is needed to tie these concepts together and make them useful for analysis.

First, it appears to be common practice, at least as indicated by the descriptions in Turvey's (1999) model and the other profiling models (Douglas, Ressler, Burgess, & Hartman, 1986; Holmes & Holmes, 1996), to classify crime scenes according to the significance of criminal acts that took place in a particular location. Unfortunately, it is not clear from the existing literature how an investigator should determine a criminal act's significance. The pitfall of defining crime scenes according to the significance or proportion of crime events that took place there is that in situations that include multiple crime scenes, it may not be clear how to measure or prioritize the criminal actions perpetrated at each crime scene. Consider the following example: An offender encounters a victim at a café and spends 2 hours conversing with her for the purpose of gaining her confidence so that he can assault her. She then agrees to walk out of the café with this offender. He takes her down a secluded alley where his car is parked, bludgeons her to death in a matter of minutes, and puts her into the trunk of his car. He then drives her body to a remote location, spends 1 hour committing postmortem acts of mutilation, steals her purse, and sets a fire to cover his activities. Which is the primary crime scene? From a legal perspective, the most serious criminal act was the murder that was committed in the alley, but that act encompassed the shortest amount of time. The largest amount of time was spent at the café, and there might be a number of witnesses there who might be able to identify the offender; however, no crime was committed at this location. The car is also a crime scene because the victim's body was transported in it, and there is likely to be evidence found in the trunk. Finally, the largest number of criminal acts were committed at the scene where the body was left, but these acts were neither the most legally serious nor the most time consuming.

It would seem that the purpose of differentiating between crime scenes is to give investigators a practical sense of where a crime was committed and what secondary or tertiary locations were involved in the perpetration of that crime. In addition, however, from the perspective of building and using a science of profiling, the purpose of understanding where a crime took place is to identify important locations from which to gather evidence and make determinations about the crime events so that they can later be related to characteristics of the offender who perpetrated them. Prioritizing crime scenes according to qualitative judgments about the criminal acts that took place there is problematic not only because of the difficulty in distinguishing between the qualities of different criminal acts but also because evidence may need to be collected before such a determination can be made. Determining the primacy of a crime scene before evidence collection therefore puts the proverbial cart before the horse and may hinder the progress of an investigation by drawing attention to locations where evidence collection may not be fruitful and away from locations that may contain important evidence.

Second, Turvey's (1999) definition of *crime scenes* (particularly *primary crime scenes*) appears to be specific to violent crimes. This is not surprising, given that Turvey indicated that profilers are primarily called to consult on "extremely violent, sexual and or predatory cases" (Turvey, 1999, p. 35). However, there is no reason to believe that profiling can be applied only to violent crimes. Although the types of evidence available will vary between violent (e.g., physical evidence, such as blood, skin, and hair) and nonviolent crimes (e.g., embezzlement might include evidence such as financial documents and computer files), the task remains to search for pathways linking evidence to offender characteristics. Whether this endeavor is fruitful would seem to depend less on the violent or nonviolent nature of a crime and more on the power of the available evidence to predict characteristics of the offender. Therefore, in the rest of this book the term *crime scenes* refers to locations where evidence of any type of crime of interest can be found, regardless of whether that evidence relates to a violent act.

Third, despite Turvey's (1999) organization, it is not clear that there are actually three categories of crime scenes. Given the criticisms previously listed, it would be more useful to define a crime scene as any location where evidence or information relevant to a crime is likely to be found. The Technical Working Group on Crime Scene Investigation at the National Institute of Justice (NIJ) discussed in its research report (NIJ, 2000a) the issue of multiple scenes, as opposed to the prioritization of crime scenes that Turvey suggested. The working group defined *multiple scenes* as "two or more physical locations of evidence associated with a crime" (NIJ, 2000a, p. 43). This concept can be applied to profiling, such that all crime scenes would be significant for the collection of evidence, and the evidence itself would be used to determine which acts (violent or not) correspond to which crime scenes. For investigators, multiple crime scenes could then be described by the acts that took place there and/or by the chronology of events indicated by the evidence. For example, in the scenario described earlier, a classification scheme of crime scenes might be the following:

- Crime Scene 1: encounter location (café);
- Crime Scene 2: homicide location (alley);
- Crime Scene 3: transport location (offender's vehicle); and
- Crime Scene 4: postmortem acts location, theft, arson, and body disposal site (remote location).

This scheme treats each location as a crime scene of importance. In addition to indicating locations from which to collect evidence, it provides information about the order in which the various locations were visited by victim and offender and about the criminal acts and other acts important to the crimes that were committed in those locations. This type of framework not only has a conceptual advantage over attempting to identify the primary and lesser scenes, as suggested by Turvey (1999) and others, but also creates a basic organizational scheme for considering the crime scene evidence itself. As discussed in the section titled "Crime Reconstruction," one element of a criminal investigation is the construction of a crime narrative and timeline. To this end, the framework of multiple crime scenes suggested earlier allows for the organization of crime scene evidence according to its location and order in the scheme of crime events.

CRIME SCENE EVIDENCE

Crime scene evidence constitutes the data with which professionals in the profiling field have to work when attempting to predict characteristics of an unknown offender. This evidence can take the form of physical evidence, such as blood, fibers, and weapons, or nonphysical evidence, such as witness descriptions about the crime events and offender and victim information, including his or her relationship to the offender, daily routine, and any other information that could lead to inferences about the perpetrator. In any crime, an investigator would ideally strive to collect as much of the relevant physical and nonphysical evidence as possible. The type of evidence that is likely to be available to an investigator for collection will vary according to the type of crime being investigated. Therefore, the type of evidence that an investigator should aim to identify and collect will depend on the type of crime at issue. For example, suppose a victim is found murdered in his home, with no sign of forced entry. During the autopsy, skin scrapings are found under his fingernails, indicating that he may have attempted to defend himself against his attacker. In this scenario, it might be important to collect DNA samples from the victim's friends and family members, or anyone to whom the victim might have opened his door voluntarily. Collecting this evidence might then indicate whether the skin found under the victim's nails came from one of these individuals, implicating that person in (at the very least) an incident of physical contact with the victim. In contrast, suppose that an individual is the victim of fraud rather than murder. In this case, even if it is believed that the fraud was perpetrated by an individual trusted by the victim, it would not seem as relevant to collect DNA samples from the victim's friends and family members.

It is clear, therefore, that the consideration of pieces of evidence that are important to a science of profiling requires a certain amount of discretion. It certainly is best to be comprehensive about evidence collection, first identifying all relevant crime scenes and then collecting whatever pieces of evidence might be informative. Unfortunately, the volume of evidence that could potentially be collected at any given crime scene could easily become prohibitive, in terms of both the time required to collect it and the time and cost of performing forensic analyses. It is therefore necessary to collect evidence that can reasonably be expected to inform an investigation of the crime at issue, as illustrated by the DNA scenario just described.

To aid in criminal investigations, the NIJ has provided guidelines for crime scene investigation in general (NIJ, 2000a) and for death investigations (NIJ, 1999), fire and arson investigations (NIJ, 2000b), explosion and bombing investigations (NIJ, 2000c), and electronic crime scene investigations (NIJ, 2001) in particular. Although these reports provide information about several aspects of crime scene investigation, including safety considerations, maintaining the evidence chain of custody, and observing professional courtesies, these guidelines vary in the degree to which they specify pieces of evidence to be collected. At one end of the spectrum, the guidelines for death investigations indicate in a very general manner that an investigator is to collect trace evidence before transporting the body. Although the likely presence of blood, hairs, and a few other types of evidence is discussed, the guidelines do not specify what individual pieces of evidence an investigator should be looking for and collecting, what that evidence looks like, why it should be collected, and what information is likely to be gleaned from it.

In contrast, the guidelines for electronic crime scene investigations are very specific. This guide details individual pieces of evidence that should be collected, describes the possible uses for each piece of evidence, and discusses what potential information might be contained in each piece of evidence. The guidelines even include pictures of each piece of evidence, to assist the investigator in correctly identifying it at the scene. For example, one piece of evidence recommended for collection in this guide is a credit card skimmer. Photos are provided of this piece of equipment in various contexts. A definition is also provided: "Credit card skimmers are used to read information contained on the magnetic stripe on plastic cards" (NIJ, 2001, p. 21). The section on potential evidence reads, "Cardholder information contained on the tracks of the magnetic stripe includes: card expiration date, credit card numbers, user's address, user's name" (NIJ, 2001, p. 21).

Although the NIJ guidelines are informative to varying degrees, it is unfortunate that they are not uniform in terms of their exhaustiveness in recommendations for evidence collection. There is no single list of evidence in the field that generalizes across crime scenes, and investigators will therefore have to rely on these and other practice guidelines to determine how to collect evidence for the types of crimes they are investigating. The degree of clarity with which investigators proceed with collecting crime scene evidence will therefore depend on the clarity and specificity of the guidelines they follow.

In terms of building a model of profiling that will relate crime scene evidence to offender characteristics, it may not be possible to rely on practice guidelines and other literature to create an exhaustive list of every possible piece of evidence that can and should be collected for every type of crime. However, it is still possible to look to this literature to ascertain the types of crime scene evidence that are likely to be collected and available for use both in investigations and for the purposes of attempting to generate predictions about offenders.

The following sections are compiled from Saferstein's (2001) chapter on physical evidence, the *FBI Handbook of Forensic Services* (Wade, 2003), and the NIJ guidelines previously discussed (NIJ, 1999, 2000a, 2000b, 2000c, 2001). They contain a descriptive list of types of evidence commonly collected and analyzed by forensic scientists and (in many cases) an explanation for why this evidence might be of interest. Although this list is not exhaustive, it represents the pieces of data that are likely to be available for use in making predictions about offender characteristics.

Abrasives

Samples from a crime scene can be analyzed to determine what kinds of abrasive materials were used to sabotage engines or other machinery.

Adhesives, Caulks, and Other Sealants

Samples of these materials can be analyzed for color and composition.

Anthropological Examination

Suspected bone fragments can be analyzed for composition, origin, and damage (e.g., bullet holes).

Audio Recordings

Recordings containing voices and signals (e.g., gunshots and telephone touchtones) can be examined, transcribed, and compared with other samples.

Bank Security Dyes

Banks have packs containing visible red or pink dyes to stain money and clothing, as well as tear gas to disable an offender. Money, clothing, and other items can be analyzed for the presence of dye and tear gas.

Blood, Semen, and Saliva

This category includes both the fluids themselves and the materials that might contain them (e.g., cigarette butts, chewing gum, and envelopes and stamps). This evidence can be collected in liquid form, through dried stains, and from materials that have been saturated with the fluids. Analysis of this evidence is conducted to determine identity and possible sources.

Building Materials

Forensic analyses can be conducted on materials such as brick, mortar, plaster, stucco, cement, and concrete to determine composition and comparison to other samples.

Codes and Ciphers

Codes are of particular interest in cases of racketeering, terrorism, foreign intelligence, violent criminals, and street and prison gangs. Materials that may contain these types of codes include drug records, gambling records, loan sharking records, money laundering records, and prostitution records.

Computers

Examinations can determine the type of data files contained in a computer, compare those files with known documents or files, determine the time when and sequence in which files were created, extract files from computers and storage media (e.g., disks, CDs), recover deleted files, convert file formats, search data files by keywords, recover passwords, and analyze and compare source codes.

Documents

Paper; ink; indented writing; obliterations; and handwritten, typewritten, burned, or charred documents can be examined. Other examples of documents include anonymous letters, extortion letters, bank robbery notes, and fraudulent checks. Photocopies can sometimes be identified with the machine that produced them. Torn edges of papers can sometimes be matched; information on burned or charred documents can sometimes be deciphered. Age of documents can sometimes be determined. Embossed or sealed impressions can sometimes be identified with the instrument that produced them.

Drugs

Substances seized in violation of drug laws can be examined in liquid, powder, pill, and solid form. They can be examined as bulk or as residue. (Although Saferstein's [2001] text does not discuss legal substances in this category, it would seem important to collect drugs that, although not illegal, might be material to an investigation. For example, if a suicide is suspected, it might be possible to look for and collect any psychotropic medications and determine whether the victim was compliant with the prescription.)

Electronic Devices

Owner- or user-entered data can be extracted from personal digital assistants, cellular telephones, pagers, and global positioning system units. Data can also be extracted from facsimile machines, stun guns, and bomb detonators.

Explosives

Devices containing explosive charges, as well as objects expected to contain residue of an explosive, can be examined. Analyses can identify the components used to construct the devices (e.g., switches, batteries, detonators, wires), identify the main charge, determine the construction characteristics, determine the manner in which the device functioned or was intended to function, and determine the specific assembly techniques used by the builder of the device.

Feathers

Analyses can determine bird species and compare crime scene feathers with other feathers.

Fibers

Both natural and synthetic fibers, including rope, twine, and cordage, can be examined. Analysis can identify the type of fiber (e.g., animal, vegetable, mineral, and synthetic), and crime scene fibers can be compared with other samples.

Fingerprints

Comparisons can be made with partial and full fingerprints and latent and visible fingerprints. Hands and fingers may also be submitted for comparison.

Firearms and Ammunition

Any firearm, bullet, cartridge, or cartridge cases can be examined. Firearms examination can assess the general condition of a weapon and whether it is functional or in a condition that could lead to an unintentional discharge. Trigger-pull examinations can demonstrate the amount of pressure necessary to release the hammer or firing pin. Analyses can determine whether a firearm has been altered to be fully automatic. Firearms can also be test-fired to obtain specimens for comparison to crime scene evidence. Fired bullets can be examined to identify general rifling characteristics such as caliber, physical features of the rifling impressions, and bullet manufacturers. Cartridge casings can be examined to determine the caliber, manufacturer, and marks of value for comparison. Unfired cartridges can be examined to determine whether the ammunition was loaded or extracted from a particular firearm. Gun parts can be examined to determine the caliber and model of gun from which they originated. Bullet jackets can be analyzed when a bullet has fragmented, preventing the comparison of individual pieces to test-fired ammunition. Bullet-lead analyses can be conducted if no firearm is recovered or bullet marks cannot be sufficiently analyzed.

General Unknowns

Powders, liquids, and stains that cannot be readily identified can be examined by forensic scientists. Even though a full identification might not be possible, it is often possible to ascertain the general classification of a substance or compare it with a known comparison sample.

Glass

Glass particles and fractures, including panes that might have holes made by a bullet or other projectile, can be examined. Analyses can determine whether particles of glass originated from a broken source. Examinations of glass fractures can determine the direction and type of the breaking force and the sequencing of shots.

Gunshot Residue

Patterns of gunshot residue can be duplicated with the firearm of interest and ammunition. By firing into test materials at known distances, patterns can be established to serve as a basis for estimating muzzle-to-target distances. Chemical analyses can also be conducted to determine the presence of gunshot residue.

Hair

Animal and human hairs can be analyzed. For human hairs, race, body area, method of removal, damage, and alteration (e.g., coloring) can be determined.

Images

Film, negatives, digital images, prints, and video recordings can be analyzed. Dimensions of individuals and objects can be derived; location, time, and date can be determined; authenticity or image manipulation can be detected; the source and age of photographic products can be determined; cameras can be examined to determine whether they produced a particular image; and automobile makes and models can be determined from surveillance images.

Impressions

Tire markings, shoe prints, depressions in soil, and other forms of tracks can be examined. Glove or fabric impressions and bite marks can also be evaluated. Casts, which are then analyzed by forensic scientists, can be made of some types of impressions. In some cases, such as shoe prints on hard surfaces, photographs are taken and dust impressions are made.

Ink

Ink can be analyzed to determine its composition and relationship to type of writing instrument. Date of ink manufacture can also be assessed.

Lubricants

Petroleum products, automotive fluids, cosmetics, and polishes can be examined to inform cases of sexual assault, vehicular homicide, and heavy equipment sabotage cases.

Metals

Metals can be examined for comparison and composition. Method of manufacturing can be determined (e.g., casting, forging, and grinding). Response of a metal to an applied force or load can be determined, and chemical composition can be examined. These analyses would be used to determine the causes of failure of or damage to metal; the temperature to which a metal was exposed; the methods used to cut or sever metal; the formation of metal fragments and nature of fragment sources; and conditions of watches, clocks, and timers (e.g., whether an appliance was on or off when an explosion occurred). Analyses can also determine whether a lamp bulb was lit when its glass envelope was broken or when it was subjected to an impact force (e.g., car accident).

Organs and Physiological Materials

Body organs and fluids (e.g., urine) can be analyzed for drugs, alcohol, and poisons. Tissues, bones, and teeth can also be examined for DNA purposes or for comparison to other materials (e.g., dental impressions).

Paint

Liquid and dried paint that might demonstrate a transfer related to a crime can be analyzed. The layer structure of a paint sample can be compared with known sources. Color, manufacturer, model, and model year of an automobile can be determined from a paint chip.

Pepper Spray and Foam

Items can be analyzed for pepper resin, dye, or tear gas.

Plastic, Rubber, and Other Polymers

Assorted manmade objects, such as plastic bags, can be examined and compared with known sources.

Serial Numbers

Stolen property can be submitted for the restoration of erased identification numbers.

Soil and Minerals

All items containing soil or minerals, such as soil embedded in shoes, or insulation found on clothing, can be submitted for examination. Color, texture, and composition can be determined and compared with known samples.

Tape

Adhesive tape pieces and suspected roll of origin can be compared. Composition, construction, and color can also be examined and compared with known sources.

Tool Marks

Examinations can be made of objects suspected of containing the impression of another object that served as a tool in the crime, such as a crowbar that produced marks when wedged against a windowsill. Lock-and-key examinations can be included.

Victim Data

Demographic information about the victim, as well as habits, lifestyle information, and history, can be compiled.

Weapons of Mass Destruction

Weapons associated with nuclear or radiological, biological, or chemical agents can be evaluated. Explosives may also be included.

Witness Statements

Interviews with witnesses can provide information about crime events that can later be compared with the physical evidence.

Wood and Other Vegetative Matter

Wood, sawdust, shavings, or other vegetation can be examined to match sides, ends, and fractures; determine wood species; and compare crime scene wood with other samples.

Once the types of crime scene evidence just described are collected, the physical evidence will likely be sent to a crime laboratory, where various forensic analyses will be conducted. The results of these analyses will then be available to investigators. In some situations, as suggested by the preceding sections, crime scene evidence can provide a direct link to an offender, whereas in other situations additional inferences have to be made to go from pieces of crime scene evidence to predictions about an offender. In the former case, crime scene evidence is used for identification and comparison purposes; in the latter case, additional inferences are incorporated through the process of crime reconstruction. Nonphysical evidence, such as victim information and witness statements, will not be analyzed in the same manner as physical evidence, but similar principles apply to its use. Investigators can compare nonphysical evidence with analyses of the physical evidence to determine whether the information is consistent. Likewise, investigators may be able to make direct inferences about the crime events and the unidentified perpetrator on the basis of nonphysical evidence (e.g., witness' physical description of offender, offender's car, and license plate).

Identification and Comparison of Crime Scene Evidence

In his text on criminalistics, Saferstein (2001) indicated that physical evidence is typically examined for two purposes: identification and comparison. According to Saferstein (2001), *identification* is "the process of determining a substance's physical or chemical identity" (p. 62). For example, if evidence of blood is found at a crime scene, it would be important to ascertain whether the blood came from a human or an animal. Likewise, if a white powder is found at the scene of a drug arrest, the crime laboratory should be able to determine whether it is a drug and identify the chemical composition of that drug. To accomplish this, criminalists use tests that compare the evidence of interest with standard materials. For example, if in the drug example it was suspected that the white powder was cocaine, then criminalists would compare a sample of the white powder with a known sample of cocaine. Conversely, the criminalist must also conduct additional tests to exclude other substances from consideration. So, for example, in addition to running a chemical comparison to determine that the white powder is cocaine, the criminalist would run a set of tests to determine that the white powder is not heroin, powdered sugar, or some other substance. Unfortunately, there are no definitive standards for determining when an identification is conclusive. According to Saferstein (2001), "it is left to the forensic scientist to determine at what point the analysis can be concluded and the criteria for positive identification satisfied; for this, he or she must rely on knowledge gained through education and experience" (p. 63).

A *comparison analysis* is "the process of ascertaining whether two or more objects have a common origin" (Saferstein, 2001, p. 63). For example, a criminalist might be able to note similarities between a carpet fiber found on a victim's body and a carpet fiber taken from the carpet of a suspect's residence. Determining whether two samples are similar involves judgment on the part of the forensic scientist. If the forensic scientist determines that the properties of the two carpet fibers, for example, do not match, then he or she would conclude that they did not come from the same source. However, if the forensic scientist determines that the two fibers are similar, this does not necessarily indicate that they did come from the same source. When conducting a comparison analysis, there are certain types of evidence that will possess individual characteristics that will increase the likelihood of determining a common source. According to Saferstein (2001), these individual characteristics are "properties of evidence that can be attributed to a common source with an extremely high degree of certainty" (p. 65). Examples of this type of evidence include fingerprint ridges, striation marks found on bullets, pieces of tape torn sequentially from the same roll, and handwriting comparisons. Another type of evidence is that which contains *class characteristics*, defined as "properties of evidence that can only be associated with a group and never with a single source" (Saferstein, 2001, p. 65). For example, given the mass production of carpets, a forensic scientist might be able to determine that both carpet fibers in a particular scenario came from a certain class of carpets, but it would not be possible to ascertain that they came from the carpet in the suspect's residence. According to Saferstein (2001), "One of the current weaknesses of forensic science is the inability of the examiner to assign exact or even approximate probability values to the comparison of most class evidence" (p. 66). A certain degree of judgment is involved in comparing pieces of evidence, and even when similarities are noted it is not always possible to indicate the probability that these pieces have the same origin. Although these comparisons can therefore be inconclusive, it is nonetheless important to note that there would be a low probability of discovering carpet fibers, for example, that came from the same crime, and were indistinguishable from each other, but originated from different sources. Thus, this type of evidence, particularly if there is a collective body of evidence with class characteristics, might still have utility in corroborating other pieces of evidence and supporting an investigative hypothesis of events.

The practice of identifying the properties of evidence and comparing pieces of evidence to each other or to a source of origin is what forensic scientists use to provide direct links between evidence and offenders. For example, the comparison of fingerprint ridges is often used to identify the person who left those fingerprints at a given location. Likewise, the advent of DNA typing has allowed scientists to match samples of blood, semen, and other materials to individual offenders. Use of these techniques makes it possible to demonstrate links such as those placing an individual offender at a crime scene, determining injurious contact between a victim and a specific offender, and determining the source of a handwritten note. These determinations require no additional inferences but can be demonstrated solely on the presence of identifying evidence and the comparison of that evidence to the offender.

Although these types of forensic procedures are commonly believed to be ironclad, and are relied on in court to demonstrate the veracity of crime hypotheses in which physical evidence is used, there are significant limitations that should be kept in mind when considering conclusions that are made about physical evidence using these techniques. First, as Saferstein (2001) pointed out, many police forces have not adopted the approach of using crime scene technicians with specialized training in evidence collection and preservation. Instead, "often a patrol officer or detective is charged with the responsibility of collecting the evidence" (Saferstein, 2001, p. 16). Depending on the training of these officers, the integrity of the evidence from the initial collection may be limited. Second, the identification and comparison of crime scene evidence involves a degree of judgment on the part of the forensic scientist. Different forensic scientists might therefore have different opinions about the identity or similarity of pieces of evidence. Third, in comparing individual and class characteristics of evidence, there are no standards for determining just when class characteristics become individual characteristics. For example, there are no guidelines that instruct a forensic scientist as to how many fingerprint ridges have to match to determine that there is a high enough probability to match a fingerprint to a particular individual. Finally, every identification and comparison is actually expressed as a probability rather than a conclusive match. Whether a paint chip matches a particular vehicle is expressed as a probability. Whether two fingerprints came from the same person is expressed as a probability. Even situations involving DNA matches are actually expressed as probabilities. Determining whether a probability is strong enough to draw conclusions about a crime is up to the forensic scientist; the investigator; and, ultimately, the court. Although these procedures are fallible, they represent the current state of the art in the use of forensic science in criminal investigations.

Crime Reconstruction

In some situations, it is not possible to go directly from pieces of crime scene evidence to characteristics of the offender. Although there are limitations to the practice of identifying and comparing pieces of evidence to draw conclusions about the offender, often the route from evidence to offender characteristics is still fairly direct and does not require more than the scientific analysis of evidence and a professional decision about whether that evidence indicates a particular offender. Unfortunately, some types of evidence (e.g., blood) might not be available at a crime scene for analysis or may not be relevant for particular types of crimes. In other cases, this evidence might be available for use once a suspect is apprehended but is insufficient for generating leads to identify potential suspects. Finally, there are types of nonphysical evidence that may be useful for predicting offender characteristics but will not be subjected to forensic scientific analysis. In these types of situations, additional inferences must be made to relate evidence to offender characteristics.

If the evidence in and of itself does not provide sufficient links to the offender, it is necessary to use a different approach for considering the available evidence and predicting offender characteristics. *Crime reconstruction* is a process already used within traditional criminal investigation (Chisum & Rynearson, 1997; Saferstein, 2001) that approaches the evidence by relating it to behavioral information about the crime, in the form of a narrative and timeline. This behavioral information can then be used to advance predictions about offender characteristics that cannot be made on the basis of the evidence itself. Crime reconstruction is not a process that bypasses physical evidence; instead, it incorporates findings regarding the physical evidence (when available) into a larger context that includes a consideration of offender behavior. For example, a victim might be found in her home, with her wrists bound by a piece of rope. It certainly is important to collect the rope as evidence and identify its properties so that class comparisons can be made in the event that a suspect is arrested and is found to be in possession of a similar product. It may even be the case that if the rope is a rare type, determinations can be made about where it was purchased or what types of individuals might have had access to it, thereby reducing the search parameters for suspects and increasing the probability of linking the rope to an offender. However, in terms of making predictions about offender characteristics, it is unlikely that the rope itself will be predictive of any particular offender characteristics. What is more likely to predict offender characteristics is the role the rope played in the context of crime events. Did the rope come from the victim's home, or was it brought to the scene? The first case might indicate an impulsive offender who committed an unplanned offense, whereas the second scenario hints at premeditation. Was the rope tied tightly enough to control the victim's movements, or was it more loosely tied, perhaps indicating some other purpose, such as the fulfillment of a sexual fantasy? Was the rope tied in an elaborate knot that would indicate a certain type of expertise on the part of the offender? To build a science that predicts offender characteristics from crime scene evidence, in cases in which the forensic analysis of that evidence is insufficient for making those predictions, one must first make inferences that relate a piece of evidence to a behavior or choice on the part of the offender, so that investigators can attempt to make predictions about the offender based on that behavior or choice. This is the essence of crime reconstruction.

An example of how crime reconstruction is used is in the area of automobile accident reconstruction. In any automobile collision, the evidence that is likely to be available would include broken glass, dents and other body damage to the automobiles involved, paint transfer from one automobile to another or to a third object, skid marks on the road, tire characteristics, witness statements, and injuries to the drivers and passengers. Taken individually, these pieces of evidence might indicate that an accident took place, but they do not necessarily provide insight into how the accident occurred and whether one or both parties is responsible. However, by combining principles of physics and other forensic sciences with logic, investigators can make determinations about the likely sequence of events involved in a given automobile accident. This process must be conducted so that the timeline and narrative both explain and are supported by the crime scene evidence.

Consider the following illustration. A woman reports a late-night hit-and-run accident in which she states that a blue truck swerved into her car, just as she had parked it and was preparing to exit the vehicle. According to this individual, the truck then drove away from the scene. The woman stated that the driver of the truck was maneuvering erratically and did not even slow down before colliding with her parked car. She is certain that the driver must have seen her because she still had her headlights on. Various pieces of evidence are collected and analyzed, including the woman's statement; broken glass; photographs of the damage to the front and side of the parked car; the parked car's headlights; and photographs and measurements of the accident scene, including tire marks and paint scrapings from the parked car. From the analysis of this evidence, investigators are able to determine the following timeline and narrative: On the basis of the time of the woman's 911 phone call, the collision occurred between 12:45 and 1:00 a.m. On the basis of the force required to produce the damage to the parked car, it is determined that the truck was traveling between 30 and 35 miles per hour at the time of impact. A paint transfer found on the parked vehicle confirms that it came into contact with a blue truck. Analysis of scrapings from the paint transfer reveal that the paint corresponds to a particular make and model of blue truck. Clear glass fragments found near the parked car are also consistent with glass used in the same make and model of truck. Contrary to the woman's description, skid marks found on the road indicate that the driver of the truck did attempt to stop before colliding with her car. Also, contrary to her statement, analyses of the woman's headlights indicate that they were not lit at the time of impact. Swerving tire marks were noted both approaching the parked car and leading away from it.

By reconstructing events from the available evidence, as just illustrated, the investigator now has a set of information that includes physical evidence (glass fragments), behaviors (swerving and skidding), and a sequence of events (driving erratically, skidding, hitting a parked car, and leaving the scene). Although the presence of any individual piece of evidence (e.g., pieces of glass) might not be predictive of the characteristics of the hit-and-run driver, it might be possible to predict relationships between the types of behaviors (leaving the scene) and choices (selection of a blue truck as the vehicle) made by the driver and other characteristics that may help to identify him.

Roles of Physical Evidence in Crime Reconstruction

To relate crime scene evidence to behavioral information for the purposes of a crime reconstruction, one must understand the various ways that evidence can inform a timeline or narrative of the crime. To some extent, the process of going from evidence to a crime reconstruction is simply the logical formation of conclusions based on information at the scene or from the analyses of forensic scientists. For example, in the hit-and-run scenario, if skid marks occur only when a driver applies the brakes, and if skid marks are found on the road before the parked car, in a trajectory consistent with the path of the moving car, one could logically conclude that the driver of the moving car applied the brakes before hitting the parked car. The evidence thus provides an indicator of the order of events (braking before collision). There are several additional roles that evidence can play in forming a crime reconstruction. One model for considering these roles is articulated next.

Chisum and Rynearson (1997) proposed a model for the adaptation of crime scene evidence to crime reconstruction, focusing on the roles that evidence can play in informing a timeline and narrative. According to this model, evidence can be sequential, be directional, describe action, define location, define ownership, and limit the crime scene. Each role is described subsequently and includes an example from the hit-and-run automobile scenario just discussed. It is important to note that evidence can serve more than one role. For example, a trail of blood drops could serve as directional evidence, by indicating a direction of travel through a crime scene, and it could serve as ownership evidence if it were analyzed for DNA and matched to a suspect with a high degree of probability.

Sequential evidence establishes the sequence of events surrounding a criminal act. In the hit-and-run scenario, the location of the skid marks would indicate that the driver applied the brakes, collided with the parked car, and then drove away, in that order. The woman's report also provides sequential evidence (albeit conflicting), indicating that the driver of the truck hit the parked car without slowing down and then drove away.

Directional evidence shows where something was going and where it was coming from. Tire tracks at the scene of the hit-and-run accident indicate the pathway of the truck as it collided with the parked car and as it left the scene.

Action evidence establishes the motion or actions of individuals at the scene. For example, the size, shape, and depth of the dent in the parked car indicates that it was hit by another vehicle, being driven by an individual who, as indicated by tire tracks, drove away after impact.

Location evidence establishes the position of individuals at a crime scene as well as the orientation of people and objects at the scene. The location of the parked car establishes where the contact occurred and the orientation of the moving truck as it struck the car. The woman's description also establishes her presence at the scene and, to the extent that her statement is reliable, the presence of an individual driving a blue truck.

Ownership evidence determines the source or identity of the evidence. Analysis of the blue paint scrapings taken from the parked car leads to the identification of a particular make and model of truck. In the case of the hit-and-run scenario, there is no physical evidence that would link the crime to a particular offender. An example of how one might be able to determine the source or identity of the evidence conclusively would be if the driver had been injured and left blood at the scene of the accident before driving away. If this individual were later apprehended (preferably while driving a blue truck with paint transfer from the parked car and a broken headlight), his or her blood could be compared with the blood at the scene to determine whether they came from the same individual.

Limiting evidence defines the parameters of the crime. In the hit-and-run scenario, the woman's description of the blue truck, combined with the matching of the paint scrapings to a make and model of blue truck, limits the search parameters for the vehicle that hit the parked car. *Limiting evidence* can also refer to physical barriers. For example, if an accident had taken place in a parking garage, and both drivers had remained at the scene, the parameters of the crime scene would be confined to that parking garage.

In addition to the roles of evidence previously described, Chisum and Rynearson (1997) discussed three other uses for evidence.

1. *Relational evidence* establishes the relationship of pieces of evidence by virtue of their location with respect to the location

of the other item. For example, yellow broken glass found on the ground near the smashed turn signal light of the parked car indicates that the glass came from the parked car.

2. *Functional evidence* describes how things work, as well as the operational condition of an item. For example, if skid marks would be expected to appear only when a driver applied sudden pressure to the brakes, then the presence of skid marks at the hit-and-run scene would be functional evidence leading to the conclusion that the driver of the truck had applied the brakes around the time he or she left the skid marks on the road.

3. *Missing or inferred information* refers to evidence that has been removed from the scene. The information has to be inferred by the investigator on the basis of the space left where that evidence would be expected to be found. For example, if the turn signal light of the parked car had been smashed by the impact of the truck during the hit-and-run accident, then investigators would expect to find pieces of yellow glass at the accident scene. If this glass were not present, investigators might conclude that either someone removed the glass or that the turn signal light had been broken at another location and was not affected by the impact of this hit-and-run accident.

Evaluation of Crime Reconstruction

It is vital to clearly appraise the strengths and weaknesses of crime reconstruction because in many cases the inferences gleaned from reconstruction are the behavioral variables that will be used to attempt to generate predictions about offenders. There currently is a paucity of research in the areas of forensic crime scene evidence analysis and crime reconstruction. First, as mentioned previously, the process of identifying and comparing crime scene evidence involves the use of individual judgment, and the degree of similarity between two pieces of evidence cannot be precisely quantified. This introduces a significant potential for error in even the most direct links between crime scene evidence and offender characteristics, such as the matching of fingerprint ridges to the fingers of a suspect. Research is needed to determine the reliability and validity of the identification and comparison procedures used by forensic scientists. Second, the extent to which crime reconstruction will be a reliable and valid process will be limited from the outset by the evidence available and the accuracy of the forensic scientific conclusions that are drawn from that evidence. Research on the accuracy rates of forensic science analyses is therefore also relevant to crime reconstruction. Third, even if determinations made by forensic scientists can be demonstrated through research to be highly accurate, there is no information about the reliability and validity of drawing logical inferences from those determinations. The reconstruction process itself must therefore also be subjected to rigorous empirical study. Until such time as sufficient research exists to assess the techniques of forensic science evidence identification–comparison and crime reconstruction, predictions generated from the use of these techniques must be made cautiously and with a clear understanding of the limitations.

In its current state, there is one other issue to be addressed regarding crime reconstruction. It is apparent, particularly as discussed by Chisum and Rynearson (1997), that crime reconstruction is intended to be used by individuals with some criminal investigative knowledge or experience. This is reflected by the fact that in cases in which the logic forming the connections between the evidence and the crime reconstruction is not obvious, there is a presumption that the individual reconstructing the crime will have the requisite knowledge or experience to understand how a particular piece of evidence supports a particular inference in a timeline or narrative. For example, if an investigator observes photographs of red glass near the rear of a dented car with a broken taillight and reads a laboratory report concluding that the composition of the red glass is consistent with the glass used in the make and model of car in the photograph, it would not require any special expertise to draw the logical conclusion that the glass probably came from the car's taillight when it was hit by something or someone. However, an individual would need to have some basic familiarity with firearm use, for example, to determine that the absence of shell casings at the site of a machine gun shooting would indicate that someone had removed them from the scene.

Building a science of forensic crime scene evidence analysis and crime reconstruction, and determining sufficient levels of proficiency or expertise for conducting these types of analyses, is beyond the scope of this book, but some guidelines can be offered. Building such a science would involve collecting data on the types of inferences that forensic scientists make in identifying or comparing pieces of evidence and attempting to approximate the probabilities involved in asserting matches or identifications as well as attempting to determine the accuracy of these inferences by comparing them to known standards or situations. For example, research could examine the process by which forensic scientists attribute fingerprints to an individual. Data could be collected on the types of characteristics that are compared (e.g., ridges, patterns), the number or percentage of characteristics that must correspond between an evidentiary fingerprint and a suspect's print before a match is declared, and the process by which this correspondence is determined. In addition, research could approximate the accuracy rate of fingerprint matching by comparing the results of the previously described process with fingerprints from known sources. These types of study would illuminate the process and success rate of the forensic science procedures that are currently in use.

With regard to crime reconstruction, a similar research process could be used to test the veracity of the kinds of inferences that are currently made by law enforcement agents when they attempt to reconstruct the timeline and narrative of a crime. Bearing in mind that the accuracy of any crime reconstruction will vary according to the strength of the available evidence, and the analysis of that evidence by forensic scientists, studies could examine the statements made in a crime reconstruction, determine the logical bases for those statements, and compare the statements and the reconstruction as a whole with known crime outcomes. For example, investigators could be provided with the same set of materials that was available to law enforcement at the time of investigation of a solved crime. Each inference made in an investigator's crime reconstruction could be evaluated and compared with the actual case outcome. Thus, an investigator might construe that the offender in a home-invasion case entered through a bedroom window and left through the back door. The investigator might then describe the basis of this inference as being the pattern and direction of a set of muddy footprints determined by the forensics laboratory to be inconsistent with the feet and shoes of every member of the household. This inference could then be compared with the narrative of the solved case to determine its accuracy, as well as whether it was properly derived from the evidence cited as the basis for the inference.

The body of research that could be generated from the types of study just described will certainly influence the task of profiling to the degree that profiling relies on forensic evidence analyses and crime reconstructions. Until this body of research is established, any crime reconstruction should simply be treated as a working hypothesis. Inferences should be checked against the results of forensic analyses and the pieces of evidence themselves and, to the extent to which findings converge, confidence in the resulting timelines and narratives can be increased. Ultimately, however, these working hypotheses will need to be compared with proven facts to confirm their validity and the validity of the process.

8

OFFENDER CHARACTERISTICS: THE CONSTRUCTS OF MOTIVES, PERSONALITY, AND BEHAVIOR

As articulated in chapter 7, crime scene evidence is likely to be the only data that a profiling investigator will have to work with when attempting to solve a crime. From these data, the investigator will have to make predictions about the characteristics of an unidentified perpetrator. In considering how to relate pieces of crime scene evidence to offender characteristics within a scientific model of profiling, the direction of causality is likely to be the reverse of the profiling process as conducted in the field. That is, rather than positing that offender characteristics are caused by the pieces of evidence that are left at a crime scene, a scientific profiling model posits that it is an offender's characteristics that lead him to leave particular pieces and patterns of evidence during the commission of his crimes. Therefore, the goal of profiling research on offender characteristics is to empirically examine on a large scale the kinds of offender characteristics that are likely to result in particular pieces or patterns of evidence. Taken together, these offender characteristics constitute three main categories: motive, personality, and behavior.

To date, no such large-scale study on offender characteristics has been undertaken. What would be required for this endeavor would be a systematic assessment of a national sample of solved cases, examining the crime scene evidence and the categories of offender characteristics just described, across a wide variety of crime types and offenders. As can be imagined, the investment required for a large-scale profiling research project would be significant in terms of costs, personnel, and time. However, given the appropriate approval and funding, the data are available for study. The storehouse of case information across federal, state, and local law enforcement agencies is likely to be vast.

With information on crime scene evidence and offender characteristics from a variety of sources, path models (Duncan, 1966; Werts & Linn, 1970) could be constructed and analyzed to determine the various pathways between offender characteristics and pieces or patterns of crime scene evidence. Chapter 11 discusses the methods involved in path analysis in more detail; in general, this technique allows researchers to estimate the magnitude of the direct and indirect links between multiple variables and use those estimates to elucidate underlying causal processes (Asher, 1983). As discussed in the following sections, the offender characteristics of interest to profiling consist of both observed and latent (i.e., unobserved) constructs. Any analytic tool that will be used in a scientific model of profiling must accommodate both types of constructs to provide a complete picture of important causal pathways. Path analysis would be well suited for this task because it considers both these observed and latent variables.

In the absence of information and analyses from such a large-scale research project, and with the hope that this book will facilitate such work, this chapter, chapter 9, and chapter 10 describe the components involved in examining offender characteristics and their relationships to crime scene evidence. This chapter describes the constructs of motive, personality, and behavior and discusses their relationship to a science of profiling. Chapters 9 and 10 discuss the relationships between motive and personality, respectively, to behavior and crime scene evidence. Examples from the criminological and psychological literature on offenders is provided in chapters 9 and 10 to illustrate how the categories of offender characteristics might interact and how findings from the extant literature might inform a more comprehensive science of profiling. Although the current offender literature consists of research conducted on a limited scale, it does provide clues for the study of offender motives, personality, and behavior and provides indicators of what scientists might find in a larger scale study.

MOTIVE

The construct of motive is concerned with the question of *why* a person engages in a behavior. The consideration of motive in profiling is based on an assumption that crimes are committed purposefully and that the motives behind the commission of an offense can be readily discerned and used to infer other offender characteristics. Thus, discussions of motive have been pervasive in the profiling literature (e.g., Canter, 2000; Douglas, Ressler, Burgess, & Hartman, 1986; Holmes & Holmes, 1996; Turvey, 1999), with regard to both inferring motives from crime scene evidence (e.g., Douglas, Burgess, Burgess, & Ressler, 1992) and inferring other offender characteristics from motives (e.g., Canter & Fritzon, 1998). *Motive* can be defined in reference to three conceptual distinctions: motive versus intent, the existence of a motive versus the ability of scientists to discern it, and the relationship of a motive to a criminal act.

First, although it is recognized that intent and motive are related, the two terms must be distinguished. *Intent* refers to whether an offender purposefully committed a criminal act, whereas *motive* refers to the offender's reasons for doing so. This distinction is important because, for the purposes of building a science of profiling, the interesting question is not *whether* an offender intended to commit a crime but *why* he or she chose to commit a crime. This sentiment is reflected in the wealth of psychological literature devoted to the study of motive across various types of criminal offense (e.g., Burgess, Hartman, Ressler, Douglas, & McCormack, 1986; Canter & Fritzon, 1998; Farrington & Lambert, 1994; Varano & Cancino, 2001).

Generally speaking, motive requires the presence of intent. If an individual does not intend to commit a criminal act, then an inquiry into his or her internal motivations for doing so is unnecessary. The reverse is also true: The presence of intent necessarily implies motive. If an individual commits an act with purpose, then there is likely to be an explanation for that purpose. Thus, the question regarding intent is merely one of presence or absence. The study of motive, however, is more nuanced, and motives can be organized from a variety of perspectives. For example, motives can be either *instrumental* or *expressive* (Feshbach, 1964). The former are those that are directed at some goal, including financial gain, political advantage, or the elimination of an adversary. In contrast, the latter are those in which the expression of anger or other emotions is paramount. Expressive motives include such things as jealousy, sexual gratification, and revenge. Similarly, motives can also be grouped according to crime type. For example, the types of motive one would expect to find underlying a sexual offense are likely to be very different from the motives one would expect to underlie embezzlement.

Second, although the presence of intent implies that there is an underlying motive, it is not necessarily the case that researchers, interviewers, or even the offender will be able to accurately identify that motive. For example, an adolescent who throws a rock through the window of an abandoned warehouse might report that she did so because she "just felt like it." One could argue that "feeling like it" represents a motive. However, discerning whether that actual motive was boredom, frustration, excitement, or impulsivity may be extremely difficult. In a more general sense, this distinction between the presence and discernment of motive reflects the difference between latent and observed variables, mentioned in the previous section. Motive is a latent variable in that it cannot be directly observed. Instead, researchers have attempted to discern motives by analyzing their more overt manifestations. For example, as discussed in chapter 9, both self-report data and reconstructive methodologies that infer motives from crime behaviors have been used to attempt to clearly discern the motives that underlie fire-setting behavior. Thus, even if a motive is determined to be present, the ability of scientists to discern its specific qualities relates to both the adequacy of scientific techniques for identifying and understanding the behavioral or self-reported manifestations of motives and the degree to which these manifestations accurately reflect the latent motives that are believed to generate them.

Third, a distinction must be made between motives to commit a crime or criminal acts and the way those motives and crimes are legally considered. In some situations, the law will view an individual as having committed a crime solely on the basis of that individual's behavior, without regard for the actor's intent and motive to commit the crime (i.e., the person's *mens rea*). For example, if an individual's home was searched, and a container of plutonium was discovered in her hall closet, that individual would be in violation of the law. Whether she intended to break the law is irrelevant, because simply possessing the plutonium would violate federal statutes. In profiling research, however, the presence of intent and the discernment of motives provide critical information, regardless of how the related acts are perceived by the legal system. With regard to the example just given, the interesting questions for profiling purposes would center around why this individual had the plutonium, where she obtained it, and what she intended to do with it—questions that might exceed the bounds of the specific law that was violated. For this reason, the presence of intent and motive are offered for their value in facilitating the discussion of profiling rather than for their accuracy as legal terms.

In addition to defining motive and making the conceptual distinctions previously described, understanding the construct of motive can be further assisted by an appreciation of its role in the commission of a crime. As demonstrated in chapter 9, the offender literature tends to treat motives as clear and separate entities, whereas in reality motives may be quite complex and changeable over even short periods of time. Although researchers strive to understand more specific relationships between individual motives and different types of crime and crime scene evidence, it may be worthwhile to devote equal time to attempting to understand the general roles that intent and motive can play in criminal behaviors. It may be that in addition to

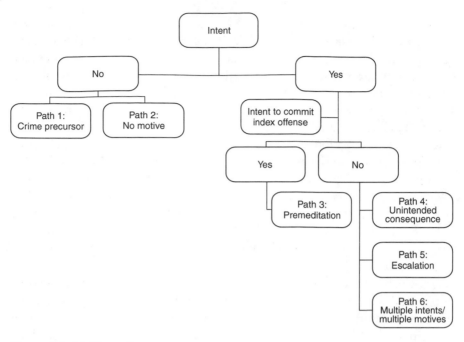

Figure 8.1. Motive pathways.

the specific content of motives (e.g., jealousy, financial gain), the timing and more general roles of motives could also differentially predict crime behaviors and crime scene features. For example, an individual whose long-standing motive of financial gain guides the premeditated murder of his brother might commit different crime behaviors and leave different patterns of crime scene evidence than an individual who, also motivated by financial gain, kills his brother in the heat of a dispute over a loan. The difference between these two crimes lies not in the specific motives, which are identical, but in the role that the motive plays in the development of the crime. In the first case, the motive appears much earlier in time and guides the offender to plan and execute the crime. In the second case, the motive arises more spontaneously and results in a more impulsive execution of the crime. The following model discusses motive in this more general context and discusses the different paths that motive may take in criminal behavior.

In the most general sense, criminal or harmful acts can be assessed according to whether there is any intent to commit a crime. Each answer, yes or no, leads to separate pathways for considering motive. This set of pathways is illustrated in Figure 8.1.

If there is no intent to commit a crime, then it remains to be determined whether there was an intent to commit some precursor to the crime. A crime precursor would involve any behavior that could and does forseeably lead to a later criminal behavior. For example, an individual might choose to stop taking medication that regulates his or her mood, despite having a history of becoming violent when experiencing agitated mood states. If, after having discontinued the medication, this individual then experiences a severely agitated mood and provokes a physical altercation with a coworker, the voluntary discontinuation of the medication would be considered a crime precursor. If there is no intent to commit a crime, but there is an intentional commission of a crime precursor, then there is potential value in attempting to discern a motive (Path 1). If the individual foresees potential harm, diminished judgment, or loss of control associated with a crime precursor, it could be fruitful to examine why this individual was willing to risk behaving in such a manner.

If there is no intent to commit a crime or crime precursor, there is necessarily no motive (Path 2). Examples of this type of situation would include true accidents, behaviors arising directly from medical conditions (e.g., seizures), and severe acute episodes of mental illness.

If there is intent to commit a crime, then one must determine whether there is an intent to commit the particular crime or crimes at issue. As can be seen in Figure 8.1, if the answer is yes, then the crimes involved are likely to be premeditated and might include such things as murder and burglary (Path 3). In these situations, because the crime has been committed purposefully the role of motive is likely to be fairly direct, as compared with the previously described situation of crime precursors.

If there is an intent to commit a crime but no intent to commit the index crime, then there are three basic scenarios to consider. The first scenario is that the offender sets out to commit one crime and there are unintended consequences that result in the commission of another crime (Path 4). For example, an offender may decide to set a fire at his workplace as an act of revenge for being fired. He does this over the weekend when the building is abandoned but, as it turns out, a fellow employee has come in to finish some extra work and is killed in the fire. In this situation, the examination of motive is likely to be most valuable in terms of considering why this individual started the fire. Looking into a motive for the death of the coworker, however, is unlikely to yield useful information because this is an unintended consequence. The second possible scenario is that the offender intends to commit one crime, and the situation escalates such that the offender commits an additional crime (Path 5). For example, an offender might decide to rob a convenience store. In the course of the robbery, the store clerk decides to resist and attempts to take the offender's weapon. The offender and clerk engage in a physical struggle, and the offender shoots the clerk. Again, this offender intends to commit one crime but ultimately commits an unintended, second crime. However, this scenario is distinct from the previous scenario because the offender engages in a second set of behaviors that result in the commission of the second crime. Whereas a single set of actions in the first scenario leads to both the fire and the death of the coworker, in this second scenario the offender commits the robbery and then willingly engages in the struggle with the clerk and shoots him. Here, therefore, there may be value in examining the offender's motive for the shooting as well as the robbery. The third scenario is that the offender sets out to commit one crime and in the course of that crime develops the clear intent to commit a second crime (Path 6). For example, an offender might decide to break into a home to steal property. On entering the home, he discovers that there is a woman sleeping in one of the bedrooms. Rather than leave with the property he has acquired, he decides to sexually assault the woman. In this scenario, although the offender arrives at the house to commit one type of offense, he later forms the intent to commit the second crime. As in the second scenario, the offender commits two separate sets of criminal behaviors, but unlike the second scenario, there is no escalation of circumstance involved. Given the opportunity to leave after the completion of one crime, the offender forms the intent to commit another.

Each pathway considers motive from a slightly different perspective. Path 2 treats the situation as being without motive. Behaviors along this pathway are either accidental or otherwise unintentional. Path 1 asks what motivations lead an offender to put himself in a situation that is likely to lead to harmful behavior. Path 3 deals with offenses that are purposeful and likely to have been planned. This pathway considers motives to have been developing over some period of time, as opposed to arising out of impulse or opportunity. Path 4 inquires into the offender's motivations for committing the initial crime. Similar to the crime precursor pathway (Path 1), it might also be valuable to examine whether the offender considers secondary consequences to his actions and whether he chooses to commit an act that might result in further harm. Path 5 asks why an offender chooses to commit the initial crime, as well as why his response to an escalation of circumstances leads to the commission of a second crime. Finally, Path 6 asks for multiple motives for multiple behaviors in a criminal event.

This model suggests that motives have different paths and can develop at different points during the commission of a crime. Thus, in addition to considering specific types of motives, an important component of understanding the construct of motive is to ask whether different motive pathways (e.g., revenge, jealousy, financial gain) differentially predict crime behaviors and crime scene evidence. To date, this type of inquiry into the construct of motive has not been undertaken. Although the literature discussed in chapter 9 addresses differences between motives that are expressive versus instrumental, or motives that involve planning versus those that are more impulsive, a more systematic and comprehensive examination of motive roles is needed to clarify the construct of motive and its relationship to criminal investigations.

PERSONALITY

Personality is perhaps the most frequently cited offender characteristic in the profiling literature. Douglas et al. (1986) described profiling as a process of "identifying the major personality and behavioral characteristics of an individual" (p. 405). Holmes and Holmes (1996) stated that "Inherent within the premise of the validity and reliability of a profile is that the person . . . has a personality that reflects pathology" (p. 2). According to Turco (1990), a crime scene is "a projection of the underlying personality" (p. 150). Turvey (1999) discussed profiling as a process that infers "distinctive personality characteristics of individuals" who commit crimes (p. 1). Also, there are numerous references to personality in the individual studies and review articles that make up the profiling research literature (e.g., Annon, 1995; Boon, 1997; Dutton, 1988; Grubin, 1995; Pinizzotto & Finkel, 1990).

Outside of profiling, the construct of personality has enjoyed a long history as a major focus of psychology research. There have been two major views of the construct of personality, each of which places a particular emphasis on either internal or external factors as essential to the definition of personality and considers personality characteristics in terms of either the person or the situation.

The Person

One view of personality, championed by Gordon Allport (1897–1967), Raymond Cattell (1905–1998), and Hans Eysenck (1916–1997), among others, holds that the essence of personality is internal to the person. According to this view, individuals have global, internal personality traits that are long-standing and stable across time, situations, and environments. For example, if an individual is said to demonstrate a high level of the trait "friendliness," one would expect that person to have been friendly for a significant portion of his or her life; to be friendly at work, home, and in recreational settings; and to be friendly to various types of people.

Researchers who approach personality from this paradigm have attempted to identify the basic personality traits important to human functioning. Allport pursued the study of traits by examining individual case histories and searching for the key traits evident in those histories (McAdams, 1990). He determined the significance of a particular trait by assessing its frequency, range of situations in which it is present, and intensity (Allport, 1961). For example, if hostility were a particularly significant trait for an individual, this would be revealed by frequent incidents of hostility, hostility across a variety of situations, and a particular intensity when that individual was being hostile.

Cattell favored a more quantitative assessment of personality traits. By conducting factor analyses of a variety of traits, he arrived at 16 basic factors, or source traits, that he believed could be used to comprehensively assess an individual's personality. He divided traits into three categories: dynamic traits, ability traits, and temperament traits. *Dynamic traits* are those that set people in motion to accomplish goals; *ability traits* are those that determine how effective people will be in achieving goals; and *temperament traits* are related to the speed, energy, and emotional reactivity of people's responses (McAdams, 1990). Subsequent research has reduced Cattell's 16 source traits into five underlying factors, typically called the *Big Five*. Researchers have had various interpretations of how to describe these five factors (Digman & Inouye, 1986; Eysenck, 1973; McCrae & Costa, 1987), but the general dimensions involved are Extraversion/Introversion, Neuroticism, Openness to Experience, Agreeableness/Antagonism, and Conscientiousness/Undirectedness (McAdams, 1990). These five traits are believed to be the most basic descriptors of human personality.

The Situation

A second view of personality considers personality characteristics to be situationally dependent. In his controversial 1968 book *Personality and Assessment*, Walter Mischel proposed that the concept of traits as internal, stable, and global was a myth and that personality was in fact malleable and specific to individual situations. Other research findings have since supported the influence of situations on personality and behavior, highlighting the importance of gender, ecological settings, race and social class, and culture and history, among other factors (Block, 1971; Bronfenbrenner, 1979; Kagan, 1984; McAdams, 1990; Miller, 1984; Moos, 1973). Mischel's critique of the concept of personality traits began a debate between the two views of personality that still has not been conclusively reconciled. Over time, the field has settled on a compromise position whereby behavior is seen as a combination of personality traits and their interaction with the environment (McAdams, 1990).

Despite the compromise position taken by scholars in the field of personality psychology, the clinical, criminal, and profiling literatures still seem to treat personality as a trait-based construct, with little discussion of situational factors. Although the person-versus-situation debate in personality is revisited after reviewing some of the offender literature in chapter 10, for now it is noted that, regardless of one's perspective, personality, like motive, is a latent construct in the study of offender characteristics. Whether personality comprises internal, stable traits, or varies according to context and situation, it is nonetheless an inner experience that is not directly observable. If one considers the various measures of personality in the field of psychology, such as projective tests and personality inventories, it is apparent that scholars have access to personality characteristics only when they are brought out of the individual and manifested in some type of directly observable statement or behavior. Thus, as with motive, the accuracy of the inferences that can be made about personality within a science of profiling will be directly related to the validity and reliability of the tools that are used to infer personality characteristics from statements and behaviors as well as the degree to which behaviors and self-reported statements accurately reflect latent personality characteristics.

BEHAVIOR

From a profiling perspective, offender behaviors are the characteristics that are likely to be of the most direct value in identifying and apprehending an unknown perpetrator. Behaviors are observable, tangible, and more easily described and used for investigation than are motive and personality characteristics. Motive and personality characteristics, although they are important to an understanding of offenders and their offenses, are limited in their utility for investigations in two main ways: (a) motive and personality are latent constructs that are not directly accessible and (b) using latent constructs in practice (i.e., investigations) is challenging, if not impossible. By focusing on behavior, however, investigators can access these two latent constructs.

ACCESSING THE LATENT CONSTRUCTS OF MOTIVE AND PERSONALITY

To understand why behavior is helpful in elucidating motive and personality, one should first consider the three possible methods of accessing the latent constructs of motive and personality. The first potential method for accessing latent motive and personality characteristics is projective testing. Projective tests, which are rooted in the psychoanalytic tradition, attempt to tap into internal motivations and personality characteristics by presenting the respondent with ambiguous stimuli, such as pictures and ink blots, and asking him or her to interpret these stimuli in some meaningful way. Examples of projective tests include the Rorschach Inkblot Test (Rorschach, 1921) and the Thematic Apperception Test (Murray, 1943). Because the stimuli used in these tests are ambiguous, the individual's responses are believed to reflect his or her subconscious motives, needs, and drives. As mentioned in chapter 5, projective tests have come under increased scrutiny by the scientific community (e.g., Lilienfeld, Wood, & Garb, 2000). Although the techniques are described briefly here because they were designed to assess latent internal states and because they continue to be used by some researchers in the study of offenders (e.g., Turco, 1990), they are not included in the discussions of motive and personality that follow in chapters 9 and 10. Criticisms of the use of projective measures in a scientific context render them unsuitable for inclusion in a scientific model of profiling.

The second method used to access offender motive and personality is self-report. Self-reported motives or personality characteristics can be direct (e.g., "I killed her for the insurance money"; "I am a friendly, outgoing person"), or they can be assessed through self-report inventories. Self-report inventories are typically paper-and-pencil questionnaires that contain a variety of questions designed to tap into various personality constructs. Examples of these inventories include the California Psychological Inventory (Gough, 1957), the Minnesota Multiphasic Personality Inventory (Hathaway & McKinley, 1983), and the Millon Clinical Multiaxial Inventory (Millon, 1982). As discussed further in chapters 9 and 10, self-report methods in research are both widely used and problematic, particularly with regard to offenders. Although numerous studies have been conducted on offenders using self-report inventories (see chap. 10), results have yielded few consistent, valid, or practical inferences that can be offered to investigators with regard to motive and personality. Thus, although self-report research should not necessarily be abandoned, it is not an ideal method with which to assess offender motive and personality. In terms of its utility for investigation, self-report is simply not a viable way to access information about offender motives and personality. This is because self-reported data are not likely to be available from an offender until after he is apprehended, at which point the investigation will have already been successful.

The third potential method for accessing latent offender motive and personality characteristics is through studying their expression in behaviors. Behaviors have an advantage over both projective and self-report measures in that they can be directly observed rather than being filtered through an offender's self-description or interpretation. To the extent that latent motive and personality characteristics are accurately reflected in behavior, behavioral observation allows an assessment of these characteristics in a more direct and tangible manner. For example, whereas hostility is an internal state that is not directly observable, the manifestation of hostility as aggression is observable. As a behavior, aggression can be observed, measured, and even further operationalized in such examples as physical fighting, verbal insults, and throwing objects.

USE OF LATENT CONSTRUCTS IN INVESTIGATION

Motive and personality are also limited in their utility for investigations because, without translating them into behavioral characteristics, the description and use of latent or internal states for investigative purposes is challenging. For example, an investigative effort directed at urging law enforcement officers and members of the community to be on the lookout for a narcissistic offender motivated by greed would not likely prove fruitful. The description and use of behavioral information, although not perfect, achieves a higher degree of precision and utility. Thus, describing the narcissistic, greed-motivated offender as an individual who primarily targets affluent homes and financial institutions, who is not likely to display empathy for victims, and who is more likely to commit suicide than surrender if cornered, brings law enforcement a step closer to identifying the offender. Furthermore, depending on the amount and quality of crime scene evidence and the strength of the relationships between internal states and offender behaviors, there is a wide range of predictable offender behaviors possible, from broader behaviors, such as social relationships and associations, to very specific choices, such as vehicle selection. Thus, behaviors represent the transformation of motive and personality into usable variables for investigation. Behaviors are external to the offender, directly observable, and can be described and used by members of both law enforcement and the public.

INFERRED BEHAVIORS AND PREDICTED BEHAVIORS

There are two different levels of offender behavior relevant to a science of profiling: inferred behaviors and predicted behaviors. At the first level, there are behaviors that can be inferred from crime scene evidence. These are the types of behaviors that are discussed in chapter 7 with regard to crime reconstruction. For example, if a portion of the crime scene evidence in a given case consists of shell casings, a victim with a bullet wound, and a bullet recovered from the victim's body, then one can logically infer that the offender's behavior included firing a gun.

Inferred behaviors have also been discussed in the existing profiling models (see chaps. 2 and 3) under the rubric of *modus operandi* (MO) and *signature*. As described by these models, MO consists of those behaviors necessary to the successful commission of a crime. For example, committing a crime at night, breaking into a home through a back window, wearing gloves, and stealing valuable items are all elements of a burglar's MO. *Signature* is described as consisting of those behaviors that fulfill some type of deeper psychological need within the offender. Examples of signature behaviors might include ritualistic posing of bodies, asking victims to say or do particular things, and choosing a particular physical type of victim. Although these other profiling models appear to treat MO and signature as special cases of behavior worthy of separate study, within a scientific model of profiling these constructs can be considered to be part of the construct of behavior previously described, for two reasons. First, as discussed in chapter 3, there is no clear evidence to demonstrate that MO and signature represent special types of behavior; neither is there sufficient information provided by the extant profiling models to effectively distinguish between the two terms. Instead, there is a commonality between existing definitions of MO and *signature* in that both terms are considered to be behaviors. Barring compelling evidence that demonstrates that MO and signature are distinct from the types of behavior discussed in this chapter, they should be considered as part of other offender behaviors. Second, another common feature of MO and signature appears to be that both are behaviors that reflect an offender's objectives and inner needs. This is consistent with this chapter's description of behavior as reflecting latent aspects of motive and personality. This book therefore considers the types of behaviors that might be considered by other profiling models to be representative of MO and signature to fall under the more general category of inferred behaviors.

At the second level there are the behaviors that can be used to identify and apprehend an unknown offender. In some cases, these will incorporate behaviors from the first level. For example, the first-level crime scene behavior, "fired a gun," predicts the second-level offender behavior, "fires gun." In other cases, personality or motive characteristics will have to be inferred from behaviors on the first level, and these characteristics will then be used to predict behaviors on the second level. For example, the first-level crime scene behavior "fired a gun" might also predict a certain degree of hostility in the offender's personality. Hostility might in turn predict a prior history of altercations with the victim or with other individuals and might predict prior convictions for assault or other arrests for public disturbances. In addition to those second-level behaviors that are inferred from first-level behaviors, or from motive and personality characteristics that are derived from first-level behaviors, it is also possible that second-level behaviors will also be predictable from other second-level behaviors, either directly or by means of other motive and personality characteristics. For example, the second-level behavior "previous conviction for assault" might lead to the further prediction that the offender will have acquired prison-related tattoos. Likewise, the second-level behavior "previous conviction for assault" might be indicative of a certain degree of impulsivity, which might in turn predict behaviors related to poor credit and financial instability.

As demonstrated by the complexity in these different levels, it is impossible to consider offender behavior as an independent construct. Instead, in the same way that motive and personality characteristics are of limited use to investigations without a consideration of behavior, behavior is also inextricably related to motive and personality and cannot be considered in isolation from the offender characteristics that generate it. Even in cases in which it is possible to go directly from a single first-level behavior to a single second-level behavior, the constellation of behaviors that would be necessary to provide a comprehensive picture of an offender that would be of value to law enforcement requires considering the plausible internal motivational and personality states of offenders and determining the plausible range of behaviors that are consistent with those states. For this reason, chapters 9 and 10 discuss motive and personality together with a consideration of their relationships to behavior, to more adequately reflect the interplay between these three offender characteristics.

9

MOTIVE AND BEHAVIOR

As discussed in chapter 8, the constructs of motive and behavior are interrelated in a scientific model of profiling. Studies of motive in the offender literature that attempt to address motive separately from behavior are somewhat useful in that they speak to some of the common motives for various types of crime, and they add to the general knowledge base regarding the possible reasons why offenders engage in criminal activity of one kind or another. However, the studies that are of the most benefit to a science of profiling are those that attempt to describe the relationships among motives, offender behaviors, and crime scene evidence. Recall that the logic of the interplay among these factors is that crime scene evidence is predicted by offender behavior, which is in turn predicted by motive and personality characteristics, or by other offender behaviors.

Within the offender literature, research that considers motive in relative isolation is quite abundant. In contrast, very few studies consider motives together with crime scene evidence and behaviors. One area of offender research that includes studies of motive with and without a consideration of behavior and crime scene evidence is the study of arson.

DISCERNING OFFENDER MOTIVES:
AN EXAMPLE FROM THE STUDY OF ARSON

Within studies of arson, the effort to discern offender motives is typically approached methodologically in one of two ways: self-report and inference. In the self-report approach, offenders are asked to report directly on their motives for setting fires. In the inference approach, researchers attempt to infer or reconstruct an offender's motive without relying on self-report. The literature on arson motives is replete with studies that have used both types of approaches.

Each approach has its advantages and disadvantages. Although self-report can provide the most direct answers to questions about why an offender committed a particular act, offenders' responses cannot always be relied on to be truthful and insightful (Hare, Forth, & Hart, 1989; Rogers & Dickey, 1991). Offenders, particularly in situations in which legal resolutions have not yet been achieved, may have incentive to portray their motivations in a more benign light than may actually be the case. In addition, even when offenders have no desire to mislead researchers, it is not clear that offenders have insight into their own behavior or that they can articulate their motivations even when they do have such insight. This has been found to be the case with arsonists, for example, who are described in the literature as uncommunicative and unable to verbalize their reasons for setting fires (Hill et al., 1982), as having difficulty in accounting for their motives (Perrin-Walqvist & Norlander, 2003), and as having limited capabilities for expressing frustration and other emotions (Canter & Fritzon, 1998).

The second approach, inferring or reconstructing motives without using offender self-report, has the benefit of avoiding offenders' intentional and unintentional distortions of their motives. It presumes that the internal experience of a motive can be accurately described by examining information external to the offender. Unfortunately, it is not clear that outside observers can be any more accurate than the offender when attempting to discern offender motives. Overall, neither approach to discerning offender motives for arson has been conclusively demonstrated to be superior to the other. Therefore, this chapter considers research findings from studies that have used both approaches.

Discerning Motives for Arson Through Offender Self-Report

The vast majority of the literature on motives for arson is based on self-report data. Some of this literature empirically examines the self-reported motives of identified arsonists, whereas other literature describes motives in a more anecdotal or clinical way.

Clinical and Anecdotal Literature

The *Crime Classification Manual* (Douglas, Burgess, Burgess, & Ressler, 1992), which is used as a standard for investigating and classifying violent crimes, contains the most detailed nonempirical discussion of arson motives. Consistent with the Douglas et al. (1986) model, which is discussed in chapters 2 and 3, the manual relies on interviews with offenders and a review of the research literature (for which no citations are provided) to identify the hypothesized motives for arson: revenge, excitement, vandalism, profit, crime concealment, and extremism. These motives are briefly described so that the relevant empirical research examining motives for arson can be compared and contrasted with them. Given that this classification scheme is used as a standard by the FBI and other law enforcement agencies in practice, it would be beneficial to determine what, if any, aspects of these motive categories are supported by the research literature. Although building a science of profiling is dependent on the accrual of findings from empirical research studies, many of the theories being tested derive from profiling practice. Part of the value of building a science of profiling lies in assessing the similarities and differences between research findings relevant to profiling and the manner in which profiling is actually conducted. These comparisons will ultimately allow profilers to build on the practices that are valid and reject those that are not.

Fires motivated by revenge are set "in retaliation for some injustice, real or imagined, perceived by the offender" (Douglas et al., 1992, p. 173). Subcategories of the revenge motive include personal retaliation, societal retaliation, institutional retaliation, group retaliation (e.g., gangs), and intimidation. Excitement-motivated fires are set because the offender "craves excitement that is satisfied by firesetting" (Douglas et al., 1992, p. 170). The subtypes of excitement-motivated arson include thrill seekers, attention seekers, desire for recognition, and sexual perversion. Arson motivated by vandalism is malicious or mischievous in nature and results in damage or destruction. Subtypes include willful/malicious mischief and peer/group pressure. Profit-motivated arson is committed for material gain. Categories of profit-motivated arson include various types of fraud, employment, parcel clearance, and competition. Arsonists motivated by crime concealment set fires secondarily, to cover up a primary crime. The types of crime-concealment arson include murder, suicide, breaking and entering, embezzlement, larceny, and destroying records. Finally, extremist-motivated arsonists are those committed to further social, political, or religious causes. Subcategories include terrorism, discrimination, and riots/civil disturbance.

Holmes and Holmes (1996) and Turvey (1999) also have discussed motivational typologies for arsonists (see chaps. 2 and 3). As the reader may recall, Holmes and Holmes (1996) described essentially the same arson typology that is contained in the *Crime Classification Manual* (Douglas et al., 1992). In addition, however, Holmes and Holmes (1996) offered some statistics on motive gleaned from an article in *USA Today* and advised that anyone who is beginning to profile an arsonist should consider these as well; the primary sources for these data are not cited and therefore are not discussed further. Turvey criticized the typology in the *Crime Classification Manual,* calling it "another re-creation of the Groth rapist typology (Groth, 1979) with some non-sexual motivations . . . and a non-motive [e.g., vandalism] . . . thrown in" (p. 276). As an alternative, he advocated for applying his behavior–motivational typology (discussed in chaps. 2 and 3) to arsonists, with the addition of a category called *precaution-oriented behaviors* to describe situations in which a fire has been set to conceal, damage, or destroy the scene of another crime.

It is unclear whether the discussion of motives for arson provided by the *Crime Classification Manual* (Douglas et al., 1992), the comments of Holmes and Holmes (1996), and Turvey's (1999) modified behavior-motivational typology are reliable and valid. Although in some instances the authors indicate that research has been reviewed and interviews of offenders have been conducted, sufficient information is not provided to evaluate the nature and quality of these sources. Although it is certainly true that creative ideas about psychological phenomena can be generated from professional practice and informal study, these ideas should be considered hypotheses to be ultimately confirmed or disconfirmed by empirical research.

Empirical Literature

The research literature on self-reported motives for arson reveals some support and some contradictory evidence relating to the categories in the *Crime Classification Manual* (Douglas et al., 1992) and the nonscientific discussions of arson motives advanced by Holmes and Holmes (1996) and Turvey (1999). First, according to the FBI's *Uniform Crime Report*, juveniles account for over 25% of arson arrests (U.S. Department of Justice, 2003), and studies suggest that their motives may differ from those of adult firesetters. Research shows that the most commonly reported motives for firesetting among juveniles are curiosity and playing/amusement (Kolko & Kazdin, 1991, 1994; Perrin-Walqvist & Norlander, 2003; Showers & Pickrell, 1987), whereas the most commonly reported motives among adults are anger and revenge (Bradford, 1982; Coid, Wilkins, & Coid, 1999; G. T. Harris & Rice, 1984; Koson & Dvoskin, 1982; Lewis & Yarnell, 1951;

Prins, Tennent, & Trick, 1985). This separation between juvenile and adult arsonists does not appear to be present in nonempirical discussions of arson motives. Although Holmes and Holmes (1996) stated that "arson is a crime that is committed almost equally often by adults and by juveniles" (p. 96), they did not acknowledge that there might be important differences between juveniles and adults that might warrant separate study. Furthermore, although there is brief mention of juveniles in the motivational arson typology contained in both the *Crime Classification Manual* and Holmes and Holmes's (1996) book (e.g., the typical vandalism-motivated arsonist is described as being a juvenile), these descriptions do not address potentially important motivational differences between juveniles and adults because they fail to discuss adults and juveniles separately and draw comparisons between the two.

Second, despite the organization of the *Crime Classification Manual* (Douglas et al., 1992) into six types of arson motives, the range of self-reported motives in the empirical literature is actually much larger. In addition to the self-reported motives mentioned thus far, juvenile and adult offenders have also reported motives of self-injury (Swaffer & Hollin, 1995), suicide (Coid et al., 1999), peer group pressure (Kolko & Kazdin, 1994; Swaffer & Hollin, 1995), accident (Coid et al., 1999; Swaffer & Hollin, 1995), distraction (Perrin-Walqvist & Norlander, 2003), fascination (Swaffer & Hollin, 1995), attention-seeking (Coid et al., 1999; Sakheim & Osborn, 1999; Schwartzman, Stambaugh, & Kimball, 1994), no motive (Hill et al., 1982), and jealousy (Hill et al., 1982). In addition, an examination of the most common arson motives for both juveniles and adults indicates that only one of the most commonly reported motives (revenge) is explicitly represented in the *Crime Classification Manual* typology. However, other frequently reported motives, such as anger, curiosity, and playing/amusement, are left out. Although one could argue that curiosity and amusement could be subsumed under the vandalism category, and that anger and jealousy are simply proxies for the revenge category, it would seem that there might be important differences in the way these motives operate in facilitating criminal behavior that are not addressed by the categories contained in the manual's typology. For example, an individual who is motivated by revenge might engage in a higher degree of planning to ensure that the target of the revenge will be harmed, either physically or by the loss of valued property. However, an individual motivated by anger might be less concerned with setting fire to a particular property and might instead want to express his anger by setting fire to the nearest available target.

Third, the delineation of motive categories is not consistent across the empirical and nonempirical literatures. Some offenders report excitement as a motive (Coid et al., 1999; Lewis & Yarnell, 1951; Perrin-Walqvist & Norlander, 2003). Although excitement is one of the categories in the *Crime*

Classification Manual (Douglas et al., 1992), it appears that the description of this motive in the empirical literature is somewhat more diffuse than in the manual. For juveniles who express excitement as a motive, the experience is described as being exciting "because it was expressly forbidden" (Perrin-Walqvist & Norlander, 2003, p. 155). However, one study of adults described the experience of "pleasurable excitement when watching the flames" (Coid et al., 1999, p. 123). Although these descriptions may be related to the Thrill-Seeking subcategory of Excitement-Motivated arsonists in the *Crime Classification Manual*, it is unclear that they are adequately described by this subcategory, because no additional descriptors are provided in the manual.

Fourth, and finally, there is controversy over the role of sexual arousal as a motive for arson. Although Holmes and Holmes (1996) described sexual gratification as "a basic motive for the crime of arson" (p. 92), and the Excitement-Motivated category in the *Crime Classification Manual* (Douglas et al., 1992) contains a Sexual Perversion subtype, there have been challenges in the literature to the assumption that sexual arousal is a fundamental motive for arson (e.g., Quinsey, Chaplin, & Upfold, 1989; Quinsey, Harris, Rice, & Cormier, 2005; Wagner, 1974). The majority of literature proposing sexual motivations for arson has been anecdotal or otherwise uncontrolled (e.g., Axberger, 1973; Bourget & Bradford, 1987; Fras, 1997; Lewis, 1966). Of the self-report studies in which offenders report a sexual motive, this type of motive is the least common, ranging from less than 1% (Coid et al., 1999) to 8.3% (Hill et al., 1982), or otherwise described as "minimal" (Yesavage, 1983, p. 128). In addition, at least one study (Quinsey et al., 1989) found the hypothesized connection between arson and sexual arousal to be unsupported. Also, some literature suggests that sexual arousal to arson is an indicator of increased pathology or severity of fire-setting behavior in both juveniles and adults (Sakheim & Osborn, 1999; Slavkin & Fineman, 2000). The prevalence of sexual motives for fire-setting, as indicated by the 1% to 8.3% range previously described, however, appears to be so low that using it as an indicator in this manner does not seem appropriate.

Taken together, the anecdotal, clinical, and empirical literatures indicate that there is a wide range of motives for arson. Within this range, it appears that there may be differences between the motives of juveniles and adults, with juveniles being motivated by curiosity or play and with adults having more aggressive motives. Although the motive categories described by the clinical and anecdotal literature provide a simple way to organize arson motives, the relationship between these categories and their relationship to the findings from empirical studies is unclear. In some cases, the empirical data appear to be consistent with the conceptualization of motives hypothesized by the clinical and anecdotal data, whereas in other cases there are contradictions. Finally, there are some instances in which it is difficult to compare the two types of literature because of a lack of consistency in terms and concepts across the literature. For example, as discussed previously, although empirical studies have treated the motives of anger and revenge separately, the *Crime Classification Manual* (Douglas et al., 1992) does not appear to do so.

Discerning Offender Motives Through Inference and Reconstruction

The second way that researchers have attempted to understand the motives of arsonists has been to use crime information to infer an offender's motives, without relying on self-report. For example, multidimensional scaling techniques have been used to examine scatter plots of crime data and infer offender motive themes. The primary group of researchers who have examined arson in this manner have relied on a model described by Canter and Fritzon (1998) that proposes to differentiate arsonists according to motivational themes. This model is consistent with the Canter model of profiling (e.g., Canter, 2000) discussed in chapters 4 and 5. In their study of arson, Canter and Fritzon used smallest space analysis (SSA) to create a visual display of 42 offense behaviors from 175 solved cases of arson. As described in chapter 4, the authors selected offense information that they believed to be important to an understanding of arson and dichotomized them according to their presence or absence. Examples of variables used include Multiple Seats of Fire, Accelerant Used, and Lives Endangered Deliberately. In place of the interpersonal-narratives themes that Canter has advanced in his other writings (e.g., Canter, 2000), Canter and Fritzon partitioned the scatter plot according to dimensions of motive. According to them, there are two dimensions of motive relevant to arson, which reflect whether the motive is instrumental or expressive in nature and whether the action is directed at an object or a person. The combination of these dimensions yields four mutually exclusive facets: Instrumental/Object, Expressive/Object, Instrumental/Person, and Expressive/Person. These facets reflect both the motive and the target of the fire. For example, the Instrumental/Object facet reflects an instrumental motive that was directed at an object. An offender who set fire to a home to conceal a burglary would be considered to be in this category. In a subsequent article, Fritzon (2001) later named these categories Damage, Display, Destroy, and Despair, respectively.

Santilla, Hakkanen, Alison, and Whyte (2003) applied this same model and method to a sample of crimes committed by 66 juvenile arsonists. The authors partitioned the juveniles' offense behaviors into the same four categories described by Canter and Fritzon (1998) and concluded that distinct structural themes are also present in the arson behaviors of juveniles.

Finally, Kocsis and Cooksey (2002), using SSA, examined a set of 71 variables from 148 incidents of solved serial arson cases. Although they used a method similar to that of Canter and colleagues, they did not use the same motive themes. Instead, they referred to their model and division of the resulting scatter plot as reflecting "behavioral themes" (Kocsis & Cooksey, 2002, p. 631), even though the content of these themes appears to be quite relevant to motive, as indicated by the following description.

Kocsis and Cooksey (2002) made two distinctions in their interpretation of the SSA scatter plot. The first is to separate the central variables that appear to be common across arsons. These variables are not thought to distinguish between types or motives for arson; instead, they are believed to typify arsons. Common variables include planning, evidence left at the scene, and relationship with the target of the arson. Second, the outlying variables are divided into four themes: Thrill, Anger, Wanton, and Sexual. In the Thrill theme, offenders create "excitement or entertainment for themselves through setting fires" (Kocsis & Cooksey, 2002, p. 648). In the Anger theme, "animosity or rage seems to find expression in the commission of an arson attack" (Kocsis & Cooksey, 2002, p. 648). In the Wanton theme, a "generalized sentiment of animosity" is "visited on a vague class of targets" (Kocsis & Cooksey, 2002, p. 649). Finally, in the Sexual theme, offenders "associate the ignition of fires with sexual excitement and/or gratification" (Kocsis & Cooksey, 2002, p. 649). It is not clear from the study what proportion of arsons are represented by each theme, or what the strength of association is between the variables contained in each theme and the theme itself. Although the authors did not identify the theme descriptions as motives, it is apparent that the content of these themes can easily be restated as motives. Offenders in the Thrill theme are motivated by excitement or entertainment. Anger-themed offenders are motivated by rage. In the Wanton theme, offenders are motivated by generalized animosity. Finally, in the Sexual theme, offenders are motivated by sexual gratification.

There are merits to the type of research just mentioned. As discussed previously, by choosing not to rely on self-report these studies avoid the biases and ambiguities that can follow when arson offenders are asked to identify and report on their internal motives for setting fires. This research also has taken advantage of the behavioral and offender-specific information contained in samples of solved arson cases, rather than relying solely on clinical and anecdotal information. Finally, as discussed in the next section, these studies have been more comprehensive than traditional studies of motive in that they have also sought to associate motives and motive categories with offender behaviors and crime scene evidence.

Despite these merits, however, there are also several limitations to the studies described. The studies by Canter and Fritzon (1998); Santilla,

Hakkanen, Alison, and White (2003); and Kocsis and Cooksey (2002) are problematic for some of the same reasons identified in chapter 5. In brief, their selection of important variables is based on their own assessment of what information would be most valuable; they dichotomized variables at the risk of losing valuable, more nuanced, information; and they used a statistical technique that allows the imposition of offender themes based on interpretation rather than on the strength of association of any set of variables to a particular motive category. There are also some additional flaws evident in this particular set of research. First, even though Canter and Fritzon (1998) referred to the Instrumental–Expressive distinction as an underlying "motivational category" (p. 73), they concluded that their findings are based on "behavioural indicators rather than inferred motives" (p. 90). This apparent contradiction perhaps reflects the fact that, rather than using the data to infer motives, the authors proceed under the assumption that their four-group classification of motives is valid, and the data are to be interpreted accordingly. This is problematic because it is not clear that this assumption is correct. Admittedly, the goal of Canter's current research is not necessarily to test or demonstrate the validity of the four-group classification; however, it is still of scientific concern that the authors seem to presume its accuracy. Second, in the study of juveniles, although Santilla, Hakkanen, Alison, and Whyte (2003) described the thematic split of juvenile arson actions as "relatively specific" (p. 14), just 33% of the arsons in the sample contain only a single theme. Approximately 21% of the arsons evidence no theme, and approximately 45% evidence two or more themes. Although Canter and Fritzon (1998) and Fritzon (2001) did not provide this information in their studies, it is reasonable to expect that there is also considerable overlap between the themes of that research as well. Again, although these studies are not necessarily designed to demonstrate the validity of the four-group classification, the difficulty that the authors seem to experience with using these groups to differentiate clearly among arsons is problematic, because it challenges the assumption that these groups represent the best way to conceptualize motive. Third, no specific motives are provided in any of the Canter studies. To explain this, Canter and Fritzon (1998) wrote that there may be a number of motives for arson but, from their perspective, "the crucial point is the source of the determination to set fires and the objective that is the target" (p. 90). Although there may indeed be important differences between crime scene and offender characteristics of arsonists in the four motive categories Canter and Fritzon proposed, this organization neglects the potential for identifying finer distinctions that might be present in an examination of more specific offender motives.

Kocsis and Cooksey (2002) addressed motives that are more specific than those discussed in the other studies (Canter & Fritzon, 1998; Fritzon,

2001; Santilla, Hakkanen, Alison, & Whyte, 2003) because they statistically examined clusters in the scatter plot of their data rather than simply partitioning the scatter plot into sections according to general motive categories that were decided on ahead of time. What is unclear, however, is how well the analytic techniques and motive themes from this research will translate to other studies of arson or to arson investigations. Although Kocsis and Cooksey indicated that theirs was a study of serial arson, they did not specify how many arsonists were involved in the study. It would be expected that motive themes might be more consistent, and the number of themes would be more limited, within the arsons of a single individual compared with what might be found across the arsons of many offenders. The larger problem with this study is in Kocsis and Cooksey's interpretation of the clusters in their data scatter plot. Although they demonstrate the presence of associations between certain variables that form clusters, there is nothing in these clusters that conclusively indicates that there are central motives that drive their association; neither is there any evidence to suggest what those motives might be. Instead, the authors speculated as to the "deeper psychological meaning" (Kocsis & Cooksey, 2002, p. 648) behind offense behaviors and the clusters of those behaviors that they identify from the data. For example, in their description of the Thrill pattern, the authors identified that offenders in this pattern are typically older and physically unattractive (which is in itself a speculation or judgment). They stated that these features may "suggest the sublimation of a possible sexual drive" (Kocsis & Cooksey, 2002, p. 648). They asserted that in the Anger pattern the destruction of household items and the use of trailers to ensure thorough spread of the fire are both expressions of the offender's anger and rage. It is not clear how these behaviors necessarily indicate rage, however, and the authors do not present any evidence that anger, and no other factor, is the motivating factor underlying these acts.

Moreover, the studies that have attempted to discern offender motives through inference and reconstruction provide no consensus on the key motives for arson. Although the Canter studies also attempt to relate motive themes to other offender characteristics (described in the next section), their conceptualization of motive itself does not offer any incremental insight beyond the discussions of motive in the self-report literature. In fact, because the Canter studies do not discuss specific motives, one could argue that this research is of even more limited utility than the self-report studies in elucidating the reasons offenders set fires. Kocsis and Cooksey (2002), although they used techniques similar to those of Canter, ultimately applied the type of interpretive speculation that is criticized in the earlier chapters on nonscientific models of profiling. Because of this, their conclusions about motive exceed the bounds of their data and remain unproven.

RELATING OFFENDER MOTIVE TO OFFENDER BEHAVIOR AND CRIME SCENE EVIDENCE

Both the sections on self-reported and inferred motives for arson address the types of motives that appear to be common to arson and discuss some of the potential differences between these motives. However, the findings reported in the previous sections fail to address the more complex relationships among motive, offender behavior, and crime scene evidence. There are, fortunately, a few studies that have attempted to study these relationships. By attempting to correlate motives with offender behaviors and crime scene evidence, these studies represent the first steps necessary to determining the pathways that could be used to predict offender characteristics from crime scene evidence in a scientific model of profiling.

There are two groups of literature on arson that discuss the relationships between offender motives and both offender behavior and crime scene evidence. The first is the *Crime Classification Manual* (Douglas et al., 1992), and the second is the multidimensional scaling research conducted by Canter and colleagues (e.g., Canter & Fritzon, 1998) and Kocsis and Cooksey (2002).

In the *Crime Classification Manual* (Douglas et al., 1992), each motive category previously described includes sections that list the crime scene indicators and forensic findings frequently noted for that category. For example, in the vandalism-motivated arson category, the common crime scene indicators are use of materials present at the site, leaving behind physical evidence; matchbooks, cigarettes, and spray paint cans present; and mechanical breaking of glass rather than heat breakage. Common forensic findings include analyses of flammable liquids and glass particles on the clothing of suspects. Each motive category also includes a section on investigative considerations. This section describes offender characteristics that are supposed to assist investigators in identifying the correct perpetrator. For example, the vandalism category states that the typical offender in this category is a juvenile with 7 to 9 years of education. This individual is described as likely to be unemployed, single, and living with his parents less than 1 mile from the scene of the arson. Although not clearly delineated as such by the authors, it is apparent that the crime scene indicators, forensic findings, and investigative considerations represent offender behaviors and pieces of crime scene evidence. For example, "mechanical breaking of glass" and "living with parents" are offender behaviors. Likewise, "spray paint cans present" and "glass particles" are indicators of crime scene evidence.

Unfortunately, in addition to the problems already discussed with respect to the validity of the motive categories, it is not entirely clear how Douglas et al. (1992) arrived at these motive–offender behavior associations and motive–crime scene evidence associations. As described previously, the authors indicate that they reviewed the literature and interviewed incarcerated arsonists, but it does not appear that any statistical analyses were undertaken. Because of this, there is no way to determine how frequent the crime scene indicators, forensic findings, and offender characteristics are in each motive category; neither is there any information about which indicators and findings are more common than others. Most important, there is no evidence to demonstrate the predictive power of the motive categories in generating these pieces of crime scene evidence and indicated offender behaviors.

For example, as can be seen from the vandalism-motivated investigative considerations, some of the offender behaviors are directly predictable from other offender behaviors or characteristics, rather than from the motives themselves. For example, if it is the case that the typical vandalism-motivated offender is a juvenile, then it can reasonably be inferred that this individual is more likely than not to be unemployed, single, and living with one or both parents. This set of associations is consistent with the discussion of levels of behavior described in chapter 8. Thus, in this scenario, the behaviors of being without employment, being single, and living with one's parents are predicted from the offender's status as a juvenile rather than from the motive category described by the authors. In attempting to build a scientific model of profiling, the pathways linking motives, behaviors, and crime scene evidence must be clear. The organization and description of motive–behavior and motive–crime scene evidence associations in the *Crime Classification Manual* confuses the distinctions between behaviors that are predicted from elements of motive and those that are predicted from other behaviors. If the motive categories cannot be used to clearly predict the correct offender behaviors and related crime scene evidence, then the value of such a manual to a scientific model of profiling is lost.

The second type of literature to associate motives with offender behaviors and crime scene evidence consists of the multidimensional scaling studies conducted by Canter and his colleagues and by Kocsis and Cooksey (2002). Canter and Fritzon (1998) associated offender behaviors and crime scene evidence with motive categories by superimposing the motive categories over the multidimensional scaling scatter plot of arson behaviors and associating each motive category with the behavioral and crime scene elements contained in that section of the scatter plot. For example, the Instrumental/Person section of the scatter plot contains the following offense behaviors: prior threats to victim, prior arguments with victim, and use of alcohol. The main piece of crime scene evidence associated with this theme was the finding of accelerant use. Santilla, Hakkanen, Alison, and Whyte (2003) found similar associations in their study of juveniles. For example, in the Instrumental/Person section of the juvenile scatter plot, Santilla,

Hakkanen, Alison, and Whyte (2003) also found the behavior of prior threats and crime scene evidence indicating accelerant use. However, there also were differences between the offense behaviors of juveniles and those of adults. The authors found the following behaviors in the Instrumental/ Person section: materials brought to the scene, multiple fire seats or locations, and the targeting of a school. These offense behaviors were not present in the same section of Canter and Fritzon's (1998) scatter plot.

It is difficult to evaluate whether the associations between motive and offender behaviors and crime scene evidence, as described by Canter and Fritzon (1998) and Santilla, Hakkanen, Alison, and Whyte (2003), are reliable and valid. Because the authors in both studies selected the partitioning of their scatter plots according to their theoretical appraisals of what clusters of behaviors fit with what motive themes, a certain amount of speculation is introduced into the analysis from the beginning. Therefore, although both of these studies suggest some degree of association among motive themes, offender behaviors, and crime scene evidence, and the results suggest that there may indeed be important differences between juveniles and adults in these areas, it would be premature to assert that motives, as described by these authors, can be used to clearly predict offender behaviors and crime scene evidence.

In a related study, Fritzon (2001) examined 156 solved arson cases to assess the relationship of motive categories to the distance traveled to commit the arson. Using the four-group classification of offender motives, she found that arsonists with Expressive motives (Display and Despair) committed their crimes very close to home, whereas offenders with Instrumental motives (Damage and Destroy) traveled slightly further. She also found that arsonists who target people travel farther than those who target objects. These findings are of interest, because distance traveled reflects an offender behavior that may have implications for predicting other offender behaviors and crime scene evidence. For example, if an offender travels a long distance to commit offenses in an area that is not served by public transportation, investigators might be able to infer that he owns a vehicle in good working condition.

Although Fritzon (2001) examined a slightly different type of crime feature (distance traveled) as related to motives, the merits and criticisms of her study are similar to those of the other Canter studies. Once again, the difficulty lies primarily in the discernment and use of the motive themes. Thus, the predictive power of any associations gleaned from comparing these themes to other data is also uncertain.

Kocsis and Cooksey (2002) also related their motive categories to offender behaviors and crime scene evidence. For example, the Anger pattern is associated with targets that are residential locations or motor vehicles, the destruction of household property prior to setting the fire, use of trailers to ensure that the fire spreads throughout the target, and the departure of the offender immediately after setting the fire. Furthermore, the authors stated that offenders in the Anger category "tend to be foreign nationals who . . . tend to possess noticeable accents" (Kocsis & Cooksey, 2002, p. 648). These offenders are also described as being financially stable, and they tend to leave the crime scenes promptly after igniting the fires. Although Kocsis and Cooksey's use of cluster analysis to identify motive categories is somewhat of an improvement over the interpretive techniques used in the Canter studies, it would be of even greater value if the authors had been able to identify and use motives as factors to determine not only that there were groups of crime scene behaviors that seemed to emerge from the data but also that the basis for these groups was driven by the proposed motives. In addition, as the authors mentioned, the sample sizes in some of their analyses were too small to use for "establishing equations for predictive purposes" (Kocsis & Cooksey, 2002, p. 636). Given that the goal of conducting this type of research is to find ways to predict crime scene evidence and offender behavior on the basis of offender motives, the small sample sizes of individual clusters is an important limitation.

NEXT STEPS

As illustrated by the research conducted on motives for arson, there is still much to be understood about the nature and role of motive in the commission of crimes, how motives can predict certain types of crime scene evidence, and how motives might be related to offender behavior. The general lesson from the various types of literature on arson appears to be that there are differences between the motives of juvenile and adult arsonists and that investigators may ultimately be able to identify some of these motives by examining crime scene evidence and offender behavior. Unfortunately, each body of literature on arson motives has its limitations. The clinical and anecdotal literature, although potentially useful for generating ideas for study from investigative practice, is not even remotely scientific. The empirical self-report literature is perhaps the most methodologically sound as a whole; however, it is potentially limited by a reliance on offenders' appraisals of their own motives. In addition, because empirical research studies tend to examine small numbers of variables at a time, the empirical self-report literature presents only a small picture of the greater world of motives, and it does not generally relate findings on motives to crime scene evidence or offender behavior. The literature that attempts to infer or reconstruct offender motives is more comprehensive in the sense that the authors of these studies attempt to present a full picture of motive that incorporates crime scene evidence as well as offender behavior, but the number of studies is small, and each is tainted by the inclusion of the authors' speculations about motives and their organization.

Although this chapter's discussion has focused on the arson literature, a review of the broader relevant literature suggests that the conceptual and methodological issues identified in the arson literature apply to the study of motive across most crimes of interest to profiling. There are essentially two types of literature on motive. First, there are studies that examine motive for the sole purpose of learning more about offender motives but without considering motive from the perspective of how it can inform investigations. These studies, although well conducted, therefore do not address some of the needs that investigators might have, such as the description of relationships between motives and other important variables, for example, behavior and crime scene evidence. Second, there are studies that are designed to examine motives for the purpose of relating the findings to profiling. Although these studies are more relevant to a scientific model of profiling, they are typically not conducted with the type of scientific rigor that is present in the research examining motives more narrowly.

Given the limitations just described, it is logical to ask about the ways in which the self-report and reconstructive methods used in profiling should be improved. First, self-report studies of motive should be improved by conducting research across a broader and larger range of offenders. In addition to using larger sample sizes from a variety of jurisdictions, samples of offenders should be broad enough to include males, females, juveniles, and adults and should include individuals who have been convicted of their offenses, paroled, given treatment-related dispositions, or hospitalized, and they should incorporate both first-time and repeat offenders. This is necessary so that motives can be assessed across a wide range of offenders, in terms of age, gender, and trajectory through the criminal justice system. At present, it is not known whether important differences exist in motives across these various groups. It may be that there are central motives common to all types of offenders, or it may be that certain subsets of offenders are characterized by different types of motives. Second, self-report studies of motive should include a wider variety of crimes, including both violent and nonviolent crimes. Again, there is at present a dearth of literature comparing motives across various groups of offenders. Third, the self-report literature should be expanded to include analyses of crime scene evidence and offender behavior and their potential correspondence to various types of motive. Although creating taxonomies of motive, or simply comparing motives across groups of offenders, may be valuable in terms of increasing an understanding of motive itself, what researchers must do is relate motives to crime scene evidence and behaviors. As discussed previously, this type of research is essential to building a science of profiling that will have utility for criminal investigations, and at present it is sorely lacking. Fourth, studies that attempt to reconstruct offender motives without self-report should use statistical means to generate motive categories rather than relying on speculation. Factor analyses should be used to identify the crime scene elements and offender behaviors that load onto various motives. As discussed previously, one of the weaknesses in the Canter studies is the derivation of motive groups based on theoretical speculation. Instead, motive groups should be derived empirically, with factor analyses conducted to assess the degree to which these groups adhere to discrete constructs. Fifth, findings from self-report measures of motive should be compared with the findings of studies using reconstruction in an effort to approach convergent validity. This is important in the building of any science, so that researchers can determine whether important findings are valid, as opposed to being an artifact of methodology. Sixth, findings from both types of literature should be used to generate predictive equations, to determine whether motives can be accurately predicted from crime scene evidence. This is the ultimate goal of studying motive, from a profiling perspective. Ideally, it will become possible to generate predictions about motive from crime scene evidence and then use those predicted motive characteristics to make further predictions about offender behavior that will assist in identifying and apprehending perpetrators.

10

PERSONALITY AND BEHAVIOR

Personality represents a second group of offender characteristics that can be used to make predictions about behavior in a science of profiling. Studies of offender personality are valuable to profiling in that they identify the range of attitudes, dispositions, beliefs, and other personality traits or states that may operate within the realm of offending and offenders. For the purpose of building a science of profiling, it is critical to relate information about personality to behaviors and crime scene evidence. Although most studies in the extant literature do not explicitly link personality characteristics to behaviors within the context of offending, there is a considerable amount of personality research available on which to build (see, e.g., the discussion in this chapter). The task at hand is to examine the current state of the personality literature on offending; identify its strengths and weaknesses; and consider ways to improve offender personality research, with a specific eye toward relating personality characteristics to behavior and crime scene evidence to produce information that will be useful to investigations. This chapter describes how to accomplish this task, using the example of personality research in sex offending.

DISCERNING PERSONALITY CHARACTERISTICS: THE STUDY OF SEX OFFENDING

Sex offending provides a good example of the use of personality characteristics in profiling. For example, the models of profiling make special note of sex offenses. Holmes and Holmes (1996) listed sadistic torture in sex assaults, rape, lust and mutilation murder, and child molesting as some of the crimes most appropriate for profiling. Likewise, Douglas, Ressler, Burgess, and Hartman's (1986) model states that rapists lend themselves to profiling techniques and that profiling has been of "particular usefulness" (p. 405) in investigating serial sexual homicides. In addition, within the clinical psychological literature, studies of sex offenders have burgeoned over the last 20 years, and a significant portion of this literature has been devoted to the study of personality characteristics (e.g., Burgess, Hartman, Ressler, Douglas, & McCormack, 1986; Canter & Gregory, 1994; Dale, Davies, & Wei, 1997; Davies, Wittebrood, & Jackson, 1997; Dietz, Hazelwood, & Warren, 1990; Gratzer & Bradford, 1995; Kaufman, Hilliker, Lathrop, & Daleiden, 1993; Ressler, Burgess, Douglas, Hartman, & D'Agostino, 1986). In general, these studies have been conducted in an attempt to differentiate among types of offenders for the purposes of planning treatment and predicting recidivism. Some of these studies, however, also attempt to relate offense behaviors to personality characteristics and relate personality to other offender characteristics.

At the outset, it is important to note that the overwhelming majority of the literature examining personality and sex offending consists of empirical studies that use self-report personality inventories, including the Minnesota Multiphasic Personality Inventory (MMPI; Hathaway & McKinley, 1983), the Millon Clinical Multiaxial Inventory (MCMI; Millon, 1982), and the Eysenck Personality Questionnaire (EPQ; Eysenck, 1973). Also within the clinical literature are reported findings from studies of researchers using projective tests such as the Rorschach Inkblot Test (Rorschach, 1921) and the Thematic Apperception Test (Murray, 1943). As discussed in chapter 5, projective tests have come under increased scrutiny, and their use within the scientific psychological community is not encouraged (Lilienfeld, Wood, & Garb, 2000). For this reason, findings from these studies will not be considered.

It is also important to recall the person-versus-situation debate within personality psychology, which is described in chapter 8. Although there has been considerable disagreement over whether personality is composed of traits or more situation-specific states, with the recent consensus being that personality is best understood situationally, much of the offender and clinical literature treats personality as a trait-based construct. The studies that are discussed in the following section are all clinical in nature, and the reader should therefore expect a bias toward the understanding of personality as a trait-based construct unless otherwise indicated.

The sex offender literature on personality described in the following section discusses and compares three main groups of offenders: juveniles, adult child molesters, and adult rapists. Some studies examined these groups separately, whereas other studies examined combinations of offender types. For the purposes of this chapter, the literature on juveniles is considered in a single section. Although it is certainly the case that juvenile sex offenders can also be subdivided into those who offend against younger children and those who offend against older individuals or peers, the majority of sex offenses committed by juveniles appears to be perpetrated against younger children (G. E. Davis & Leitenberg, 1987). In addition, the empirical study of juvenile sex offending is still in its infancy, particularly compared with the study of adult sex offending, and the primary task in the study of juveniles has been to conduct research to validate clinical impressions. For this reason, the literature on juvenile sex offender personality is considerably smaller than that of adult sex offender personality, with few studies differentiating or comparing offenders according to victim age.

Juvenile Sex Offenders

The sex offender literature indicates that juvenile sex offenders are a heterogeneous population across many dimensions of assessment (Becker, 1998; Becker, Harris, & Sales, 1993; G. E. Davis & Leitenberg, 1987; Hunter, Hazelwood, & Slesinger, 2000; Worling, 1995). Because of this variability in juvenile sex offender characteristics, researchers have attempted to identify subgroups of offenders to facilitate treatment planning and assist in dispositional decision making. Juvenile sex offenders have thus been distinguished by demographics (Graves, Openshaw, Ascione, & Ericksen, 1996), crime type (Hagan & Cho, 1996), psychopathology (Kavoussi, Kaplan, & Becker, 1988), and family environment (Kaplan, Becker, & Cunningham-Rathner, 1988).

In addition, juvenile sex offenders have been described according to personality. Personality studies that have used a variety of self-report inventories have elicited clusters of personality traits that reportedly distinguish juvenile sex offenders from nonoffenders as well as from other types of juvenile offenders. For example, structural equation models examining the influence of personality on juvenile-perpetrated child molestation show adolescent child molesters to have deficits in self-confidence, independence, assertiveness, and self-satisfaction. Adolescent sex offenders appear to be more pessimistic and self-blaming compared with nonperpetrating youth (Hunter & Figueredo, 2000). Adolescent sex offenders also show higher scores on the Schizophrenia and Psychopathic Deviate scales of the MMPI than do non-sex offenders (Losada-Paisey, 1998). On Cattell's High School Personality Questionnaire (Cattell & Cattell, 1969), compared with oppositional-defiant adolescents, adolescent sex offenders have been found to be detached, self-indulgent, followers of others, and frustrated (Moody, Brissie, & Kim, 1994). These adolescent sex offenders have also been characterized as being impatient, demanding, and impulsive.

Other measures of personality have also elucidated clusters of traits that distinguish among different types of juvenile sex offenders. For example, adolescents who offend against younger children have demonstrated higher scores on the Schizoid, Avoidant, and Dependent scales of the MCMI, whereas adolescents who offend against peers show more narcissistic traits. Thus, adolescents who offend against children may have more difficulty with social interactions with peers and may be more comfortable relating to younger children, in contrast to offenders who target peers and are more exploitative (Carpenter, Peed, & Eastman, 1995). Structural equation models indicate a similar set of personality traits. Hunter, Figueredo, Malamuth, and Becker (2003) found that juveniles who offended against young children showed more *psychosocial deficits*—which they described as problems with self-esteem and self-efficacy as well as negative attributional styles, pessimism, depression, and anxiety—than those who offended against pubescent females. Offenders against children were further characterized by a lack of social confidence, feelings of social alienation, and a preference for the company of younger children.

On the MMPI, a sample of juveniles who committed sodomy behaviors scored higher on the Schizophrenia and Psychopathic Deviate scales than juveniles who committed rape and other types of sex abuse. Juveniles who committed sodomy behaviors also appeared to show more deficits in social skills than other juvenile sex offenders (Herkov, Gynther, Thomas, & Myers, 1996).

In the Netherlands, youth who committed solo sex offenses (i.e., without group participation) had significantly higher scores on scales of neuroticism and impulsivity and lower scores for sociability on a variety of instruments, including the Junior Netherlands Personality Questionnaire, the Adolescents Temperament List, the Amsterdam Biographical Questionnaire, and the Netherlands shortened MMPI (Bijleveld & Hendriks, 2003). In contrast, however, youth who committed sex offenses as part of a group had average, nondeviant scores on personality measures. Solo offenders were also three times more likely than group offenders to have committed previous sex offenses.

Within the literature that has attempted to distinguish among different types of juvenile sex offenders, there are two studies that have identified typologies for juvenile sex offenders based on personality traits. An early MMPI study designed to identify groups of adolescent sex offenders used MMPI factor scores to classify 178 adolescent sex offenders into four groups. Group I was described as shy, emotionally overcontrolled, and having few friends; Group II was narcissistic, demanding, insecure, and argumentative;

Group III was socially outgoing, honest, and prone to emotional out-bursts; and Group IV exhibited poor self-control and judgment and was mistrustful and undersocialized (Smith, Monastersky, & Deisher, 1987). An attempt to replicate this study using the California Psychological Inventory (Gough, 1957) revealed four similar groups in a sample of 112 adolescent male sex offenders: (1) Antisocial/Impulsive, (2) Unusual/Isolated, (3) Overcontrolled/Reserved, and (4) Confident/Aggressive (Worling, 2001). The Antisocial/Impulsive group was the largest. These offenders were characterized as having delinquent and impulsive personality traits and were most likely to have received criminal charges for their most recent offense. In addition, they were the most likely group to have been physically abused by their parents. Both the Antisocial/Impulsive and the Confident/Aggressive juveniles were most likely to be living in some type of residential setting. The two most pathological groups were the Antisocial/Impulsive and the Unusual/Isolated groups. They were most likely to have separated or divorced parents, and they were the most likely to have recidivated (sexually or nonsexually) at a 6-year follow-up assessment.

There are similarities among the sets of four groups identified in these studies. In both studies (i.e., Smith et al., 1987; Worling, 2001), two relatively healthy groups emerged. One group was emotionally overcontrolled and socially reserved (Smith et al.'s Group I and Worling's Overcontrolled/Reserved group), and the other was a group of honest, outgoing offenders prone to aggression (Smith et al.'s Group III and Worling's Confident/Aggressive group). In addition, two more pathological groups emerged in both studies. First was a group of antisocial and impulsive adolescents (Smith et al.'s Group IV and Worling's Antisocial/Impulsive group), and second was a group of emotionally disturbed, insecure youth (Smith et al.'s Group II and Worling's Unusual/Isolated group). These studies therefore suggest the presence of at least four clusters of personality characteristics for juvenile sex offenders. An examination of the remaining literature also indicates support for some, if not all, of these four clusters.

For the purposes of building a science of profiling, the value of discerning these personality characteristics lies not only in identifying types of sex offenders but also in linking personality characteristics or types with crime scene evidence and offender behaviors that are relevant for investigation. In this regard, there are two points of interest in the previously reviewed body of literature.

First, there appears to be a general distinction between the personality characteristics of adolescents who offend against young children and those who offend against peers or adults, such that offenders against children seem to display avoidance, a negative affective style, social skills deficits, and a preference for socializing with younger children. As noted earlier in this section, however, the limited number of studies that have differentiated juvenile sex offenders according to victim age warrants caution in interpreting this finding. However, if this distinction can be validated, it is significant because of its potential use in making predictions about unknown offenders. For example, if a young child reports to investigators that she has been molested by a teenager who is unknown to her, the inference that this perpetrator might be somewhat socially inept and prefer to socialize with children might lead to a different investigative strategy than if a teenage girl reported that she was raped by a same-aged peer. In both cases, an investigative strategy might be to interview teachers or counselors at the nearby high school, but in the first case it might be more fruitful to search for individuals who might present as more withdrawn or anxious, whereas in the second case the perpetrator may be more likely to have a more normal (although possibly delinquent) social circle.

Second, it is also apparent from the literature that at least a small subgroup of adolescent sex offenders will present as having average, nondeviant personality characteristics. Both of the typology studies (Smith et al., 1987; Worling, 2001) indicated two groups of relatively healthy personality clusters, and the study on solo versus group offenders (Bijleveld & Hendriks, 2003) also indicated that adolescents who commit sex offenses in groups show nondeviant personality characteristics. For profiling purposes, it would be useful to discern the types of crime scene evidence and offense behaviors that might be associated with these "normal" personality profiles.

Adult Sex Offenders

The literature on adult sex offenders divides offenders into child molesters/pedophiles and rapists. Some studies have examined the two types of offenders separately, whereas others compare them with each other.

Child Molesters

The literature on personality characteristics of child molesters seems to indicate a cluster of traits similar to those of juvenile sex offenders who offend against young children, discussed previously. The essential features of this cluster appear to be social ineptness, anxiety, avoidance, depression, and pessimism. Finkelhor and Araji (1986) proposed a model to explain this cluster of traits, suggesting that the "typical" child molester is socially and emotionally immature, with deficits in social skills and impulse control. The personality characteristics of child molesters are thus congruent with the developmental stage of their victims.

Studies using the MMPI and MMPI–2 (Butcher, Dahlstrom, Graham, Pellegen, & Kremer, 1989) have yielded some support for this cluster of traits and its specific relationship to child molesting. In terms of using personality traits to identify child molesters, clinical scales on the MMPI–2 have been used to distinguish child molesters from control respondents with an 81% degree of accuracy (Ridenour, Miller, Joy, & Dean, 1997). Studies have also used the MMPI to describe clusters of traits within samples of child molesters. For example, in a sample of 97 Roman Catholic priests and religious brothers alleged to have committed sex offenses against children, four clusters of personality traits were identified using the MMPI–2 along with other measures (Falkenhain, Duckro, Hughes, Rossetti, & Gfeller, 1999). The largest cluster, which constituted 42.3% of the total sample, indicated a pattern of social discomfort, insecurity, passivity, submissiveness, and deficits in emotional development. This is consistent with the model of child molester personality traits described earlier. Shealy, Kalichman, Henderson, Szymanowski, and McKee (1991) also found four MMPI profile subtypes in their sample of 90 incarcerated child molesters. Similar to the findings from the two typology studies of juveniles discussed in the previous section (Smith et al., 1987; Worling, 2001), Shealy et al.'s study elicited two less disturbed groups and two more pathological groups. The two more disturbed groups showed traits indicating anger, anxiety, poor judgment, and suicidal ideation. Finally, a study that compared the MMPI scores of child molesters with those of offenders against adolescents and adults (Kalichman, 1991) found that the scores of child molesters on the "neurotic triad" (Kalichman, 1991, p. 193) were higher than those of the other sex offenders. These score elevations suggest significant difficulty with developing interpersonal relationships, feelings of social alienation, immaturity, anxiety, and emotional disturbance.

Despite the previously mentioned support for a cluster of personality traits typifying child molesters, other researchers have had more equivocal results and have launched criticisms against research that claims to demonstrate accurate and reliable MMPI profiles for child molesters. For example, although some studies have found similar patterns of personality traits on the MMPI, as described earlier, several authors have pointed out that the percentage of offenders accounted for by these traits is rather modest. Mann, Stenning, and Borman (1992) found MMPI scale elevations indicating low social skills, discomfort, and submissiveness in their sample of pedophiles who were in sex offender treatment programs at state, federal, and military prisons. Unfortunately, this elevation was present in only 18% of their sample, leading the authors to conclude that there is no characteristic profile of a pedophile. Another study found that the most common MMPI profile in a sample of child molesters accounted for only 7% of the total and was not significantly more frequent than any other profile (Hall, Maiuro, Vitaliano, & Proctor, 1986). A larger study of 403 convicted sex offenders elicited 43 of the possible 45 MMPI code types (Erickson, Luxenberg, Walbek, & Seeley, 1987). For child molesters, the most common subtype accounted for only 12.6% of the total. These findings, indicating the heterogeneity of individual MMPIs for pedophiles, led the authors to state that the findings "do not support descriptions of any MMPI profile as typical of any sort of sex offender" (Erickson et al., 1987, p. 569). They further stated that attempts to identify individuals as sex offenders on the basis of the MMPI were "reprehensible" (Erickson et al., 1987, p. 569). This assertion is further supported by findings that the error rate for classifying child molesters using the MMPI is substantial. One study that compared MMPI scores and results from penile plethysmographs in a sample of 90 alleged child molesters found that even though scores on the MMPI separated child molesters who had deviant arousal from those who did not (McAnulty, Adams, & Wright, 1994), use of MMPI scores alone still resulted in the misclassification of one third of the individuals.

In addition to the failure of the studies discussed previously to identify a clear cluster of personality traits typifying the child molester, other studies that have used the MMPI have failed to find clusters of personality traits that distinguish child molesters from other types of sex offenders or that discriminate among different types of child molesters. For example, Quinsey, Arnold, and Pruesse (1980) found no differences among child molesters, rapists, violent offenders, and property offenders on the MMPI, and MMPI scores have also failed to distinguish between intrafamilial versus extrafamilial child molesters (Panton, 1979) and outpatient intrafamilial child molesters versus nonoffenders (Scott & Stone, 1986).

Other measures of the personality traits of child molesters have yielded similarly equivocal results. Studies that have used the 16 Personality Factors Questionnaire (Cattell, Cattell, & Cattell, 1993; Langevin, Hucker, Ben-Aron, Purins, & Hook, 1985; Langevin, Paitich, Freeman, Mann, & Handy, 1978) to examine pedophiles from clinical and forensic samples have failed to confirm the cluster of pedophilic personality traits proposed in the Finkelhor and Araji (1986) model described earlier. Although pedophiles were found to be more shy and reserved than control participants, there were no significant differences between pedophiles and other sexually deviant respondents. In Langevin et al.'s (1985) study, pedophiles were not found to be significantly more shy than the comparison group, and the authors also concluded that there was no support for the idea that pedophiles are unassertive, particularly as compared with other sex offenders.

Studies of pedophiles that have used the EPQ reported findings that support a cluster of traits consistent with the "typical" child molester described earlier, but a closer examination of the results seems to cast doubt on these findings. Wilson and Cox (1983) reported finding higher indicators of depression, loneliness, shyness, isolation, and sensitivity to social situations in a sample of 77 child molesters versus control respondents. Unfortunately, although pedophiles scored higher than controls on indicators of social deficits, the authors reported that there was no marked lack of social skills overall. In addition, the measures of depression and loneliness comprised face-valid items (e.g., "I feel lonely") and not valid clinical measures of depression or other mood disorders. Gingrich and Campbell (1995) found increased neuroticism in fixated pedophiles compared with regressed pedophiles, exhibitionists, and rapists. The division of individuals into the categories of fixated and regressed pedophiles, however, makes the interpretation of findings problematic, as there have been challenges to the validity of the fixated–regressed dichotomy of child molesters (e.g., Simon, Sales, Kaszniak, & Kahn, 1992).

More recent studies have used the MCMI to attempt to discern personality characteristics of child molesters. Similar to the studies that used the EPQ, these studies have reported promising findings that become problematic on closer examination. For example, one study (Cohen et al., 2002) found interpersonal deficits, lack of assertiveness, shyness, avoidance, narcissism, and self-doubt in a sample of pedophiles compared with control respondents. It is unfortunate that because the pedophile sample was not compared with rapists or any other type of offender, it is difficult to determine how particular this set of characteristics is to pedophiles or child molesters. It could be that these characteristics are also common to rapists and thus typify sex offenders as a group rather than being specific to child molesters. Other studies have found a higher degree of anxiety, depression, dependence, and avoidance in child molesters compared with rapists. Although the presence of comparison groups is helpful in demonstrating that the cluster of traits may be particular to child molesters, these traits represent only a portion of the cluster that has been discussed with regard to the "typical" child molester. The other characteristics measured by the MCMI that would be expected to occur in this cluster (e.g., negativism, self-defeating traits, and histrionic traits) were not found. Thus, these studies offer only partial support for a cluster of pedophilic personality traits (Ahlmeyer, Kleinsasser, Stoner, & Retzlaff, 2003; Chantry & Craig, 1994).

Other, isolated studies also have reported findings consistent with Finkelhor and Araji's (1986) model, but these have also been sufficiently problematic as to render their findings equivocal. For example, one study reported finding "anxiety neurosis" in a sample of pedophiles but did not explain how this was assessed (Bradford, Bloomberg, & Bourget, 1988). Fisher (1969) used the Edwards Personal Preference Schedule to compare individuals who offended against minors with control respondents. Although the results indicated that offenders against minors were more passive, insecure, and unassertive than control respondents, there was not as much difference between offenders against minors and other types of offenders. A study that used the Kelly Repertory Grid (Kelly, 1955) to compare pedophiles and control respondents determined that the pedophiles were lacking in social skills (Howells, 1979). Unfortunately, this was the only significant finding in the study, and a later project failed to replicate it (Horley, 1988).

Thus, an examination of the personality literature on child molesters does not reveal unequivocal support for any single profile of a typical child molester; neither does it show any consistent set of personality characteristics that distinguish child molesters from other types of offenders. However, the lack of consistent findings may have to do with the problems in the research more than with the lack of the existence of a personality profile. Aside from the criticisms levied against the individual studies of child molester personality just described, there are three overarching problems worth noting. First, there are no consistent definitions across studies of what a pedophile or child molester is. In some cases, *pedophile* and *child molester* are used interchangeably, despite the possibility that pedophiles may not have committed any illegal acts (see the discussion of the Holmes & Holmes [1996] model, chap. 2). There may be important differences in personality traits between offenders who act on their inappropriate sexual urges toward children and those who do not, but the overlap in definitions may obscure these differences. Also, differences in legal and social definitions of *child victims* may also create a certain degree of confusion, such that researchers using a legal definition of *child* might include victims up to age 18, even though such individuals might be considered by societal standards to be sexually mature (Okami & Goldberg, 1992). There may be important differences in personality between individuals who offend against prepubescent children and those who offend against teenagers that may not be clearly identified without a consistent definition of *child* that takes into account the multiple characteristics that define maturity (e.g., age, mental development, emotional status, physical development).

Second, few of the studies previously described have used nonoffender or non-sex offender control samples. This is an important issue because to show that there is a characteristic set of personality traits for child molesters, the research must not only demonstrate that child molesters consistently exhibit these traits but also clearly show that other types of sex offenders and general offenders do not exhibit these traits. If child molesters are shown to be socially inept, anxious, and depressed, but rapists and burglars show the same set of traits, then this cluster of traits cannot be said to exclusively describe child molesters. Instead, the cluster might more generally describe all sex offenders or all offenders. The failure to include control groups, or the appropriate control groups, in the existing studies thus makes it unclear whether the personality traits identified by these studies are more characteristic of specific or general groups of offenders (e.g., pedophiles, sex offenders, all offenders).

Third, there are data to suggest that sex offenders display substantial response bias on psychological tests (Grossman, Haywood, & Wasyliw, 1992; Lanyon, 1993; Wasyliw, Grossman, & Haywood, 1994) and that child molesters show more impression management than rapists (Nugent & Kroner, 1996). When completing self-report instruments, sex offenders, particularly pedophiles, may not answer questions honestly but instead may answer in such a way as to make themselves appear either more psychologically healthy, or more pathological, than they actually are. Because the vast majority of personality inventories have a self-report format, this tendency toward manipulating self-presentation is of significant concern. Depending on how successful offenders are at manipulating their personality profiles on these instruments, and depending on the direction in which they bias their answers (e.g., health vs. pathology), the results of studies that use these instruments to evaluate sex offenders are unlikely to reflect offenders' personality traits.

Rapists

The study of personality characteristics in rapists has been approached in a manner similar to that of child molesters. Efforts have centered primarily on the use of the MMPI, MCMI, and other personality inventories in an attempt to elucidate clusters of characteristics that typify rapists and distinguish them from other types of offenders.

A series of studies has identified five clusters of rapist personality characteristics using the MMPI (Kalichman, 1991; Kalichman, Craig, et al., 1989; Kalichman, Szymanowski, McKee, Taylor, & Craig, 1989). In the first of this set of studies (Kalichman, Szymanowski, et al., 1989), 120 incarcerated rapists were administered the MMPI, and the following clusters of personality emerged: Profile Type 1 contained no significant elevations. This was the least disturbed group, and their profiles were similar to those of other types of offenders. Profile Type 2 was characterized by antisociality and aggression. The authors described this type of offender as the "proto-typical rapist" (Kalichman, Szymanowski, et al., 1989, p. 153) who victimizes strangers. Profile Type 3 was described as antisocial and hostile, and offenders in this type were likely to commit rapes during the course of committing other crimes. Offenders in Profile Type 4 were said to show poor adjustment to incarceration. They were described as highly deviant, with a wide range of deviant personality characteristics. Finally, Profile Type 5 was characterized as the most deviant, with the greatest amount of psychological disturbance.

In a subsequent study (Kalichman, Craig, et al., 1989), a sample of 127 incarcerated rapists was administered the MMPI in an effort to replicate the earlier findings. Analyses resulted in the presence of the same five clusters. In an effort to cross-validate these findings, the authors reclassified respondents into cluster subgroups using the classification rules from the earlier study. Using this procedure, the authors were able to correctly reclassify 59% of the rapists into their clusters. Finally, in a study that compared rapists with child molesters and with offenders against adolescents, Kalichman (1991) used the MMPI to conclude that the rapists were the least disturbed of the three groups and evidenced emotional restraint and antisociality.

A more recent study that used the MMPI (Curnoe & Langevin, 2002) examined 228 offenders, comparing a variety of types of sex offenders and nonviolent, non-sex offender control respondents. The authors found considerable overlap between the mean scores of sex offenders and control respondents. Although they also stated that there were some group differences in levels of depression and persecutory ideation, the authors admit that this effect was not statistically significant (Curnoe & Langevin, 2002).

Research on rapists using the MCMI does not provide any clear insights into rapist personality traits. For example, one study found that rapists tended to show elevations on measures of dysthymic, posttraumatic stress disordered, and depressive traits; however, they determined that there were very few differences between rapists and non-sex offenders (Ahlmeyer et al., 2003). Likewise, another study that compared rapists, child molesters, and non-sex offenders reported that rapists' personalities were more similar to those of non-sex offenders than to those of child molesters (Chantry & Craig, 1994).

Studies that have used other measures of personalities have been similarly equivocal. For example, a comparison of semistructured interviews conducted with elderly sex offenders and elderly non-sex offenders found that the sex offenders tended to show more schizoid and avoidant traits. Unfortunately, the sample comprised a combination of child molesters and rapists, and findings were not reported separately for rapists (Fazel, Hope, O'Donnell, & Jacoby, 2002). A study of rapists and child molesters that used the Clinical Analysis Questionnaire and an additional semistructured social history questionnaire reported that rapists evidenced more inadequacy, insecurity, and passivity than did child molesters (Hillbrand, Foster, & Hirt, 1990), whereas another study found, conversely, that rapists were more extraverted than exhibitionists and pedophiles, as measured by the EPQ (Gingrich & Campbell, 1995). Unfortunately, both of these studies suffered from small sample sizes. Hillbrand et al.'s (1990) study used a sample of 29 patients in a forensic hospital, and Gingrich and Campbell (1995) based their conclusions on only seven rapists.

Compared with the child molester literature, the number of articles devoted to the description of rapists is small, and their findings are much less cohesive. The child molester literature primarily centers on the dispute over whether there is a cluster of personality characteristics, reflecting insecurity, passivity, fear, and avoidance that typifies child molesters. Although the findings have varied, the child molester literature nonetheless reflects a collective effort on the part of researchers in the area to address similar questions about the personality characteristics of child molesters. Studies using various personality inventories have thus provided both support and disconfirming evidence for the cluster of child molester personality characteristics previously described. In contrast, the literature on rapist personality has not seemed to settle on any one cluster of traits to either support or refute. As with the literature on child molester personality, the literature on rapists does not indicate any profile of a typical rapist; neither does this literature provide convincing support for the idea that there are distinct personality clusters that can be used to distinguish among different types of rapists or differentiate them from child molesters. However, as with the literature on child molesters, this may be because the literature on rapist personality contains many problematic studies that include limitations such as small sample sizes, lack of nonoffender control groups, and a scattered representation of a seemingly infinite variety of personality traits across samples of rapists. These difficulties render it virtually impossible to draw any reliable and valid conclusions about the personality traits of rapists based on the use of personality inventories and the studies discussed earlier.

RELATING OFFENDER PERSONALITY TO CRIME SCENE EVIDENCE AND OFFENDER BEHAVIOR

With respect to the relationship among sex offender personality, crime scene evidence, and offender behavior, the previously reviewed literature is of very limited use to a science of profiling, for two main reasons. First, the literature itself is unclear and imprecise. Across both juvenile and adult studies, the literature consists of very general conclusions about sex offender personality. These conclusions center on a search for clusters of personality characteristics that will describe child molesters and rapists and distinguish them from other types of offenders. Unfortunately, as already noted, it is not clear that such clusters of characteristics can be consistently found. It is also not clear that where clusters of personality characteristics appear to exist, they describe sex offenders and not offenders in general. It is also unclear that certain personality characteristics describe child molesters or rapists specifically, rather than sex offenders in general. Attempts to make these finer distinctions and clear demarcations between sex offenders and other offenders, as well as among different types of sex offenders, appear to have been largely unsuccessful.

Second, the literature has failed to demonstrate relationships between personality characteristics and crime scene evidence and behavior. Most of the studies that are reviewed in this chapter do not explicitly link personality characteristics with crime scene evidence or offender behaviors at all. Instead, most of these studies relate personality traits to each other. For example, one of the juvenile sex offender personality clusters identified by Smith et al. (1987) describes a constellation of traits that includes narcissism, demandingness, insecurity, and argumentativeness. This suggests that the four offender characteristics described are related to each other in some way and can be expected to occur together. Thus, from a profiling perspective, when one finds a juvenile sex offender who is narcissistic, one may also find that same offender to be argumentative. Another example can be seen in Falkenhain et al.'s (1999) clusters of alleged child molesters. The most prevalent cluster of alleged offenders in that study indicated a pattern encompassing the traits of social discomfort, insecurity, passivity, submissiveness, and deficits in emotional development. Thus, if one can determine that a child molester is insecure, it is also likely that he will turn out to be passive and submissive. Unfortunately, these types of relationships are not sufficient to be of use in an investigation because they do not refer to behavior. As described in chapter 8, the value of having information about personality traits lies in what they can predict about behavior and, consequently, crime scene evidence. For example, if the traits of insecurity, passivity, and submissiveness described by Falkenhain et al. could be described in terms of how they predict how a child molester will behave during the commission of a crime and, thus, what kind of evidence he will leave behind, they would be of increased value to the field of profiling. It may be that a child molester who possesses these three traits would be hesitant to approach a child, would seek reassurance from the child, and would withdraw on rejection from that child rather than use any kind of physical force. Thus, the evidence that would be left might include verbal statements to the victim asking for reassurance or approval, lack of physical injury to the victim, and a cessation of sexually inappropriate behavior on a refusal from the victim. Unfortunately, the majority of studies of personality and sex offending have not used personality characteristics to make predictions about offender behavior such as these.

A small number of studies in the reviewed literature have attempted to link offender personality traits or clusters to offense behaviors. For example, in an MMPI study of rapists, the Profile Type 2 (antisocial and aggressive) rapist was described as being likely to attack strangers, and Profile Type 3 (antisocial and hostile) rapists were described as being more opportunistic and likely to commit sex offenses during the course of committing other crimes (Kalichman, Szymanowski, et al., 1989). From an investigative perspective, associations such as this suggest that certain personality traits may predict variations in offense behaviors. Unfortunately, even if these inferences and relationships are valid, they would still not be specific enough to narrow down a pool of suspects to a single individual. The process of relating a somewhat generalized cluster of personality traits (antisocial and aggressive) to a generalized description of offense behaviors (offends against strangers) is not rigorous enough to be a useful tool to law enforcement and is somewhat reminiscent of the kinds of investigative inferences suggested by the nonscientific profiling models. For example, in the nonscientific profiling models it is also not uncommon to see generalized descriptions of personality (e.g., organized) related to equally generalized descriptions of offense behaviors (e.g., plans the offense). These limited studies are therefore too vague to advance the state of knowledge with regard to relationships between personality characteristics and sex offense behavior. In addition, the validity and reliability of associations such as those previously described remains to be seen. In future research, offender personality characteristics and offense behaviors should be separated into discrete variables to be measured and related to each other through statistical analyses. For example, rather than describing a profile of antisocial–aggressive or antisocial–hostile personalities (which appear on the face to be very similar personality types), the individual personality characteristics proposed as composing these groups could be measured and compared with specific offense behaviors, such as breaking into a victim's home, hitting her, or stealing her property.

Despite the shortcomings of the personality literature on child molesters and rapists, there is an area of personality research that has demonstrated some promise in elucidating important personality traits among sex offenders. This area of study is psychopathy. *Psychopathy* is a clinical construct that encompasses a variety of interpersonal, affective, and lifestyle characteristics (Cleckley, 1976; Hare, 1999). Interpersonally, psychopaths are "grandiose, arrogant, callous, dominant, superficial and manipulative" (Hare, 1999, p. 183). In terms of affect, they are "short-tempered, unable to form strong emotional bonds with others, and lacking in guilt or anxiety" (Hare, 1999, p. 183). Their lifestyles are socially deviant, such that psychopaths tend to ignore social conventions and engage in impulsive and irresponsible behavior.

Although not all psychopaths are criminal offenders, the constellation of traits central to psychopathy is certainly consistent with increased contact with the criminal justice system. In particular, the prevalence of psychopathy in sex offenders is noteworthy. Among rapists and individuals who offend against both children and adults, the prevalence is estimated to be between 40% and 50% (Hare, 1999). One study that compared sex offenders with incarcerated non-sex offenders ($n = 329$) found that 64% of the mixed offenders (offenders against both children and adults) were psychopaths (Porter et al., 2000).

Psychopathy is also a robust predictor of both sexual and violent recidivism, particularly when paired with deviant sexual arousal. Psychopathy has been found to be a general predictor of both violent and sexual recidivism (Quinsey, Harris, Rice, & Cormier, 2005; Quinsey, Rice, & Harris, 1995). Within 6 years of release, 80% of psychopaths recidivated violently (which included many instances of sexual recidivism as well), compared with 20% of nonpsychopaths. High scores on the Psychopathy Checklist (Hare, 1991) have been found to predict violent recidivism and, when paired with deviant sexual arousal as measured by the penile plethysmograph, high scores also predicted sexual recidivism (Rice & Harris, 1997). Furthermore, psychopathy paired with deviant sexual arousal appears to predict not only increased recidivism but also faster recidivism (Serin, Mailloux, & Malcolm, 2001).

Of particular relevance to profiling are the findings that link psychopathy to certain crime scene evidence and offender behaviors. Currently, there are three sets of findings that may inform a science of profiling in this regard. First, psychopaths are more likely to have convictions for non-sex offenses than for sex offenses (Hare, 1999). Therefore, if there are indicators of psychopathy during the investigation of a sex offense, it would not be fruitful to limit offender searches to individuals who have exclusive convictions for sex offenses. Second, there is substantial evidence to suggest that the sex offenses of psychopaths are more violent and sadistic than those of other sex offenders (Barbaree, Seto, Serin, Amos, & Preston, 1994; Quinsey et al., 1995; Serin, Malcolm, Khanna, & Barbaree, 1994). Pending the outcome of more comprehensive data sets demonstrating the validity of this finding, it may eventually become possible to use these crime features (evidence of excessive violence or sadism) to predict psychopathic personality traits and thereby narrow the pool of potential suspects in an investigation. Finally, A. J. R. Harris and Hanson (1998) found that high scores on the Psychopathy Checklist (Hare, 1991), combined with deviant sexual arousal, predicted more prior sex offenses, more kidnapping and forcible confinement, more non-sex offenses, and more violent recidivism than in other sex offenders. Once again, pending the appropriate empirical validation of these findings, it may be possible to use this research to make predictions about psychopathic offenders based on certain crime behaviors.

In terms of relating findings on sex offender personality to other information that is relevant to investigations, the body of literature on psychopathy and sex offending shows the most promise for informing a science of profiling. This literature uses the constellation of traits associated with the construct of psychopathy to successfully make predictions about crime behaviors (e.g., increased violence), past behavior (e.g., varied criminal record), and future behavior (e.g., likelihood and speed of recidivism). Future studies of personality and sex offending that are conducted with investigative goals in mind should therefore incorporate psychopathy in attempting to make predictions about offenders and their offenses.

PERSONALITY AND PROFILING

Aside from the psychopathy literature, the limitations evident in attempting to relate the sex offender personality literature to a science of profiling are not uncharacteristic of the problems with other types of literature on personality. However, the specific limitations evident in much of the extant personality research can be remedied to make the application of personality to studies of offenders more suitable for profiling across a wide variety of offenses.

First, few studies on personality characteristics of offenders have been designed or carried out with profiling in mind. The goal of linking personality traits, crime scene features, and other offender characteristics is specific to an investigation and is not necessarily shared by researchers who conduct their studies with treatment or diagnostic concerns in mind. This disparity in goals makes it difficult to find studies on personality that attempt to associate their findings with other crime and offender characteristics.

Second, the literature on offender personality, like the clinical literature on sex offender personality, generally considers personality characteristics to be global, stable traits rather than conceiving of them as malleable and situation dependent. This is especially the case in discussions of personality within the profiling literature. Pinizzotto and Finkel (1990) stated that profiling "focuses attention on individuals with personality traits that parallel traits of others who have committed similar offenses" (p. 216). Ressler and Shachtman (1992) distinguished among types of offenders who "have very different personalities" and argued that these distinctions are "important to unraveling a crime" (p. 137). Holmes and Holmes (1996) discussed "the personality traits necessary to mold a criminal mind" (p. 28). Rossmo (2000) similarly wrote that the "interpretation of crime scene evidence can indicate the personality type of the individual(s) who committed the offense" (p. 68). It has thus been long assumed in profiling that offenders have distinct, discrete, stable, and predictable personality traits that can be determined by examining the crime scene evidence.

However, as discussed in chapter 8, the view of personality as dispositional rather than situational is no longer an uncontested or predominant paradigm among personality theorists. Alison, Bennell, and Mokros (2002) identified the personality paradox first articulated by Bem and Allen (1974) that is now evident in the offender and profiling personality literature. According to the original authors, a paradox exists whereby individuals persist in inferring global and stable traits from the behaviors of others, even though empirical evidence demonstrates that trait constructs fail to predict behavior accurately across time and situations. This position has been supported by a number of other studies (Cheek, 1982; Dudycha, 1936; Kenrick & Stringfield, 1980; Mischel & Peake, 1982; Underwood & Moore, 1981). The roles of situational influences and the interactions between person and situation have thus been increasingly favored over traditional trait approaches (e.g., Bowers, 1973; Cervone & Shoda, 1999) in the personality and social psychology literature.

Given the inadequacy of the personality trait approach for investigative purposes, as highlighted by the equivocal findings from studies of sex offending, it seems that a science of profiling would more likely be advanced by viewing personality characteristics in the context of situational factors. As Alison et al. (2002) pointed out, this will be a challenging task. It is rare that contextual information on crimes, aside from items such as the time, date, location, and victim information, is available for study. As a starting point, Alison et al. recommended conducting interviews with both non-offenders and offenders to assess what situational factors they consider to be relevant to certain behaviors. For example, some offenders may become hostile if they encounter victim resistance. Likewise, other offenders may become controlling in high-risk situations. By turning these into if–then statements (e.g., "If the victim resists me, then I become hostile") and cluster-analyzing the contingencies, it may be possible to generalize from one if–then contingency to another within the same taxonomic group (e.g., sex offenders).

Alison et al.'s (2002) approach to the application of personality to profiling is a promising starting point. There are four additional considerations that might enhance these ideas. First, the offender interviews suggested by Alison et al. should be conducted on a large scale, using a comprehensive population of offenders across a variety of states and jurisdictions. Second, in addition to conducting interviews, there may be additional value in using self-report instruments such as the MMPI and MCMI. Although there are certainly limitations to using these instruments, their utility may be increased if they are administered in various contexts and at multiple points in time. For example, instruments could be administered at arrest, pre- and post-conviction, and after the appellate process and subsequent adjustment to incarceration. Although caution must be exercised in that the validity of results may be affected if this retesting occurs at intervals that are too brief, it may be possible to use results from multiple test administrations to determine whether the personality traits that are evident nearer to the time that a crime is committed are consistent with the personality traits that emerge once crime events have been resolved. Currently, personality inventories are typically administered only after an offender is incarcerated or in treatment. The offender's attitudes, dispositions, and beliefs may therefore bear little resemblance to those he held at the time of the commission of the offense as well as to the behaviors that may have been generated from those attitudes, dispositions, and beliefs. Thus, to generate the types of if–then contingencies described by Alison et al. and relate offender statements of personality to predictions about behavior, one must discard the assumption that the personality characteristics identified by self-report instruments are global and stable in favor of an approach that permits variations in personality across situations.

Third, as mentioned in the discussion of offender motives, self-report data can be problematic for a variety of reasons, particularly when dealing with criminal offenders. Therefore, in addition to garnering offenders' own appraisals of their behavior and personality characteristics in various contexts through self-report inventories, it would be wise to investigate ways to measure personality traits without relying on self-report. This would likely require behavioral assessment but, unlike the studies mentioned earlier that have approached behavioral assessment of personality traits in an effort to demonstrate trait consistency and stability, newer studies might consider the influence of situations and environments on personality assessment and provide more context-specific appraisals of offender personality traits (e.g., behavioral assessments conducted at both the home and the workplace).

Finally, personality characteristics per se are not likely to be directly useful for profiling and criminal investigations, even when situational factors are taken into account. Understanding that an offender is shy in social situations, for example, will not necessarily assist police in identifying and apprehending him. Instead, the value of personality lies in its potential to predict characteristics that are of greater use to law enforcement, such as crime scene evidence and concrete offender behaviors. Therefore, in addition to conducting analyses on patterns of personality characteristics, studies of offender personality should reference the immense databases of collateral materials that have been collected across various law enforcement jurisdictions, to compare data gleaned from interviews and other personality assessments with crime scene information and crime behaviors. For example, information about the personality traits of a sample of burglars could be compared with crime scene evidence and police reports of offender behaviors from the offenses of those same burglars. On the basis of these comparisons it may be possible to make predictions about the offense behaviors and pieces of crime scene evidence that would be left by burglars with particular personality traits. Note that consideration should be given to the validity of testing contained in collateral materials, as this testing may not have been conducted with the rigor that would be expected in a scientific study. Where appropriate, testing may need to be conducted prospectively to ensure validity.

It is clear that there is much to be done with regard to creating a new literature of personality that can inform a science of profiling. Although the study of personality has been long-standing, and the basic tenets have been in place for decades, as Alison et al. (2002) pointed out, the adaptation of these tenets to profiling requires a paradigm shift and a new body of research that examines personality and offending in the light of situational and contextual factors. Although the challenge of building this body of research will be great, the potential benefits will be increased specificity and precision in relating offender personality characteristics to various offense situations and behaviors through the thorough study of personality across a wide variety of offenders and offenses. With adequate research, it may eventually be possible to use personality characteristics to make reliable and valid predictions about crime scene evidence and offender behavior that will enhance criminal investigations.

11

A SCIENTIFIC MODEL OF PROFILING

Thus far in this book, on the basis of the investigative and forensic science practice literature, the types of crime scene evidence that are typically available and submitted for analysis by law enforcement investigators have been described. The process of crime reconstruction, in which attempts are made to translate these pieces of crime scene evidence into a narrative of crime events and offender behaviors has been discussed and evaluated. Next, the examination of crime scene evidence, offender motives, personality, and behavior in chapters 7 through 10 identified pieces of the science that can be used to build a new scientific model of profiling. Chapters 8 through 10 further demonstrate the primacy of behavior as an expression of both motive and personality. Finally, using arson and sex offending as examples from the psychological and criminological literature, relationships between motive and behavior and personality and behavior have been selectively examined.

Consistent with much of the empirical literature in the fields of psychology and criminology, the arson and sex offending literatures have approached the study of motive and personality, respectively, by examining limited, often bivariate relationships between variables of interest (e.g., personality type and type of sex offense; motive and age). The isolated cases in which these relationships have described situations relevant to investigation (e.g., increased violence in the sexual offenses of psychopaths), along with select findings from the multidimensional scaling research specific to profiling, have provided a promising although modest look into what a scientific model of profiling may be able to offer to the practice of criminal investigation.

Even the most promising findings, however, represent only pieces of profiling. For example, the prediction that an offender who kidnaps a victim and commits an uncharacteristically violent sexual offense is likely to have personality characteristics consistent with psychopathy, although potentially useful, represents only a portion of what investigators would need to know to successfully identify and apprehend the correct perpetrator. Likewise, the findings of differences in motive types between juvenile and adult arsonists are still insufficient for advancing investigative practices because they do not provide a comprehensive set of offender characteristics that would narrow down a suspect pool sufficiently to identify and apprehend the correct perpetrator.

To a great extent, the lack of comprehensiveness in the profiling literature on offender characteristics is simply an artifact of empirical study. In science, knowledge about a phenomenon is achieved through the gradual accrual of studies examining manageable, precise relationships between aspects of the phenomenon of interest. Thus, studies in the offender literature have related individual offender characteristics (e.g., motive) to individual behaviors (e.g., fire setting) and small sets of personality characteristics (e.g., a proposed cluster of pedophilic personality traits) to subsets of behavior (e.g., child molestation vs. rape) in the hope that these individual findings will eventually produce a collective body of literature that will describe the larger world of offenders and their offenses. Although the process of conducting these individual studies of the relationships between small numbers of variables will gradually add to the knowledge base of criminal offending, a scientific model of profiling requires the conceptualization and investigation of a broader picture of profiling-related variables. This is because the task of making the kinds of investigative predictions necessary to profiling requires understanding the relationships and pathways that link multiple sets of variables rather than the simple bivariate relationships predicted by many offender studies. Indeed, as demonstrated by chapters 8 through 10, the offender characteristics of motive, personality, and behavior do not lend themselves easily to simple bivariate analyses. Instead, multiple variables, some observable and some latent, are proposed to interact in the commission of a given crime.

This chapter describes in greater detail what this proposed broader picture of profiling involves, in preparation for a discussion of the steps necessary to begin empirical testing. First, a conceptual scientific model of profiling is proposed. This model incorporates the components of crime scene evidence, motive, personality, and behavior and describes their interaction. Second, the homicide research conducted by Canter and colleagues is reviewed to describe and evaluate the only other current scientific approach that studies variables of offender motive, personality, and behavior simultaneously. This research will be evaluated to assess its relationship to the proposed scientific model of profiling and to identify contributions that can be made to a science of profiling from this literature. Finally, the role of situational factors in crime is discussed, and their incorporation into the proposed scientific model of profiling is described.

MODEL OF CRIME SCENE EVIDENCE, MOTIVES, PERSONALITY, AND BEHAVIOR

In chapters 7 through 10, the components of a scientific model of profiling are described, and bivariate relationships among crime scene evidence, motives, personality, and behavior, are discussed and illustrated with examples from the offender literature. As previously mentioned, however, these types of relationships do not comprehensively represent the multiple relationships between variables that are at work in any given crime. Instead, they illustrate only pieces of a larger model of offending. This larger model of offending, using the same variables described in chapters 7 through 10, is presented in Figure 11.1. This model includes the same types of bivariate relationships already discussed but also allows for more complex interrelationships among variables that are currently unaccounted for by much of the offender literature. The same model of offending, using an example of a murder to illustrate the relationships among variables, and to assist the reader with the following description of the model's components, is presented in Figure 11.2.

There are three important points to note before discussing this model. First, although the model and example described in Figures 11.1 and 11.2 are more comprehensive in terms of the types of relationships described, they are nonetheless pared-down versions of what an investigator would see in an actual crime. The model is presented in its simplest form to clearly describe the components and the proposed relationships among components. Thus, in the murder example, the crime scenario contains only three pieces of crime scene evidence—a fraction of what would be expected in a true murder investigation. Second, depending on the type of crime, the nature and quality of crime scene evidence, and the reliability and validity of the relationships linking the model's variables, a model of profiling could take multiple forms. A more complex model and example is presented after this initial description to illustrate how the models for different crime scenarios may differ. Third, the predictors and relationships between variables provided in the murder example (and in the burglary example that follows

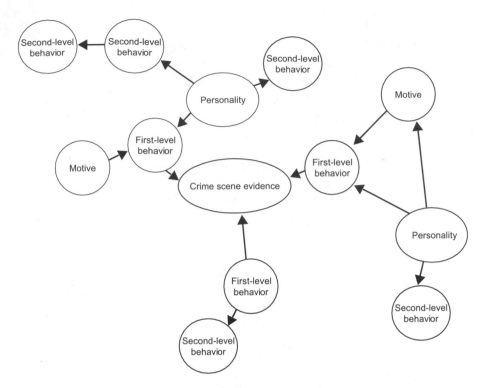

Figure 11.1. Basic structure of a scientific model of profiling.

later) are hypothetical. Given the current paucity of research providing reliable and valid links among behaviors, motive, and personality, as described in chapters 8 through 10, there is currently no basis on which to assert clear predictors and specific relationships between variables (e.g., hostility predicts previous assaultive behavior). Thus, the predictors and relationships in the examples, although they have face validity and are logically derived, have not yet been borne out by research. As discussed in chapter 12, this is an area that requires further empirical study.

As demonstrated by Figure 11.1, the basic structure of a scientific model of profiling is that of a branching cluster of variables that can be organized into tiers of predicted relationships. The relationships specific to the commission of the crime of interest point inward toward the most central set of variables: the crime scene evidence. The relationships specific to the behaviors of the offender that may assist in identifying and apprehending him branch outward from the crime-related variables, with the terminal point of each branch being an investigation-relevant offender behavior. Organized around this structure, the most basic profiling model can be described in three tiers as follows.

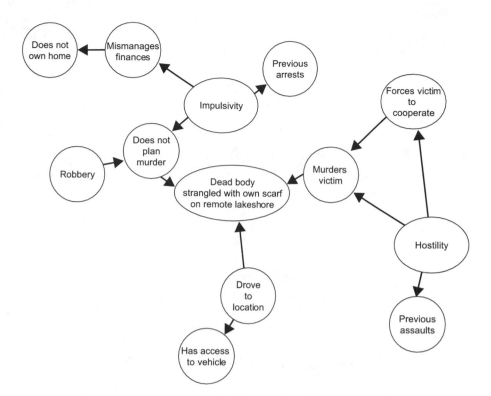

Figure 11.2. An illustration of the application of Figure 11.1.

Tier 1: Crime Scene Evidence and First-Level Offender Behaviors

As illustrated in Figure 11.1, crime scene evidence is at the center of this model of profiling, representing the only available information that an investigator is likely to have to use in solving a crime. In the hypothetical murder scenario described in Figure 11.2, this crime scene evidence consists of a dead body found on a remote lakeshore that has been strangled with the victim's own scarf and is missing its identification. One possible narrative of this example that would be consistent with the modeled variables is that the offender approaches the victim to rob her, but the situation quickly escalates to murder. During the attempted robbery, the victim refuses to comply with the offender's demands, and through his attempts to force the victim to cooperate, the offender strangles the victim with her own scarf. The offender then takes the victim's purse and drives to a remote lakeshore, accessible only by car, to dispose of the victim's body and facilitate his escape.

According to the model in Figure 11.1, the crime scene evidence is directly predicted by first-level offender behaviors. Recall from chapter 8 that first-level behaviors have also been referred to as *inferred behaviors*. This is because, for the purposes of investigation, the direction of the predictions in this portion of the profiling model is reversed through the process of crime reconstruction, such that the behaviors are inferred from the crime scene evidence. When considering how these relationships operate in the commission of a crime, however, it is the offender's behaviors that predict the evidence that will be left behind. These behaviors are referred to here as *first-level behaviors* because they are directly related to the criminal act and, hence, the crime scene evidence. These behaviors are to be distinguished from *second-level behaviors*, which are the investigation-relevant behaviors that can be predicted from variables in the model but are not necessarily related to the commission of the crime. In the murder example, the first-level behaviors that predict the crime scene evidence are murdering the victim (predicts the presence of a dead body), committing an unplanned offense (predicts that the victim was strangled with her own scarf, rather than being killed by a weapon that was brought to the scene by the offender) and driving to the body dump location (predicts the body's remote location).

Tier 2: Motive, Personality, and First-Level Offender Behaviors

In the second tier of variables, aspects of motive and personality predict the first-level offender behaviors that predict crime scene evidence. In Figure 11.2, the offender's motive to rob the victim (motive variable) as well as his impulsivity (personality variable) predict the unplanned commission of the murder. Likewise, the offender's hostility (personality variable) and motivation to force the victim to cooperate (motive variable) predict the murder of the victim. These relationships thus represent the manifestation of the latent constructs of motive and personality as behavior described in chapter 8. These links, from motive and personality to first-level offender behaviors, are also the subject of the studies reviewed in chapters 9 and 10. Those chapters examine the types of predictions that could potentially be generated about crime behaviors by looking at aspects of motive and personality. Again, these predictions represent the proposed direction of causality in the commission of the crime; that is, aspects of motive and personality are thought to cause the crime behaviors that, in turn, lead to the crime scene evidence. In an investigation, profilers would use information gleaned from research on motive and personality to make predictions in the reverse—using first-level offender behaviors to draw inferences about motives and personality characteristics.

Tier 3: Motive, Personality, and Second-Level Offender Behaviors

In the third tier of variables, the proposed direction of causality changes away from predicting crime scene evidence to predicting the behaviors that will assist in identifying and apprehending an unknown perpetrator. This shift in direction reflects the hypothesis that the same motive and personality characteristics that predict crime-related (first-level) behaviors will also predict the offender's non-crime-related (second-level) life behaviors. It is also proposed that certain crime-related behaviors will directly predict life behaviors without the consideration of motive or personality. Thus, in this tier of variables second-level offender behaviors are predicted by both motive and personality characteristics and by first-level offender behaviors. For example, in Figure 11.2, the same impulsivity (personality variable) that predicts the offender's crime-related behavior of committing an unplanned murder also predicts that he will have acted in such a way as to have an arrest record and to have mismanaged his finances (second-level life behaviors). For investigative purposes, although impulsivity may not be of great utility in identifying and apprehending a perpetrator, the manifestation of impulsivity as an arrest record and poor credit history may help narrow down the suspect pool. Likewise, in Figure 11.2, the first-level crime-related behavior of driving to a remote location to dump the victim's body predicts the second-level behavior of accessing a vehicle. This prediction is made without a consideration of motive or personality and is thus more similar to the types of logical inferences made in crime reconstruction.

In addition to predicting second-level behaviors, in the third tier of the profiling model, motive and personality can also become predictors of each other. Thus, in Figure 11.2, the offender's hostility (personality variable) may make him more inclined to want to force the victim's cooperation in the robbery (motive variable). These variables may then act in concert to result in the offender murdering the victim. The relationship between motive and personality, and their mutual relationship to behavior, is a further area that has thus far been neglected in the profiling literature and requires future research.

Branches of Predictions Beyond Tier 3

Once the direction of causation shifts away from crime-related behaviors, and aspects of motive, personality, and first-level behaviors are used to make predictions about second-level behaviors, the pattern of relationships continues to branch outward toward predicting additional second-level behaviors. Figures 11.3 and 11.4 depict a more complex profiling model, in

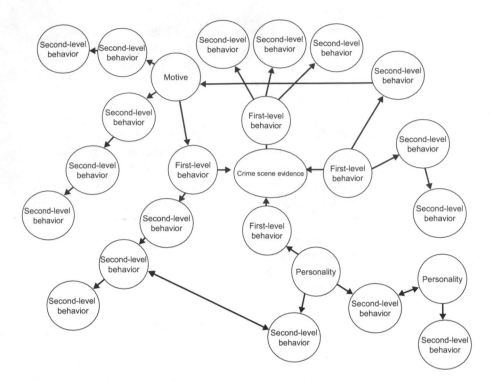

Figure 11.3. A more complex structure for a scientific model of profiling.

which relationships among variables continue to branch away from the crime-related behaviors, with each branch terminating in a second-level behavior.

The hypothetical scenario represented in Figures 11.3 and 11.4 is a home burglary. The resident comes home from work at lunchtime and discovers the house in disarray. Valuables have been taken, and when the police arrive they find no fingerprints at any point of entry to the house. As with Figures 11.1 and 11.2, Tier 1 comprises the crime scene evidence at the center of the figure and the first-level behaviors (striking during the day, vandalizing the home, taking valuables, and wearing gloves) that directly predict the evidence. In Tier 2, aspects of motive and personality predict the crime-related first-level behaviors. For example, the motive for financial gain predicts the stealing of valuables; likewise, the presence of hostility in the offender's personality predicts the vandalizing of the house. In Tier 3, motive, personality, and first-level offender behaviors predict second-level offender behaviors. For example, the same motive for financial gain that predicts the stealing of valuables also predicts that the offender has not secured gainful employment or that he has a drug problem that causes him

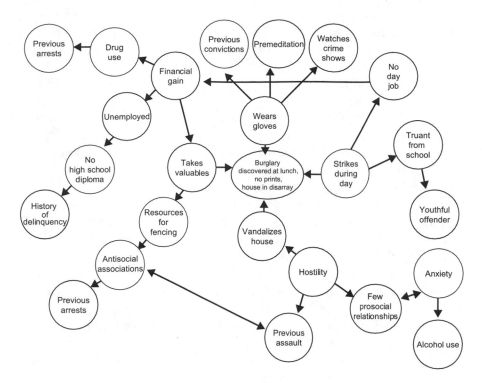

Figure 11.4. An illustration of the application of Figure 11.3.

to spend money beyond his means. Likewise, the same hostility that predicts the vandalizing of the house also predicts that the offender has engaged in previous assaultive behavior and has formed few prosocial relationships. In addition, the first-level offender behavior of striking during the day predicts that the offender is not employed during the day, or, if enrolled in school, is truant.

These types of relationships in Tiers 1, 2, and 3 depicted in Figures 11.3 and 11.4 are similar to the relationships described in the previous section and represented by Figures 11.1 and 11.2. However, in Figures 11.3 and 11.4 the branches of relationships beyond Tier 3 continue to predict second-level offender behaviors. In some cases, these behaviors are predicted directly from the second-level behaviors in Tier 3. For example, the first-level behavior of taking valuables predicts the second-level behavior of securing resources for fencing those valuables. That behavior in turn predicts that the offender will have formed antisocial associations, which in turn predicts that he is likely to have had previous contact with law enforcement, in the form of prior arrests. In other cases, the second-level behaviors in Tier 3 may predict aspects of motive and personality, which in turn predict other second-level behaviors. For example, the second-level offender behavior of engaging in few prosocial relationships predicts (and is predicted by) anxiety, which in turn predicts alcohol consumption. Thus, second-level behaviors may continue to branch from other behaviors and from aspects of motive and personality.

The model of profiling just described requires scientific findings to link the variables of motive, personality, and behavior and generate predictions about offenders. Although the network of predictions and variables contained therein may therefore strike law enforcement investigators and profiling practitioners as an exclusively empirical exercise, the goal of this model is to identify offender behaviors that have relevance to investigations and that will assist law enforcement in identifying the correct perpetrator. Thus, each branch of the model terminates in a second-level behavior, describing a piece of information that law enforcement can use in an investigation. Science is required because the utility of the model for investigators depends in great part on the number and strength of the predictions that can be made to link aspects of motive, personality, and behavior together. The greater the evidence, and the more reliable and valid predictions that science can provide, the more that the model of any given crime example will branch. Because each branch terminates in a second-level behavior, and because the second-level behaviors are the behaviors most relevant to investigation, additional branches of predictions will increase the number of behaviors available for investigators to use in narrowing down the field of potential suspects in a crime.

LITERATURE INTEGRATING CRIME SCENE EVIDENCE, MOTIVES, PERSONALITY, AND BEHAVIOR

Although chapters 9 and 10 already discussed the state of the literature linking pairs of variables (e.g., motive and behavior) from the scientific profiling model, it would also be useful, and consistent with the concept of the model presented in this chapter, to consider any available literature that integrates all three of these variables (motive, personality, and behavior) in research on offending. Such literature would provide some clues as to how to further refine the scientific profiling model, by identifying the types of interrelationships among variables that have already been established. For example, literature that integrates these variables might be able to demonstrate how psychopathy (personality) and greed (motive) might act in concert to predict both violence toward a bank teller during a robbery (first-level behavior) and a parasitic living situation with a family member (second-level behavior). It is unfortunate that there is a paucity of research that approaches profiling by integrating variables of motive, personality, and behavior in the manner described by the previous model. Research in the offender literature has failed to describe how motive, personality, and behavior work together in crime, and there are currently no reliable and valid findings that would allow investigators to use information about motive, personality, and first-level offender behaviors to make inferences about the types of second-level behaviors that might lead to the apprehension of a perpetrator.

One exception to this deficit in the offender literature is the homicide research conducted by Canter and his colleagues (e.g., Santilla et al., 2001). Canter's studies, although not entirely consistent with the previously described model of profiling, provide some clues about the types of predictions that might result from a simultaneous consideration of motive, personality, and behavior.

Multidimensional Scaling and Geographic Profiling Research

Research conducted by Canter and colleagues has attempted to address the offender characteristics of motive, personality, and behavior in combination and to use the findings to make investigation-relevant predictions. Some of these studies were reviewed in chapter 9 to illustrate findings relevant to motive (e.g., Canter & Fritzon, 1998; Fritzon, 2001), and Canter's work was discussed in greater detail in chapters 4 and 5. The following section reviews the multidimensional scaling and geographic profiling research on homicide offenders conducted by Canter and colleagues, to describe the available research combining aspects of motive, personality, and behavior (Canter, Coffey, Huntley, & Missen, 2000; Godwin & Canter, 1997; Salfati & Canter, 1999; Santilla, Hakkanen, Canter, & Elfgren, 2003) and to compare it with the previously described scientific model of profiling.

Multidimensional Scaling Research

There are two main studies that have used multidimensional scaling to simultaneously study homicide behaviors, aspects of motive and personality, and offender behaviors that might lead to the identification and apprehension of the perpetrator (for a more detailed description of Canter's methods, see chaps. 4 and 5). Salfati and Canter (1999) plotted 36 crime behaviors from 82 single-offender, single-victim homicides in a two-dimensional space using smallest space analysis (SSA), and the resulting scatter plot is divided into three sections according to the authors' theoretical determinations about motive themes, also called *interpersonal narratives*. The three themes of crime scene behaviors identified are Instrumental Opportunistic, Instrumental Cognitive, and Expressive Impulsive. The authors then attempted to link offender background characteristics to the

TABLE 11.1
Offender Themes, Crime Actions, and Offender Characteristics

Offender themes	Crime actions	Offender characteristics
Expressive (Impulsive)	Multiple wounds distributed across victim's body: limbs, torso, face Different types of wounds: slash/cut, stab Bring weapon to scene Use weapon from scene	Previous violent offenses Previous offenses for public disorder Previous offenses for damage to property Previous sexual offenses Previous traffic offenses Previous drug offenses Married at time of offense Previous marriage Female offender
Instrumental (Opportunistic)	Female victim Old victim Property of value taken Crime at victim's premises Manual infliction of injury Face hidden Sexual assault Partially undressed Neck injuries	Previous offenses for theft Previous offenses for burglary Previous vehical theft offenses Previously came to police notice Unemployed Familiar with the area of the crime Knew victim
Instrumental (Cognitive)	Body hidden Crime committed/body disposed outside Body left face up Transported body Stealing nonidentifiable property Removal of forensic evidence	Served in the armed services Served a prison sentence

Note. From "Differentiating Stranger Murders: Profiling Offender Characteristics From Behavioral Styles," by C. G. Salfati and D. V. Canter, 1999, *Journal of Behavioral Sciences and the Law, 17*, p. 404. Copyright 1999 by John Wiley and Sons, Ltd. Adapted with permission.

crime scene themes by conducting a second analysis that included 18 offender background variables in the SSA of the 36 crime scene actions. The resulting scatter plot is divided into the three offender themes just identified, and associations between crime scene actions and offender characteristics are asserted on the basis of their mutual presence in the same theme section of the scatter plot.

The three offender themes identified in this study, and the crime scene actions and offender characteristics that are associated with each, are shown in Table 11.1. According to Salfati and Canter (1999), the Expressive Impulsive theme represents a "collection of frenzied and eclectic impulsive behaviors" (p. 401). Examples of crime actions contained in this theme are multiple and varied types of wounds inflicted on the victim and the use of a weapon. The associated offender characteristics include a history of a variety of violent and nonviolent offenses, marriage or a previous marriage, and being female. The Instrumental Opportunistic theme is "a distinct theme of opportunistic victims being targeted . . . where the offender used the victim as an object through which to attain an ulterior motive such as money or sex" (Salfati & Canter, 1999, p. 401). The crime actions found in this theme include the targeting of older female victims, committing the crime at the victim's home and taking property, committing sexual assault, and manually inflicting injury through methods such as strangulation. Associated offender characteristics include being familiar with the victim and the area, being unemployed, and having a previous history of burglary and theft. Finally, the Instrumental Cognitive theme has "a highly cognitive emphasis" (Salfati & Canter, 1999, p. 401), and offenders in this category attempt to hide their actions and remove incriminating evidence. Examples of crime actions include transporting and concealing the body, removing forensic evidence, and committing the murder or disposing of the body outdoors. Offenders in this theme have a history of having been in prison or the armed forces.

In a similar study, Santilla, Hakkanen, Canter, and Elfgren (2003) identified three themes of offender characteristics and one core set of offender characteristics in a set of 502 homicides, using SSA (see Table 11.2). The core set of offender characteristics are those that are common to a majority of the sample of homicides, in this case, greater than 50%. The variables in this core set of offender characteristics include being male and being familiar with the victim and with the area in which the crime was committed. These characteristics represent those that are thought to typify homicide offenders rather than distinguish among them. The three offender themes in the sample are Instrumental, Expressive (Intimate), and Expressive (Blood). According to the authors, the Instrumental theme describes "a maladjusted, antisocial lifestyle in conditions of relative social deprivation" (Santilla et al., 2003, p. 112). Associated offender characteristics include previous violent, property, and sexual offenses; being homeless or residing in government housing; and being single and abusing alcohol. The Expressive theme represents "relationship issues concerning both intimate and family relationships and problems in them" (Santilla et al., 2003, p. 113). The Expressive theme is divided according to whether the relationship between offender and victim is intimate or familial. The Expressive (Intimate) theme describes offenders who are "reacting against perceived frustration and threats to self-esteem" (Santilla et al., 2003, p. 114). Examples of offender characteristics in this theme include having an intimate relationship with the victim, being gainfully employed, owning a home, and having a weapon permit. In contrast, the Expressive (Blood) theme represents offenders who "are likely to have some sort of psychiatric problem . . .

TABLE 11.2
Offender Themes and Offender Characteristics

Offender theme	Offender characteristics
Core variables	Male Familiar with area Knew victim
Instrumental	Divorced Multiple convictions for violence Homeless Council housing Previous property offense conviction No weapon permit for gun used in homicide Previous sexual offense conviction Alcoholism Single
Expressive (Intimate)	Weapon permit for gun used in homicide Owns own home Intimate relationship with victim Higher level occupation (professional/entrepreneur)
Expressive (Blood)	Blood relative of victim Education beyond middle school Psychiatric problems

Note. From "Classifying Homicide Offenders and Predicting Their Characteristics From Crime Scene Behavior," by P. Santilla, H. Hakkanen, D. Canter, and T. Elfgren, 2003, *Scandinavian Journal of Psychology, 44*, pp. 107–118. Copyright 2003 by Blackwell Publishing. Adapted with permission.

[and] problems in creating or maintaining long-term relationships" (Santilla et al., 2003, p. 113). Offenders in this theme tend to be educated beyond middle school, be related to the victim by blood, and have a history of psychiatric problems.

To relate crime scene actions to offender characteristics, Santilla, Hakkanen, Canter, and Elfgren (2003) correlated the themes of the crime scene actions from the set of homicides (derived by Santilla, Canter, Elfgren, & Hakkanen, 2001) to the themes of offender characteristics. Across crime scene actions and offender characteristics, these themes are not identical. Whereas the offender characteristics comprise the three themes just described, the crime scene actions consist of five themes: Instrumental/Sex, Instrumental/Resources, Expressive/Firearm, Expressive/Body Parts Removed, and Expressive/Body Hidden. Correlational analyses between themes revealed that, "generally speaking, instrumental crime scene themes were associated with instrumental background characteristics and expressive crime scene themes were associated with expressive background characteristics" (Santilla, Hakkanen, Canter, & Elfgren, 2003, p. 117), with significant correlations ranging from .08 (Expressive/Body Hidden × Expressive/

Intimate) to .28 (Instrumental/Resources × Expressive/Intimate, for victims over age 56).

The two studies described previously (Salfati & Canter [1999], and Santilla, Hakkanen, Canter, & Elfgren [2003]) attempted to make predictions about offender background characteristics on the basis of crime scene actions through offender themes. Although the techniques used to associate offender characteristics and crime scene actions differ slightly, in both cases the relationship of offender themes to both offender characteristics and crime scene actions appears to be paramount. Findings from both studies suggest that determinations about interpersonal-narratives themes, namely, differences between expressive and instrumental motivations, can be used to relate crime scene actions to the kinds of offender background characteristics that may help identify the perpetrator.

Geographic Profiling

A second group of homicide studies conducted by Canter and colleagues involves geographic profiling. Although geographic profiling was briefly mentioned in the discussion of Holmes and Holmes's (1996) model in chapter 2, and mentioned in the discussion of the Canter model in chapters 4 and 5, much of this discussion was confined to Holmes and Holmes's (1996) limited description of a technique first articulated by Rossmo (1995a, 1995b, 1997). According to Rossmo, geographic profiling is a procedure that examines the spatial behavior of offenders with regard to the locations of their crime scenes and the spatial relationships between those scenes. Although geographic profiling involves quantitative measures that allow for the interpretation of spatial patterns, Rossmo (1997) also emphasized a subjective component involving the psychological profiling of the offender to reconstruct and interpret his "mental map" (p. 161). Rossmo did not describe procedures for this profiling component; neither did he specify how it interacts with the quantitative analyses of location patterns (Rossmo, 1997).

Geographic profiling, according to Rossmo's (1997) model, is based on a model of crime location selection put forth by Brantingham and Brantingham (1981). This model proposes that victim selection is spatially biased toward an offender's home location. As a result, criminal acts follow a decay function, such that the farther an offender is from home, the less likely he is to commit a crime. The model also articulates, however, that there is a buffer zone, such that offenders will avoid committing crimes too close to their homes, to avoid incriminating themselves. Rossmo's model integrates these two principles into a mathematical model, using the locations where a serial killer dumps his victims' bodies to identify the location of the offender's home. Although Rossmo has described the utility of his technique, he has not specified the details of his algorithms, and there is currently no research demonstrating the validity of his model.

Unlike Rossmo's (1997) approach, which considers spatial behavior to be the product of some unspecified set of offender characteristics, Canter and colleagues have attempted to incorporate aspects of motive and personality in their concept of offenders' spatial behavior. These aspects of motive and personality are embedded in Canter's interpersonal-narratives theory and explain the principles that underlie offenders' choices regarding crime and home locations. Using SSA, Godwin and Canter (1997) attempted to model the spatial behavior of serial killers without the incorporation of the subjective profiling techniques advocated by Rossmo. The authors used SSA to plot two types of crime locations: the "point of fatal encounter" (Godwin & Canter, 1997, p. 27), where offenders apprehend their victims, and the locations where the offenders dump the victims' bodies. Using solved cases in which the offender's home location is known, the authors then attempted, on the basis of Canter's interpersonal-narratives theory, to assess the relationship between the crime locations and the offender's home. Recall that the main tenet of this theory is that crime is a product of the more general lifestyle of the offender. As applied to spatial behavior, this theory proposes that the home "acts as a structuring device for the development of criminal activity" (Godwin & Canter, 1997, p. 26). Thus, according to Canter, if crime develops out of an offender's daily activities, then the home location will also necessarily be central to his offenses. The predictions generated from this model of geographic profiling are somewhat consistent with the distance-decay and buffer principles that guide Rossmo's (1997) model, but there are also some differences. First, Godwin and Canter (1997) predicted that the home will operate as a base for the activities of the offender. This prediction is similar to the distance-decay hypothesis in the Rossmo model, which suggests that an offender's crimes will radiate out from the central home base. Second, Godwin and Canter predicted that there will be differences in the distances traveled to acquire victims and dump their bodies. They suggested that the body dump location is likely to contain the most forensic evidence and is therefore likely to be farther from the offender's home. This prediction incorporates the buffer principle from the Rossmo model but applies it only to the body dump location. Third, they predicted that the body dump locations will change over time, whereas the points of fatal encounter will not. This prediction is consistent with interpersonal-narratives theory, which suggests that acquiring victims will be an outgrowth of the offender's daily activities, whereas the body dump locations will change so that the offender can avoid incrimination.

Godwin and Canter's (1997) results indicate that offenders indeed tend to operate from a home base and acquire their victims closer to home than the locations where they dump their victims' bodies. Over 10 offenses, the mean distance from offenders' homes to the point of fatal encounter in a sample of 54 serial offenders was 1.46 miles, whereas the average distance to the body dump location was 14.3 miles (Godwin & Canter, 1997). Contrary to what was predicted, however, the body dump locations became progressively closer to offenders' homes over the course of 10 offenses, rather than gradually being farther away. The authors proposed that this finding suggests that the offenses became increasingly integrated into the offenders' daily lives, but they admitted that future research is necessary to clearly identify the factors involved.

Subsequent studies have supported Godwin and Canter's (1997) findings and have demonstrated success at modeling offenders' home locations on the basis of information about the locations of their crimes. A study of 126 U.S. and 29 British serial killers (Lundrigan & Canter, 2001) used the circle hypothesis (Canter & Larkin, 1993) to correctly predict that serial killers' home locations can be found within a circle defined by the two disposal sites that are farthest from each other. Using this heuristic, 89% of U.S. serial killers' homes and 86% of the British serial killers' homes were found to be contained within the identified circles. In addition, the location of the home was not necessarily in the center of the circle, which would indicate random movement in a variety of directions to commit crimes; instead, the relationship between home and crime locations was biased along routes that were related to other activities in the offender's life (e.g., work).

Other studies have used a geographical decision support tool based on the principles of spatial behavior articulated in Canter's geographic profiling model to model offenders' home locations from the locations of body disposals. This decision support tool (Dragnet) was used on a sample of 79 U.S. serial killers (Canter et al., 2000) to assess the cost-effectiveness of various search area sizes. The offenders' home addresses as well as the addresses of body dump locations were entered into the computerized tool as raw coordinates. All 79 of the serial killers' home addresses were located within the search parameters defined by Dragnet for the sample of offenses. In terms of cost-effectiveness, 51% of offenders' homes were found within the first 5% of rank-ordered locations specified by Dragnet, and 87% of homes were found within the first 25% of locations, placing the optimal search cost of the entire sample at 11% of the defined search area. A subsequent study demonstrated that, given two relevant heuristics (the circle hypothesis and the distance-decay principle), study participants with no knowledge of geographic profiling achieved predictions of offender home locations that were not significantly different from those generated by Dragnet (Snook, Canter, & Bennell, 2002). Thus, it appears that although Dragnet can generate efficient predictions about offender home locations from information about body dump sites, human judges can, with minimal training, achieve comparable success by eyeballing data plots of body dump locations.

Evaluation of the Research by Canter and Colleagues and Its Relationship to a Scientific Model of Profiling

The research conducted by Canter and colleagues constitutes perhaps the only body of literature to simultaneously address offender motives, personality, and behavior and to attempt to describe the interrelationships among these variables. The homicide studies described in the previous section represent two areas of research—multidimensional scaling of offender characteristics and geographic profiling—that have generated relationships between crime actions and offender characteristics that may be of use to investigations.

There are three basic types of variables in the multidimensional scaling research: crime scene actions, offender themes, and offender background characteristics. A comparison between these components of the multidimensional scaling research and the components of a scientific model of profiling described earlier in this chapter reveals several similarities between the basic variables involved.

First, the crime scene actions described in the studies of Canter and colleagues appear to represent a combination of crime scene evidence and first-level offender behaviors as described by the current model. For example, the presence of neck injuries (Salfati & Canter, 1999) is more consistent with crime scene evidence, whereas the variable indicating manual infliction of injury appears to represent a first-level, crime-related offender behavior that might predict the presence of neck injuries. Canter and colleagues have not addressed the distinction between crime scene evidence and the behaviors that would be discerned from that evidence using crime reconstruction. Instead, using police files from solved cases, they extracted crime-relevant variables that seem to contain both pieces of evidence and crime behaviors. In the geographic profiling studies, the only crime scene actions focused on are the acquisition of the victim and the dumping of the body. Again, Canter and colleagues have not distinguished between the crime scene evidence (e.g., locations of point of fatal encounter and body dump) and the behaviors that predict the evidence (e.g., acquiring a victim and dumping the body); however, the crime scene actions in geographic profiling appear to be more analogous to first-level offender behaviors than to pieces of crime scene evidence because of the authors' emphasis on the locations as indicating a choice on the part of the offender.

Second, the offender themes, guided by interpersonal-narratives theory, appear to address aspects of motive and, to a lesser extent, personality, as a way of relating crime scene actions to offender background characteristics.

As discussed in chapter 9, the instrumental and expressive themes described by Canter and colleagues refer to offenders' motivations and purpose for committing crimes. The instrumental themes reflect the pursuit of some type of secondary gain, whereas the expressive themes seem to indicate a desire to release a certain degree of hostility or aggression. For example, Santilla, Hakkanen, Canter, and Elfgren (2003) described offenders in the Instrumental theme as using aggression as a problem-solving technique. Conversely, Salfati and Canter (1999) described the Expressive theme as evidencing a "very emotional attack" (p. 401). The presence of characteristics such as hostility and impulsivity in the descriptions of these themes also implies the influence of aspects of personality; however, this was not directly addressed by the authors.

In the geographic profiling studies, the role of interpersonal-narratives theory is much more embedded than in the homicide studies conducted by Salfati and Canter (1999) and Santilla, Hakkanen, Canter, and Elfgren (2003). Instead of dividing homicide offenders according to offender themes, the geographic profiling studies appear to consider the spatial patterns of offenders as deriving from a common theme, or motive. According to interpersonal-narratives theory, the motivation for offenders to commit crimes grows out of their daily activities. The motivation to acquire victims thus appears to reflect a certain degree of opportunism and, potentially, impulsivity, with the choice of body disposal site reflecting the motivation to avoid incrimination but still occurring within the area circumscribed by the repertoire of the offender's noncriminal activities.

Third, the offender background characteristics described by the multi-dimensional scaling studies appear to be analogous to second-level offender behaviors. Salfati and Canter (1999) described background characteristics such as offense histories, the use and abuse of alcohol and drugs, and being unemployed, whereas Santilla, Hakkanen, Canter, and Elfgren (2003) described such characteristics as involvement in relationships, educational achievement, and acquisition of weapon permits. These types of characteristics are similar to the types of second-level behaviors, described in Figures 11.1 through 11.4, that may assist in identifying and apprehending the perpetrator. The geographic profiling studies focus on a single second-level behavior: the offender's selection of a home location. As evidenced by studies of geographic profiling, home location may be one of the most efficient second-level behaviors currently available in terms of narrowing down the suspect pool. As further studies of geographic profiling are conducted, it may be possible to increase the accuracy and efficiency of home location for identifying the correct perpetrator.

Although the multidimensional scaling and geographic profiling research uses some of the same theoretical components as the model of profiling proposed in this chapter, its findings are limited with regard to informing a science of profiling in two major ways. There are limitations related to the conceptual criticisms made of the Canter model, described more fully in chapter 5, such as inconsistencies in interpersonal-narratives theory and the consequent problems with the resulting hypotheses. Because the studies described previously derive from the Canter model and interpersonal-narratives theory, they necessarily lack a certain degree of conceptual clarity and scientific rigor, which makes it difficult to have unqualified confidence in the validity of the findings. In addition, although the difficulties with using multidimensional scaling techniques were already discussed in chapter 5, it bears repeating that SSA does not allow one to make causal predictions that link elements of motive and personality to either first- or second-level behaviors, represented in the Canter studies by offender themes, crime scene actions, and offender background characteristics, respectively. Instead, what SSA allows the Canter studies to demonstrate is the co-occurrence of certain first- and second-level behaviors in a section of a visual scatter plot whose properties have been defined by the theoretical proposals of the authors. Although the practice of identifying behaviors that co-occur is not without value to a scientific model of profiling, the determination of co-occurrence in SSA is, to a great extent, made subjectively by the authors. SSA may plot the relationships between variables, but it is the authors who determine the delineation between one group of variables and another. This is a significant limitation, because the use of subjective judgment is not scientific, and determinations made through subjective judgment therefore do not add to a science of profiling.

Considering both the limitations to the research conducted by Canter and colleagues and its conceptual similarities to the scientific model of profiling proposed in this chapter, there are three contributions that this body of literature can make to the advancement of a science of profiling. First, the studies by Canter and colleagues demonstrate that it is possible to incorporate motive, personality, and behavior into a single model of profiling and identify associations between first- and second-level offender behaviors. According to the Canter studies, this is accomplished through a consideration of offender themes, much in the same way that the model of profiling described in this chapter considers the roles of motive and personality in generating first- and second-level behaviors. From here, what is required for a scientific model is to re-examine these relationships as causal pathways and to attempt to measure the influence of motive and personality as latent variables rather than subjectively determining their relationship to behaviors. Second, as described in Table 11.1, the Canter research has identified certain co-occurrences of first- and second-level be- haviors. Although the degree of association between these behaviors, and the nature of the variables linking them, has yet to be determined, as just described, it would seem reasonable to incorporate these co-occurrences into a scientific model of profiling as hypotheses to be tested once the appropriate data sets are obtained. For example, Salfati and Canter (1999) reported the co-occurrence of removing forensic evidence (first-level behavior) and a history of being in prison (second-level behavior) within the same offender theme. With the appropriate data, one could test whether there is a predictive relationship between these two variables, such that the absence of evidence such as fingerprints and DNA indicates that the offender has spent time in prison, a hypothesis for which there is already some support (Davies, Wittebrood, & Jackson, 1997). Third, the geographic profiling research conducted by Canter and colleagues provides a seemingly robust predictive relationship between homicide locations (first-level behavior) and offender home locations (second-level behavior). Although this relationship is valuable as a heuristic, it is also consistent with the scientific model of profiling described in this chapter. Homicide locations and home locations, as first- and second-level behaviors, are potentially linked by aspects of motive and personality. On the basis of the findings of Canter and colleagues (e.g., Snook, Canter, & Bennell, 2002), these aspects of motive and personality may relate to comfort in familiar areas (e.g., obtaining victims near the home location) as well as the motivation to avoid apprehension (e.g., disposing of bodies farther from home). Further empirical testing of the relationships between spatial behavior and aspects of motive and personality may greatly enhance a scientific model of profiling as well as its consequent investigative inferences.

Because of the limitations described here and in chapter 5, it does not appear that the research of Canter and colleagues can supplant the scientific model of profiling proposed in this chapter. There appears to be considerable agreement, however, between the two approaches in terms of identifying important components or variables and attempting to relate them to each other. Although the more subjective elements of the Canter model and its related studies are problematic for reasons already detailed, there is still a contribution to be made by the research of Canter and colleagues to a science of profiling. Specifically, their findings have provided some promising directions for the testing of hypotheses linking aspects of motive and personality to both first- and second-level behaviors, and the studies on geographic profiling have been quite convincing with regard to the potential for using spatial (first-level) behavior to predict offender home location (second-level behavior).

ROLE OF SITUATIONAL FACTORS

There remains one type of variable to consider in a scientific model of profiling that has, thus far, not been explicitly accounted for by the tenets or analyses of any other model of profiling: situational factors. A scientific model of profiling is ultimately concerned with predicting offender behavior. The purpose of profiling as a practice is to attempt to ascertain crime events (first-level offender behaviors) and use that information to make predictions about the offender (second-level behaviors) that will allow law enforcement to identify and apprehend him. A scientific model of profiling proposes that motive and personality (and their expression as behavior) are the important variables that can be used to assist in making these predictions. As articulated by Alison, Bennell, and Mokros (2002), however, and as discussed in chapter 10, there are indications in the personality literature that various environmental and situational conditions affect the expression of personality characteristics. Similarly, the model of motive described in chapter 8 indicates that there is every reason to predict that motive is also susceptible to situational influence. Thus, the variables important to predicting offender behavior do not exist in a vacuum but instead change with context. A complete understanding of a science of profiling therefore requires a consideration of that context.

Addressing the role of situational factors within a scientific model of profiling requires two trajectories of scholarship. As touched on in previous discussions of motive and personality, more research must examine the influence of situational factors on motive and personality characteristics themselves, to identify any consistent patterns that might be of assistance to investigative practice. While such research is underway, a scientific model of profiling also must consider how the construct of situational factors might operate in offending and how that construct might be related to variables of motive, personality, and behavior.

To successfully carry out these two types of scholarship, researchers must first address two considerations. First, what are situational factors? Second, how do they come into play during the course of an offense? In the current scientific model of profiling, it is proposed that situational factors are elements related to the context or environment of the offense. They can include such components as location, time, weather, victim response, and unexpected obstacles to the completion of an offense. Situational factors can also include some types of events that are internal to the offender (e.g., the sudden onset of a migraine). These types of offender states must be specific to the context of the crime to be situational factors rather than long-standing internal traits. Situational factors are not offender motives, personality characteristics, or behaviors.

In a scientific model of profiling, situational factors are identified and described through crime reconstruction. To the extent that crime scene evidence permits the logical reconstruction of crime events and their temporal order, situational factors will also be derived from this crime scene evidence and included in the timeline and narrative. For example, a crime location can be reconstructed with a physical description of the crime scene. The time of a crime can be determined by such pieces of evidence as estimated time of death, the state (lit or extinguished) of broken lights, victim and witness statements, and alibi information from suspects. A sudden downpour of rain may be ascertained by observing wet objects outside the crime scene, water damage, and cross-references with weather reports. Unexpected reactions from victims may be evidenced by victim and witness statements, evidence of escalation in violence, or the failure to complete an offense. An unexpected obstacle, such as a large animal darting out in front of a getaway car, may be evidenced by skid marks on the road or the presence of animal remains on the vehicle. Whatever the scenario, a situational factor is simply another element of the crime event that can be reconstructed from the crime scene evidence. As such, the description of situational factors is included within the narrative and timeline of a crime reconstruction.

The second important consideration is that although situational factors do not fall under the rubric of offender characteristics, they do interact with offender motive and personality characteristics in the manifestation of first-level offender behaviors. Although the possible range of situational influences in offending may seem limitless, it is in fact possible to account for situational influences within this current scientific model of profiling if these situations are considered from the perspective of their relationship to offender motive, personality, and behavior rather than being considered as individual scenarios.

For example, consider the narrative of the scenario depicted in Figure 11.2. In this crime scenario, an unpleasant situational factor is presented to the offender, such that the victim resists the offender's initial attempts to rob her. The model indicates that the presence of hostility as a personality variable, together with the motive to force the victim to comply, results in a violent response from the offender. Now consider how the offender's response might differ depending on the manner in which the victim resists. If the victim resists aggressively, by hitting or kicking the offender, screaming, or threatening to call the police, the offender's response might be expected to be very similar to the scenario in Figure 11.2. However, if the victim resists more passively, by holding on to her belongings, crying, and turning away from the offender, he might be less inclined to respond violently. Thus, the specific situation of victim resistance appears to be less important than the impact that the resistance has on the offender. In the first version of victim resistance, the offender might feel challenged or threatened. The violence would therefore be a response to feeling threatened, taking into account the motive, personality, and behavioral variables already in place.

In the second scenario, the offender might feel less challenged by the victim and might therefore not feel inclined to use as much force as he would use with a more aggressive victim.

If one considers other situational factors that might influence offender behavior, it becomes equally apparent that the details of any given situation are less relevant than the impact of the situation on the offender. For example, what is the value of rain as a situational factor unless one knows the impact of rain on the offender? Will an offender feel frustrated and angry if it begins to rain during the commission of an arson? Or will the offender simply walk away and decide to come back another time? Could rain be perceived as beneficial to other types of offenders who want evidence to be washed away? The presence of rain itself carries no inherent meaning. Instead, it is the offender's perception of rain that has an influence on his subsequent actions.

In addition, however, the offender's perception is not the sole influence on his subsequent actions. Rather, the situation and the offender's perception of that situation interact with existing motive and personality variables to produce first-level behaviors. For example, if an offender were hostile and motivated to set a fire for revenge, he might respond differently to bad weather than would a more passive offender who was motivated by boredom.

Recall that in proposing ways to study a situation-specific model of personality, Alison et al. (2002) suggested developing if–then contingencies through interviews with offenders to identify common sets of relationships between situations and personality characteristics (e.g., "When a victim resists me, I become hostile"). As described in chapter 10, the development of these if–then contingencies is a strategy that may assist in the consideration of situational factors in assessing offender personality. However, if one further considers that offenders respond not to individual situations but that, instead, the impact of situations influences offending behavior, finding categories of if–then contingencies for situations and personality, as well as motive and behavior, becomes a much more manageable task. In this framework, the task is not to find contingencies between, for example, the presence of rain and some aspect of offender personality, because rain can make some offenders happy and others frustrated, and because a wide variety of other weather conditions can make offenders happy or frustrated. Instead, the task is to use the crime reconstruction to ascertain the impact of the situational factor on the offender and relate that impact to motive, personality, and first-level behaviors. A science of profiling is concerned not with whether it rained during the course of an offender's crime but with how the rain, snow, a resistant victim, or a malfunctioning gun affected the offender and how that relates to his motive, personality, and behavior.

12

STEPS TOWARD TESTING A SCIENTIFIC MODEL OF PROFILING

The scientific model of profiling presented in chapter 11 demonstrates how aspects of motive, personality, and behavior can be integrated to generate predictions about offender behavior that will assist law enforcement investigators in identifying and apprehending unknown perpetrators. Research conducted by Canter and colleagues has also considered an integrated approach to the study of offender behavior. Consistent with the criticisms of the Canter model levied in chapter 5, however, there are limitations to that approach, and the findings of that research therefore require reexamination. Nonetheless, if the relationships asserted by Canter and colleagues (e.g., Santilla, Hakkanen, Canter, & Elfgren, 2003) between crime actions (first-level behaviors) and offender characteristics (second-level behaviors) are treated as hypotheses to be tested within the framework of the current scientific model of profiling, they do serve as indicators of potentially fruitful directions for profiling research. In addition, chapter 11 noted the importance of assessing situational factors to achieve a complete understanding of offenders and offenses. The current model of profiling accounts for the inclusion and description of situational factors through crime reconstruction, with further research being required to understand the relationships between situational factors and aspects of motive and personality.

The next phase in developing a science of profiling is to consider the steps necessary to test the scientific model of profiling proposed in chapter 11. This chapter describes these steps by considering populations from which to collect data, the types of data that should be collected, the generation and testing of hypotheses important to profiling, and strategies for analysis.

DATA

The first steps in testing a scientific model of profiling are to identify the appropriate population from which to collect data and to carefully consider the types of data that should be collected. Although it may be ideal to collect as much information as possible from as many respondents as possible, the limits of empirical research necessitate that investigators use sampling procedures, which involve collecting information from a limited number of participants in an effort to understand the larger population of interest. Although a discussion of basic research methodology is beyond the scope of this book, there are several considerations regarding the composition of samples and selection of data specific to a study of profiling that are addressed here.

Population

Because the intent of profiling is to generate predictions about the motives, personalities, and behaviors of individuals who have committed criminal acts, the appropriate population with which to conduct profiling research is criminal offenders. There are several choices with regard to selecting a sample to represent this population, with each potential sample reflecting a different phase of the criminal justice system. There are suspects, individuals who have been arrested, individuals who have been selected for prosecution, and convicted offenders. Of these choices, the sample that best taps into the population of criminal offenders is composed of individuals who have been convicted of crimes. Samples of convicted offenders can be found in both state and federal prison systems, and offenders who have conviction records but who are not currently incarcerated may also be found in parole and probationary supervision settings. Other formerly incarcerated offenders may be found elsewhere in the populace; however, additional effort to locate and recruit these individuals for study participation will likely be required.

The selection of convicted offenders as the relevant group for testing the profiling model has one significant advantage and three potential drawbacks. First, the selection of convicted offenders has the advantage over the other proposed samples in that, unlike individuals who have been suspected, arrested, or acquitted, the guilt of convicted offenders has been confirmed by the criminal justice system, and their cases can therefore be considered to be solved. The determinations of the justice system, although certainly not infallible, are currently the best indicators available with regard to the resolution of case facts and, particularly in cases in which offenders have pleaded guilty or admitted to their offenses, the case events and outcomes can be presumed to be accurate. This is not necessarily the case with samples of individuals who might be selected from cold case files, arrest records, or unsuccessfully prosecuted cases. The guilt of individuals in these samples has not been established, and one therefore cannot assume that they have committed any crimes.

There are three possible drawbacks, however, to limiting research to samples of convicted offenders. These drawbacks take the form of questions that currently have no clear answers. First, are convicted offenders representative of offenders in general? If there are biases in the way that individuals are arrested, prosecuted, convicted, and sentenced, it may be that some offenders go undetected or unpunished while specific types of offenders are disproportionately apprehended and subsequently convicted. These biases may be inherent to the criminal justice system (e.g., prejudice, availability of law enforcement in particular neighborhoods), or they may be offender specific (e.g., more intelligent offenders avoid detection). If such biases are indeed present, then researchers must give consideration to the possibility that their research findings will apply only to other convicted offenders, and not necessarily to the larger offender population.

Second, if convicted offenders are in fact different from offenders in general, can profiling research still generate predictions that will be of use in the field? As discussed in earlier chapters, profiling as an artful practice has typically been reserved for cases in which traditional law enforcement strategies have been unsuccessful. For study findings to be of use to profiling, convicted offenders would therefore need to be sufficiently similar to offenders who avoid detection. Whether this is the case has yet to be determined, and researchers should therefore use appropriate caution when making recommendations for practice based on data from convicted offenders.

Third, can offenders be relied on to be truthful or insightful about their criminal acts? On the one hand, researchers must consider that any self-report studies of offenders may be biased such that individuals may malinger psychopathology or attempt to present themselves in an unduly favorable light. On the other hand, even offenders who are truthful when providing self-reported information may not possess adequate insight to comment on the motives and personality characteristics that underlie their behavior. Researchers should consider this when reporting on findings gleaned from self-report methods, and they should consider supplementing self-reports with objective measures (see the following "Data" section) whenever possible.

Any studies of profiling should consider and attempt to address these questions, particularly when discussing the generalizability of study findings gleaned from offender data. In terms of choosing a sample to represent the population of offenders, however, these same questions would prove relevant to samples of suspects, arrestees, and unsuccessfully prosecuted individuals and thus do not prohibit one from choosing a sample and beginning the profiling research process.

Although no sample resembles perfectly the population it is intended to describe, to the extent that profiling researchers can compose a sample that approximates the true offender population, findings from research using appropriate samples will have greater application in practice. For example, the larger and more varied that samples of convicted offenders are, the more likely it is that research will be able to capture variations in offender characteristics that may relate to the larger offender population. Thus, to maximize representativeness, samples of convicted offenders used for profiling research should include a wide variety of demographic characteristics (e.g., age, ethnic background, gender, socioeconomic status), geographic locations and characteristics (e.g., East coast, Midwest, urban, rural), jurisdictions (e.g., federal, state, local), and offenses (e.g., violent, nonviolent, sexual).

Data

There are two basic types of data that can and should be collected for profiling research in samples of convicted offenders. First, there are self-reported data. As indicated in the preceding section, this type of data should be treated with caution, as offenders may manipulate their self-presentations or be unable to offer accurate information on their own internal psychological processes. When valid, however, self-report methods are also the most direct way to collect information about latent variables such as motive and personality, because they use the report of the offender himself rather than relying on the observations of a third party. Self-report assessment of offenders can take the form of paper-and-pencil tests or interviews. There are standardized paper-and-pencil instruments and interview protocols for various types of assessment, but self-report data can also be collected in unstructured interviews and questionnaires tailored for recording offender histories and case information.

Second, researchers can review collateral materials that can support, contradict, or supplement information provided by offenders. A wide variety of collateral materials should be considered from a variety of sources, to allow for the most comprehensive picture of the offender and his criminal acts. Examples of collateral materials include juvenile records; medical and mental health records; school records; employment records; police reports; victim, witness, and offender statements; medical examiner reports; court transcripts; correctional institution records; and interviews with family members, spouses, clergy, friends, coworkers, neighbors, and any other individuals with whom the offender may have had important relationships. Both types of data to be collected—self-report and collateral material—should relate to aspects of motive, personality, and behavior, consistent with the scientific model of profiling described earlier in chapter 11.

Motive

Collecting data in preparation for studies of motive largely limits researchers to the use of self-report methods because, as discussed in chapter 8, motive is a latent variable that reflects states internal to the offender. There is certainly a role for collateral materials in the study of motive, in that certain types of records and interviews with individuals close to the offender may reveal information that supports or contradicts the offender's self-reported motive. For example, an offender might report that he murdered his wife because he discovered that she was having an affair. Financial records, however, might indicate that prior to the murder, the offender took out a life insurance policy on his wife, for which he was made the sole beneficiary. This information might indicate either that the offender's self-reported motive is false or that there was an additional, financial motive for having committed the murder. Thus, collateral information may be useful as a tool to guide interview questions and challenge offenders' statements about motive. It is unfortunate that even though this additional collateral material might allow the researcher to infer, for example, that financial gain was a motive for murder, and the offender might be questioned further as to whether this was indeed the case, the offender will ultimately either confirm or deny the motive, and any determination contrary to the offender's report will necessarily be speculative. When such a conflict arises, the study investigator can choose to rely on collateral materials rather than offender report; however, the choice to exclude one type of data in favor of another would need to be clearly explained and defended.

There are two kinds of self-reported data that should be collected with regard to motive in scientific studies of profiling. These follow from the analysis of motive and behavior conducted in chapter 9. First, offenders should be asked to report on their motives for committing crimes, across a wide variety of crime types. Offenders' responses should be as descriptive as possible, rather than being limited to choices between motives that have been preselected by the researchers. This is because, as evident in the arson studies described in chapter 9, the range of motives even within a single type of crime can be quite variable. Valuable information may be lost if offenders are not permitted to elaborate on all of their perceived reasons for committing a particular crime. Self-reported data on motive should be sufficiently comprehensive as to allow researchers to assess the variation of motives within a single offender, the variation of motives within a single crime type, and the variation of motives across crime types. It should also be kept in mind that, per the discussions of chapters 8 and 9 and the structure of the profiling model described in chapter 11, data on motive will be collected with the purpose of relating it to offender behavior. Therefore, when presenting questions to the offender regarding the commission of crimes, these crimes should be described in behavioral terms. Thus, asking an offender "Why did the victim have to die during the robbery?" is likely to make it much more difficult to relate his response about motive to behavior compared with asking "Why did you kill the victim during the course of the robbery?"

Second, information should be collected that will facilitate a better understanding of the structure of motive. Recall the model of motive presented in chapter 9. This model proposes that there are various points during the commission of a crime at which motive may develop or change. Thus, in addition to collecting data on specific motives for various crimes, offenders should be asked to reconstruct the development and evolution of their motives throughout the planning (if applicable) and execution of their criminal acts. This reconstruction must also be descriptive but can be aided by questions such as "When did you first decide to commit your offense?", "What were you thinking and feeling when you decided to commit your offense?" "When did you actually commit your offense?" "What were you thinking and feeling at the time when you committed your offense?" and "Was there ever a time when your reasons for committing your offense changed?" These types of questions will allow researchers to collect information on the trajectory of an offender's motive as well as any changes in motive that may have occurred over the course of the crime.

Personality

Like motive, personality is a latent construct that is not directly observable but is instead internal to the offender. Thus, profiling research on personality will also rely heavily on self-reported information, with collateral material helping researchers to elicit and challenge self-reported information. As discussed in chapter 10, a number of personality assessment instruments are available. The recommendations at the end of chapter 10 suggest that although these assessment instruments may continue to be useful for offender research, it may be advantageous to use them in conjunction with a greater consideration of situational factors.

Given the discussion of situational factors in chapter 11, there are two types of modifications that can be made to current personality assessment approaches that may make them more suitable for profiling. Offenders can be asked to report on their personality characteristics separately for various situations. For example, an offender could be asked to complete a personality assessment inventory in a manner that reflects what he is like when he is at work. He could then complete the same instrument with instructions to report on what he is like with his parents. This could be repeated for a variety of contexts and situations, to identify characteristics that are consistent across situations and those that appear to fluctuate depending on context. Such an approach is not limited to paper-and-pencil inventories. For example, offenders could also be interviewed with regard to their personality characteristics in various contexts and situations, to construct the types of if–then contingencies suggested by Alison, Bennell, and Mokros (2002). Offenders could be presented with partial statements such as "When I am around my boss, I act like . . ." or "When I am with my children, I am . . ." and be asked to respond by completing the sentences. In this way, open-ended questioning could be used to allow offenders to generate their own personality descriptors, rather than simply endorsing the predetermined characteristics contained in personality inventories.

Offenders could also be questioned as to the significance of various types of situations to them, and attempts could be made to relate the significance of these situations to the personality characteristics that are elicited. An offender might indicate that when he is around his boss, he feels nervous. He might then indicate that when he feels nervous he becomes introverted, anxious, and quiet. Thus, data might be collected regarding potential relationships both between individual situations and personality characteristics and between the impact of situations and the personality characteristics that are elicited as a result.

As described in chapter 10, the study of personality has a long history, and much research has been invested in the construction and validation of various personality assessment inventories. The goal with regard to collecting data on personality is therefore not to reinvent personality assessment but to attempt to collect information that is more relevant to a criminal investigation. As previously described, one way to accomplish this is to assess personality with a greater consideration of situational factors. In addition, as with motive, researchers should keep in mind that the purpose of collecting data on personality is to use this information to make predictions about behavior. Thus, it would be advantageous to use instruments or measures that will allow the collection of data on separate personality characteristics, such as hostility, introversion, or impulsivity (e.g., Personality Assessment Inventory), rather than using measures that yield information on broader personality types (e.g., the Minnesota Multiphasic Personality Inventory [Hathaway & McKinley, 1983], the California Psychological Inventory). Although it may be that groups of personality characteristics can be combined to make predictions about behavior, it would also be valuable to be able to identify the individual characteristics that relate to both first- and second-level behaviors.

Behavior

There are two main realms of offender behavior for which data must be collected in a scientific model of profiling: criminal behavior and noncriminal, life behavior. These two realms of behavior correspond to the first- and second-level behaviors of the profiling model described in chapter 11. Self-report measures may be used to collect data on offender behavior, in a manner similar to that suggested for motive and personality. Paper-and-pencil questionnaires can be administered to offenders, inquiring about their criminal and noncriminal activities; likewise, interviews with offenders can be conducted to elicit narratives of criminal acts and other life behaviors. Unlike the assessment of motive or personality, however, behavior is an observable construct, and researchers therefore need not rely solely on self-report that is supplemented by collateral information. Instead, objective accounts of offender behavior should be available from a variety of collateral sources, and in the absence of self-report, behavioral data can still be collected from these sources.

First-level offender behaviors are those involved in the commission of the offender's crimes. In addition to the offender's report of these behaviors, collateral sources likely to contain data relevant to first-level behaviors include police reports, victim and witness statements, and court transcripts. A wide range of crime-related behaviors should be considered to gain a comprehensive assessment of the acts involved in committing the offense of interest. For example, consider a case in which an offender kidnaps a child for ransom. Some obvious data to collect with regard to first-level behaviors might include the snatching of the child and the placement of a phone call demanding ransom. In addition to these behaviors, data should be collected on other first-level behaviors that relate to the planning and execution of the crime, such as the surveillance or stalking of the child, the acquisition of the parents' telephone number, and the preparation of a location to house the child while awaiting payment. Although chapter 7 discussed the need for further research into forensic analysis and crime reconstruction, to the extent that these sources of information are included in collateral case materials they may assist researchers in ascertaining these types of first-level offender behaviors, especially given that solved cases will be used. For example, forensic analyses might trace the origin of telephone calls placed to the parents' home back to the telephone number of the offender's workplace. Crime reconstruction might then identify a temporal pattern, such that the calls occur only on the offender's shift, with no overlap with coworkers occurring across the total timeline. From this information, it could be inferred that the offender telephoned the parents of the kidnapped child.

Second-level offender behaviors are life behaviors, not necessarily crime related, that may assist in identifying or apprehending an offender. When dealing with offenders who have already been apprehended, there are two ways to approach the collection of these data. The first approach is to actually attempt to ascertain those behaviors that resulted in the offender's apprehension. For example, an offender who murders a victim might come to law enforcement attention because he attends her funeral. Likewise, an offender might be apprehended because he brags to a friend about his crime. In a more complicated situation, such as the husband's murder of his wife, described earlier, the second-level offender behaviors that result in an offender's arrest might include a combination of a history of violence toward the victim, the collection of insurance benefits, and the initiation of a relationship with another woman immediately following the wife's death. With the exception of the bragging behavior, these second-level behaviors do not necessarily implicate the offender conclusively, but they do represent the behaviors that could allow law enforcement to successfully narrow the subject pool down to the correct perpetrator.

The second approach to ascertaining second-level behaviors is to collect a broader range of data on life behaviors with the goal of ascertaining their relationship to aspects of motive, personality, first-level behaviors, and other second-level behaviors. Data to be collected in this category might include social and offense histories; substance use patterns; financial behavior; relationships with family, friends, and coworkers; and marital and sexual histories. These data can be collected from the offender, as well as from official records and interviews with individuals with whom the offender has had relationships. If the offender is incarcerated, data on current second-level behaviors can also be collected from institutional records and interviews with fellow inmates, correctional officers, and individuals who conduct prison programs.

Generating and Testing Hypotheses

Together, the data collected from self-report and collateral sources should reflect a comprehensive body of information that will prepare profiling researchers to test predictions about motive, personality, and behavior. The next step is to consider the types of hypotheses that will be tested with these data and how to test them.

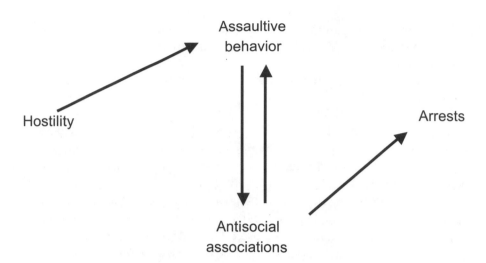

Figure 12.1. Path diagram of variables predicting arrest history.

Causal Modeling

It would be ideal, ultimately, to test a complete scientific model of profiling all at once or, at the very least, examine the relationships contained within large sections of the model. For example, recall Figures 11.3 and 11.4. In one section of this model, hostility predicts a previous history of assaultive behavior, which predicts, and is predicted by, having antisocial associations, which in turn predicts a prior arrest history. If this entire section of the model could be tested, it might be possible to determine the strength of each variable as an ultimate predictor of arrest history. Perhaps hostility is the main predictor of arrest history, with assaultive behavior and antisocial associations acting as intervening variables through which hostility exerts its influence. Or perhaps prior assaultive behavior is the primary predictor of arrest history, with hostility and antisocial associations acting as only minimal influences.

One way to approach a simultaneous analysis of the variables just described is to use causal modeling to posit and then test their relationships to each other. Causal modeling is a heuristic device that can be used to map out the causal relationships between variables and construct arrow diagrams, or path diagrams, similar to those presented in chapter 11, to reflect these processes. If the section of Figure 11.4 that deals with hostility and arrest history is separated from the rest of the robbery example, it can be represented as the path diagram seen in Figure 12.1. In this diagram, the arrows depict the proposed causal relationships among the variables of interest. Thus, hostility is proposed to cause assaultive behavior, assaultive behavior and antisocial associations cause each other, and antisocial associations cause arrests. In addition, the arrows indicate that hostility causes arrests, when assaultive behavior and antisocial associations are also taken into account.

These statements expressed by the path diagram may initially seem strange, because of the use of the term *cause*. In the common vernacular, *cause* typically indicates a one-to-one relationship between an action and its effect. For example, pouring water on something will cause it to get wet. In a similar way, blowing on a candle flame will (in most cases) cause it to extinguish. Thus, it may seem like an overstatement to suggest that having antisocial associations will cause someone to engage in assaultive behavior, or to be arrested. In causal modeling, however, the term *cause* is treated somewhat differently. When expressing relationships between two variables, Variable X is considered to be a cause of Variable Y in two basic situations (J. A. Davis, 1985). First, X is a cause of Y if changes in X produce changes in Y. This is the sense in which it is proposed that antisocial associations cause arrests. If, for example, an offender increases the number of fellow offenders with whom he associates, it may increase the attention paid to him by law enforcement and result in more frequent arrests. If he decreases his antisocial associations, he may be less noticed by law enforcement and be arrested less frequently, even though he might still engage in the same amount of illegal behavior. Thus, changes in the offender's antisocial associations may lead to changes in the frequency and number of his arrests. Second, because some Xs remain constant, X is also a cause of Y when Ys "tend to line up with fixed values of X" (J. A. Davis, 1985, p. 9). For example, if hostility is viewed from the trait perspective in personality, such that it is a relatively unchanging personality characteristic, a causal relationship between hostility and assaultive behavior could be proposed such that hostile people tend to assault others whereas nonhostile people do not. In this example, hostility does not change, but different levels of assaultive behavior are associated with the fixed presence or absence of hostility.

It should also be noted that the proposals contained in causal models reflect averages or tendencies (J. A. Davis, 1985). Individual exceptions to the predictions of the model are to be expected. So, for example, law enforcement investigators may encounter individual offenders in the field who have a lengthy arrest history but do not associate with other law-breakers. Likewise, there are certain to be individuals in the population who associate with antisocial groups but have never been arrested themselves. In addition, proposing that antisocial associations, for example, are a cause of arrests does not imply that antisocial associations are *the* cause of arrests. Indeed, as is evident in Figure 12.1, there may be multiple causes of arrests. Causal modeling thus represents a set of hypotheses that propose how a set of variables might work together to cause a phenomenon of interest. Determining the actual magnitude of the relationship between variables in the model may or may not be possible in any given situation, but modeling phenomena causally represents an improvement over "simply correlating independent and dependent variables in a relatively unthinking fashion" (Asher, 1983, p. 9).

Path Analysis

Once causal models have been constructed, it is possible to use empirical data, such as those described earlier in this chapter, to solve for a numerical value for each arrow in the causal model that will indicate the strength of that causal influence (Loehlin, 1998). *Path analysis* is the process of constructing and solving these path diagrams. If the variables in the model are all observable, path analysis is accomplished by calculating the intercorrelations of the variables in the model and using them to calculate the path coefficients. In Figure 12.1, the paths among antisocial associations, assaultive behavior, and arrests could be solved for in this manner, using data from convicted offenders that would include information about previous arrests, history of violent behavior, and the arrest histories of known associates of the offender.

Figure 12.1 also contains a latent variable: hostility. Recall from chapter 8 that the variables of motive and personality cannot be directly observed. Investigators instead must depend on the manifestations of aspects of motive and personality as observable behaviors to determine their presence and role in a given crime. As an aspect of personality, hostility cannot be directly observed. Instead, hostility may manifest itself as assaultive behavior, antisocial associations, and arrests—variables that can be observed and measured according to this model. Solving for the causal pathways in a model containing one or more latent variables is somewhat different from the process just described for observed variables. This is because latent variables and observed variables cannot be correlated with each other. It is possible, however, to solve for the causal paths that involve the latent variable if the model specifies the relationship between the latent and observed variables, and if the correlations between the observed variables are available. Thus, it may be possible to solve for the influence of hostility, given the appropriate data about the observed variables that are contained in the same causal path.

Path-Analyzing a Scientific Model of Profiling

In summary, then, path analysis provides a method for testing the causal pathways proposed by a scientific model of profiling. It accounts for both observed and latent variables and allows for the examination of relationships among variables in a causal context, rather than attempting to conceptualize a model ad hoc after calculating a piecemeal assortment of correlations between variables of interest. This represents an advantage over the bivariate studies of motive and behavior, and personality and behavior, described in chapters 9 and 10, because it allows for the simultaneous study of multivariate relationships. Path analysis is also more informative than the multidimensional scaling methods used by Canter and colleagues (and Kocsis and colleagues; e.g., Kocsis & Cooksey, 2002; Salfati & Canter, 1991) because it describes the magnitude of causal relationships between variables rather than being limited to associations made by eyeballing data scatter plots with no determination of the strength of those associations or their causal relationships to each other.

Although some aspects of a scientific model of profiling appear ready to be tested by investigators using path analysis, other aspects of the model are not. This is because path analysis requires that the investigator have substantial confidence in the proposed linkages between the variables of interest (Asher, 1983). If there is little confidence in the links between variables, then causal modeling and the resulting path analyses become "fishing expeditions" in which the investigator is repeatedly constructing different combinations of variables without a clear purpose, in the hope of identifying a model that is plausible. In addition, causal modeling and path analysis techniques will not determine the direction of causality between variables (Asher, 1983). Instead, if there is a causal relationship, the investigator must specify this ahead of time, on the basis of sound theory and, ideally, findings from existing research.

The difficulty in applying path analysis to the scientific model of profiling is that, largely owing to the paucity of relevant offender research, many, if not most, of the proposed relationships between variables are not established by the literature. This is why the examples of the scientific profiling model depicted in Figures 11.2 and 11.4 are entirely hypothetical scenarios, and the position of the variables (and hence the direction of causality) in many of the proposed relationships could easily be changed. For example, Figure 11.4 suggests that hostility causes the presence of few prosocial relationships. However, it could just as easily be that having few prosocial relationships would cause an individual to become hostile. Although the structure of the overall model, representing the prediction of crime scene evidence from first-level offender behaviors and the subsequent prediction of second-level behaviors through aspects of motive, personality, and behavior, may remain intact, the details contained in the examples given in chapter 11 might turn out to be quite different if they were based on a body of sound empirical literature.

Research Plan for a Science of Profiling

Given the state of the offender literature related to investigation, and the basic requirements of causal modeling and path analysis just described,

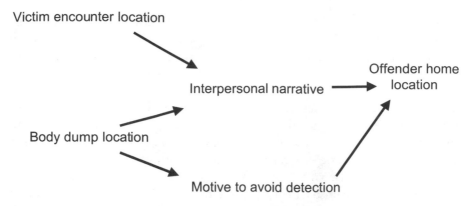

Figure 12.2. Proposed causal model for geographic profiling.

there are two research pathways one can take when embarking on a science of profiling. First, those relationships that have sound theoretical underpinnings and sufficient support in the literature to be causally modeled and path-analyzed should be identified and tested. Currently, there are two main areas in the profiling field for which this would appear to be an appropriate step. Both relate to research from the Canter model: geographic profiling and multidimensional scaling research. Second, in those areas of profiling for which there is not yet sufficient information for constructing and testing causal models, steps should be taken to improve and strengthen offender research in preparation for causal modeling.

Geographic Profiling. The first area in which causal modeling and path analysis could be applied is geographic profiling. As a heuristic technique, geographic profiling has already demonstrated utility in predicting offenders' home locations from certain crime locations, as described by the research of Canter and colleagues (Canter, Coffey, Huntley, & Missen, 2000; Canter & Larkin, 1993; Fritzon, 2001; Godwin & Canter, 1997; Lundrigan & Canter, 2001; Snook, Canter, & Bennell, 2002). In describing geographic profiling and proposing its mechanisms, Canter and colleagues have, in essence, posited a set of causal pathways, such that aspects of interpersonal-narratives theory predict the offender's selection of crime locations in a manner consistent with the locations (including the offender's home) that are part of the offender's daily life. In addition, for cases of serial murder, Canter proposes that the locations at which offenders dispose of their victims' bodies are predicted in part by a motivation to avoid detection but are also consistent with the parameters of an offender's daily life.

Figure 12.2 represents a possible causal model that could be constructed from the principles articulated by Canter and colleagues and the results already obtained in studies of geographic profiling. According to this model of serial killings, the two types of crime locations (point of victim encounter and body dump location) predict the offender's home location. The victim encounter location predicts offender home location through the aspects of interpersonal narratives that relate to the offender's proclivity for operating within a familiar area. The body dump location predicts home location not only by means of this same variable but also by means of the motive to avoid detection. To test this model, one would need to collect data on offender crime and home locations, similar to Canter and colleagues' previous studies. Unlike previous studies, however, testing the causal model in Figure 12.2 would also involve examining the mechanisms through which crime locations are proposed to predict home locations. Because the variables representing these mechanisms—namely, the aspects of motive and personality contained in interpersonal-narratives theory—are latent variables, consideration would have to be given to how to measure them. As discussed earlier in this chapter, measuring motive will involve relying in great part on the offender's self-report. In addition, however, because the motive of interest is the motive to avoid detection, case materials could be reviewed to assess whether the offender demonstrated this motive in other ways, such as removing forensic evidence or taking precautions such as wearing gloves. Measuring the interpersonal-narratives variable may pose more difficulty. Although the concept of this variable is not entirely clear, it appears to represent the offender's comfort or habitual operation within an area of familiarity. One way to approach the measurement of this variable would therefore be to ask offenders questions related to their familiarity with the victim encounter and body dump locations. Questions such as "Why were you at Location X the day you encountered the victim?" or "Had you ever been to Location Y before that day?" as well as an assessment of the locations that are part of an offender's daily activities might help establish the repertoire of locations in which an offender is comfortable. These questions may only approximate the interpersonal-narratives variable, however, and additional consideration should therefore be given to clarifying the operational definition of the interpersonal-narratives variable and validating whatever measures are ultimately used to assess it.

Once the appropriate data have been collected, the magnitude of the pathways between variables in the causal model can be calculated. This procedure would advance the current state of knowledge about geographic profiling by reinforcing the relationship between crime and home locations already observed in previous research as well as by evaluating the strength of the mechanisms that are posited to explain this relationship.

Multidimensional Scaling Research. The second area of profiling in which it would be appropriate to begin causal modeling and path analysis is the body of multidimensional scaling research conducted by Canter and colleagues. One of the criticisms levied against Canter's model in chapter 5 was that the methods used to test the interpersonal narratives theory and,

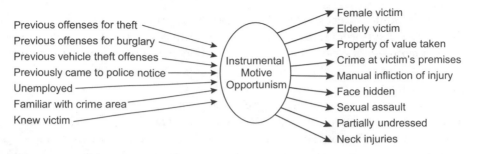

Figure 12.3. Proposed causal model for stranger homicide.

consequently, the aspects of motive and personality contained therein, did not allow the inference of causation or establish an empirical basis for the associations asserted to exist between various crime actions and offender characteristics (first- and second-level behaviors). Causal modeling would allow investigators to test these relationships between crime actions and offender characteristics along with the variables that are proposed to cause them.

For example, Figure 12.3 is a causal model that could be constructed from the portion of the smallest space analysis scatter plot posited by Salfati and Canter (1999) to represent the Instrumental Opportunistic theme within a set of stranger homicides. Recall that Salfati and Canter (1999) reported that this is "a distinct theme of opportunistic victims being targeted . . . where the offender used the victim as an object through which to attain an ulterior motive such as money or sex" (p. 401). The causal model in Figure 12.3 proposes that the offender characteristics identified by the authors predict the presence of this Instrumental Opportunistic theme, which in turn predicts the crime actions evidenced in the sample of homicides. To test·this model, an investigator would need to collect two types of data. First, one would need to collect information on the first- and second-level behaviors of homicide offenders, to determine the crime actions and offender characteristics Salfati and Canter described. Second, similar to the previous example of geographic profiling, aspects of the Instrumental Opportunistic theme would need to be operationalized as aspects of motive and personality and measured. One approach to this might be to assess the level of opportunism involved in the commission of the crime, in an attempt to discern aspects of motive. Was the murder committed during the course of another crime? Is there evidence of the type of lack of planning that might accompany an opportunistic offense? Another approach, which could be used in conjunction with an assessment of opportunism, might be to assess instrumental aspects of the offense. Is there evidence of secondary gain? Do offenders report that they committed murder with the motive of acquiring money or achieving some other benefit? Once the Instrumental Opportunistic theme has been adequately described in terms of motive and personality and has been measured, the model could be tested to determine the relationship between offender characteristics and crime actions, as well as the strength of the Instrumental Opportunistic theme as a mechanism for relating offender characteristics to crime actions. Other offender themes from interpersonal-narratives theory could also be examined in this manner, across the various types of offenses that have been examined with regard to the Canter approach thus far.

Together, the geographic profiling and multidimensional scaling research appear to represent the only current body of profiling principles for which it would be appropriate to begin constructing causal models and conducting path analyses. Although the associations between crime actions and offender characteristics reported by Canter and colleagues have been previously questioned because of the methods used to determine these associations, constructing causal models and solving for the relationships between variables in the models will constitute significant progress toward addressing some of the criticisms levied against findings gained by using the Canter model. The main challenge will be finding ways to measure the offender themes proposed by Canter's interpersonal-narratives theory. Some aspects of these themes are not clearly defined, as discussed previously, and because the elements of motive and personality inherent to these themes are latent, the construct validity of any measures used to assess offender themes must be carefully examined and addressed.

Strengthening Offender Research. There are many areas of profiling for which it is not yet appropriate to construct and test causal models. For example, the literature on personality and sex offending, described in chapter 10, appears to be so equivocal that one would have significant difficulty in asserting confidence in any personality type or characteristic as being a cause of a given sex offending behavior. This is not to say that no relationship between personality and sex offending exists—in fact, the scientific model of profiling described in chapter 11 views aspects of personality (as well as motive) as being essential to every type of criminal behavior. However, because of many of the limitations described in chapter 10, the links between personality and sex offending have not yet been established to the degree that it would be appropriate to include them in a causal model.

For areas of the literature such as this, steps should be taken to strengthen offender research in preparation for future causal modeling. With this in mind, a second research pathway for a science of profiling would be to use data from convicted offenders to attempt to build on the kinds of offender studies of motive, personality, and behavior described in chapters 9 and 10 in an attempt to identify and propose causal relationships between variables in which substantial confidence can be asserted. So, for example, incorporating the criticisms and recommendations from chapter 10 and the data collection segment of this chapter, personality characteristics could be assessed in a manner that considers situational factors. The personality data could then be compared with data on the first-level, crime-related behaviors of convicted sexual offenders to yield relationships between specific aspects of personality and specific crime-related sexual offense behaviors. Whereas previous research attempted to relate global personality types or clusters (e.g., antisocial/aggressive) to broad categories of offenses (rapists), the type of analysis proposed in this chapter would allow a more precise determination of individual personality characteristics (e.g., impulsivity) and their relationship to types of offense behavior (e.g., father–daughter incest behaviors) and particular settings or situations (e.g., in a stepparent relationship). Findings from this type of research on personality and behavior, along with findings from similar studies of motive and behavior, will assist in building the appropriate research base for the development and testing of new causal models for profiling.

13

CONCLUSION: RECOMMENDATIONS FOR PRACTICE

Although the development and testing of a science of profiling, described in chapters 11 and 12, will add to the existing body of offender literature and allow a better understanding of the role of motive, personality, and behavior in the commission of crimes, the immediate concern for profiling practitioners is how to use this information to improve criminal investigations in the field. There are two sets of answers to this question. First, there are recommendations for profiling practice that will apply once findings from the scientific model of profiling are available. Second, there are recommendations to assist profiling practitioners while studies of profiling are underway.

APPLICATION OF FINDINGS FROM A
SCIENTIFIC MODEL OF PROFILING

There are two main ways to apply findings from profiling research to profiling practice. The first method involves combining known data and then making decisions or predictions based on experience, judgment, or discussion with others. This is quite similar to what goes on in college admissions committees. Profiling professionals have used this type of clinical judgment in the past to assess individual cases and make recommendations to law enforcement agencies. The second way to make decisions related to profiling is to apply actuarial methods to cases to generate predictions about offenders that may inform investigations. Actuarial (or statistical) methods use formal algorithms or equations to make decisions or predictions, without involving clinical judgment.

As described in Part I of this book, reliance on the first approach to profiling (i.e., clinical judgment) is fraught with problems, not the least of which is its low rate of accuracy (Holmes & Holmes, 1996; Copson, 1995, cited in Canter, 2000). Despite these problems, however, intuitive judgments have been tolerated and even embraced in profiling because of the creative and artful nature of the field's origins and because there has been no scientific alternative available. As findings from a science of profiling become available, it will be possible to construct actuarial tools for making predictions about offenders rather than relying on impressionistic judgment.

The decision to choose actuarial methods over clinical methods is not without controversy. The argument for using actuarial methods was thoroughly articulated by Grove and Meehl (1996), who demonstrated the superiority of actuarial over clinical methods in generating accurate predictions. The reader is referred to their article for a comprehensive discussion and convincing resolution of the actuarial–clinical controversy, but there are two points Grove and Meehl raised that should be considered here because they are particularly relevant to profiling.

First, a distinction must be made between *data collection* and *data combination* (Meehl, 1996). Profiling practitioners may feel that if they are confined to using equations or algorithms to make predictions about an offender, then important qualitative information gleaned from the case information or crime reconstruction will be excluded from analysis and predictions about offenders. This need not be the case. As described in chapter 12, the data recommended for use in testing a scientific model of profiling includes a range of information. Some of this will consist of quantitative information (e.g., number of arrests), but much of it is related to qualitative aspects of motive, personality, and behavior. The clinical–statistical distinction relates, then, not to the nature of the information that is collected and deemed relevant to investigation but rather to the manner in which that information is combined to generate predictions about second-level behaviors. Many of the qualitative variables that have been historically important to profiling (e.g., staging, modus operandi behaviors, interaction with victim) can and should be included in causal models to determine their relevance to predicting second-level offender behaviors. The weight of that information and the nature of its relationship to other information about motive, personality, and behavior, however, are best determined by actuarial methods in any given profiling case.

The second point from Grove and Meehl's (1996) discussion that is related to profiling addresses a concern that profiling practitioners may have with regard to applying statistical figures that deal with aggregate information (i.e., group or nomothetic data) to predictions that relate to individual offenders (i.e., idiographic data). If the type of research proposed in chapter 12 involves studying groups of offenders, how can those findings be applied to individual offenders? Would it not be more accurate to consider each individual's case information and make decisions without relying on these general statistics? And are there not particular offense characteristics—such as the unique posing of a body at a crime scene—that would be so significant to a profiler that it would trump the more general predictions that would be generated by a statistical tool?

The first two questions reflect the faulty assumption that whereas statistics can give only probabilities or aggregate results, dealing with a unique individual and applying clinical judgment will allow profilers to predict exactly what that individual will do. This is simply not the case. As discussed in chapter 6, even nonscientific profilers describe their profiles as reflecting a more general type of individual that may have committed a given crime. These profiles are then almost invariably applied to individuals to demonstrate the accuracy of the predictions contained in them. Thus, even in profiles that are derived from individual cases, predictions are made in terms of the likely characteristics of the offender, and these likelihoods or probabilities are then applied to the individual offender. If actuarial methods and artful profiling methods are essentially using the same procedure, the question becomes whether these predictions about offenders are best generated by an actuarial tool or by an individual profiler. As indicated previously, research suggests that actuarial predictions are equal or superior to individual, clinical judgments the vast majority of the time (Grove, Zald, Lebow, Snits, & Nelson, 1996, cited in Grove & Meehl, 1996).

The third question addresses the issue of whether there are certain facts about an individual that might be so rare but so important that actuarial tools may not account for them, and their presence would override any actuarial predictions. For example, an actuarial tool might predict that an unknown offender who has committed five rapes over the past month has an 80% chance of committing a sixth rape today. However, on the basis of a crime reconstruction from the fifth offense, the profiler knows that the offender was unsuccessful in completing the fifth rape because the victim defended herself by using her car keys to inflict injuries on the offender's eyes that rendered him blind. Faced with this information, it would certainly be a mistake to rely on the actuarial prediction. The problem is that most predictions regarding aspects of motive, personality, and behavior do not contain the types of near-certainties in the previous example. Predictions of second-level offender behavior involve a consideration of motive, personality, other behaviors, and situational factors. In this context, clinicians are not adept at selecting situations in which a variable is sufficiently rare and important as to override the relevant actuarial equation, and actuarial methods are thus still superior to clinician judgment in generating accurate predictions (Grove & Meehl, 1996).

The scientific model of profiling described in chapters 11 and 12 represents a significant departure from current profiling practice, and the application of its findings through actuarial methods is likely to meet with a certain degree of resistance. Profiling practitioners, however, will not be the first group to respond with skepticism to the assertion that actuarial methods are almost always superior or equal to clinical judgment. As Grove and Meehl (1996) pointed out, objections are raised by practitioners across many branches of social science, and these objections often stem from a lack of understanding of the principles involved in actuarial prediction and a reluctance to depart from the traditional theories and approaches of their disciplines. If the goal of profiling, however, is to generate accurate predictions about offenders to assist in identifying and apprehending them, profilers must be willing to embrace a science of profiling and consider the evidence in support of actuarial prediction. Given the potential impact of the accuracy and inaccuracy of profiling predictions on both victims and offenders, it is time to improve profiling through the application of science.

RECOMMENDATIONS FOR THE CURRENT ART AND SCIENCE OF PROFILING

As the field of profiling awaits findings from the testing of a relevant scientific model, law enforcement investigators must continue to investigate crimes to the best of their ability, and profiling practitioners must still attempt to contribute to these criminal investigations. Given that there is currently very little science on which to rely, what can profiling practitioners do to maximize their contributions to investigation and reduce the negative consequences that can result from error? The main recommendation that can be made is for profiling practitioners to follow the scientific model of profiling described in chapter 11, using it as a road map for how to think about profiling inferences in an organized fashion. At each tier of the profiling model there are different sets of hypotheses that can be generated and offered to law enforcement for consideration in an investigation. Although profilers must be careful to state the limitations of these hypotheses, because the science to support definitive predictions about offender characteristics is still largely unavailable, offering law enforcement investigators a structured way to relate evidence, behavior, motive, and personality to generate leads for investigation may represent a significant advance over the current, artful state of profiling.

Tier 1: Crime Scene Evidence and First-Level Offender Behaviors

According to the scientific model of profiling, Tier 1 represents the inferences involved in crime reconstruction. This tier of inferences is crucial to any criminal investigation, because in essence it provides a determination of what happened during the course of the crime. The basis for inferences in Tier 1 should therefore be clearly rooted in the forensic evidence and the analyses of evidence provided by forensic scientists and witness accounts. In addition, the logic linking inferences about evidence and first-level offender behaviors should be as precise as possible, because the determination of first-level behaviors will guide subsequent predictions about motive, personality, and second-level behaviors. Profiling practitioners should rely on this logic to attempt to create a narrative of first-level behaviors and a timeline that describes the temporal order of the first-level behaviors in a given crime. These inferences should be cross-checked so that each inference both explains, and is explained by, the evidence. For example, returning to Figures 11.2 and 11.4, if the evidence includes a body that is left on a remote lakeshore accessible only by car, a logical inference would be that the offender must have driven the body to the dump location. Likewise, if there is a complete absence of fingerprints at a burglary crime scene, a logical inference would be that the offender wore gloves during the offense. These inferences both explain the location of the dead body and the absence of fingerprints, respectively, and the inferences are supported by the available evidence. It is also important, however, to consider any plausible alternative inferences and make law enforcement agents aware of these alternatives. For example, it could be that the offender in the murder scenario traveled from one side of the lake to the other by boat, rather than driving from the nearest town straight to the area of shore where the body was found. In a similar manner, it could be that the offender in the burglary scenario did not wear gloves but was instead careful to wipe his fingerprints from every surface he touched before leaving the scene. In the case of plausible alternatives, the profiler should consider the types of evidence that would be required to support the relevant inferences. For example, if the offender in Figure 11.2 transported the body by boat, one might expect to see evidence on the shore of a boat having come and gone. Likewise, if the offender in Figure 11.4 wiped his fingerprints, one might expect to find evidence of at least one smeared print, or other oily residue from the fingers that might have remained on surfaces in the house. Where there are alternative scenarios, the profiler can certainly communicate an opinion about which seems more correct, while presenting to law enforcement all plausible scenarios for their consideration.

Tier 2: Motive, Personality, and First-Level Offender Behaviors

Once logical determinations have been made about first-level offender behaviors through crime reconstruction, profiling practitioners should consider the potential relationships of these behaviors to aspects of motive and personality. What kinds of hypotheses can be generated with regard to the influence of motives and personality characteristics on first-level crime behaviors? In the murder example, the offense might be motivated in part by the desire to force the victim to cooperate with a robbery. In addition, the personality characteristics of the offender might include a certain amount of hostility and impulsivity, particularly because the murder was unplanned. Because of the limitations of the current profiling research literature, the inferences made in Tier 2 must be stated as hypotheses. Nonetheless, practitioners should still make an effort to derive these hypotheses logically and ensure that they are consistent with the inferences made in Tier 1. For example, it would not be logical to predict that the offender in the Figure 11.2 murder scenario had passive personality characteristics. Although it might be possible that the offender is less aggressive in other realms of his life, the evidence and first-level behaviors do not support this as a viable hypothesis in the context of Tier 2 of this offense.

Tier 3 and Beyond: Motive, Personality, and Second-Level Offender Behaviors

Given the first-level offender behaviors and the hypotheses about motive and personality generated from the information in the crime reconstruction, what predictions might be made about second-level offender behaviors? If the steps leading up to Tier 3 have been logical, and if the information contained in the inferences about first-level behaviors (i.e., motive and personality) have been correct, what other offender behaviors might follow from these inferences? For example, if the offender who committed the robbery depicted in Figure 11.4 was indeed motivated by financial need and had hostile personality characteristics, what might this individual do in his noncriminal life that would assist law enforcement agents in identifying and apprehending him? Perhaps his motive of financial need would predict the second-level behavior of being unemployed, which might in turn predict not having graduated from high school and having a history of delinquency as a juvenile. In addition, perhaps his hostility would predict the second-level behavior of having committed assaults in the past, which may in turn predict the second-level behavior of arrest history. As with the predictions in Tier 2, these predictions must be stated as hypotheses because there is currently no research literature to demonstrate many, if not most, of the relationships that would link aspects of motive and personality to second-level offender behaviors. As previously discussed, however, the hypotheses in Tier 3 must still derive logically from the predictions in Tiers 1 and 2. Thus, in the robbery example depicted in Figure 11.4, it would not be logical to predict that the offender would be gainfully employed at a 9-to-5 job, with no experience or knowledge about police investigations. The fact that the offense was committed during the day appears to refute the former prediction, and the care taken to avoid leaving fingerprints belies the latter prediction.

Applications of the Scientific Model of Profiling for Practice

Across the three tiers described previously, the scientific model of profiling can be used as a road map to generate hypotheses for investigation in a logical and organized manner. By following the structure of the model, one can organize profiling inferences into three main tiers, with each tier reflecting a particular type of relationship between crime variables. Tier 1 contains hypotheses linking crime scene evidence to first-level offender behaviors. Tier 2 relates first-level behaviors to aspects of motive and personality. Finally, Tier 3 involves the derivation of second-level behaviors from motive, personality, and other behaviors.

Use of the three-tier model and the presentation of profiling inferences to law enforcement agencies in the context of this model has three main benefits over current nonscientific profiling practices. First, by using an organized system for considering hypotheses and providing the logical links between the hypotheses and inferences leading up to second-level behaviors, profiling practitioners will assist law enforcement agents in understanding the relevance and role of behavioral and psychological information to a conceptualization of crime. By organizing inferences into the three tiers of the scientific model, profilers will be able to demonstrate to law enforcement where and how aspects of motive and personality become important and how to use information about crime events to make predictions about the second-level offender behaviors that may assist law enforcement in capturing the offender.

Second, by making the steps involved in generating predictions about second-level behaviors explicit, profiling practitioners will be able to track the trajectory of their hypotheses through the three tiers of the scientific profiling model and make adjustments in the face of new information. For example, in the murder example from Figure 11.2, the remote location of the body led to the prediction of the first-level behavior of driving to the body dump site. This first-level behavior subsequently led to the prediction of the second-level behavior of having access to a vehicle. Suppose that new information became available to suggest that a boat had been used to bring the body to the remote area of shore from across the lake—an area that is populated with homes. This would contradict the inference that the offender had to drive to dump the body and thus must have had access to a car. Because the progression of inferences has been described explicitly, however, it is possible to go back to the source of the inference about having access to a vehicle and change it. Thus, the first-level behavior of navigating a boat would be added to the crime reconstruction. This would in turn lead to different predictions about second-level offender behaviors. For example, one might predict that the offender has sailing experience or owns a boat. One might also predict that the offender lives in the neighborhood on the opposite lakeshore. The benefit of using the scientific model of profiling as a road map is that the paths of inferences can be traced and adjusted in the event that new information becomes available.

Third, by conceptualizing profiling predictions as hypotheses and making the derivation of those hypotheses as logical and explicit as possible, profiling practitioners will be providing profiling researchers with important empirical questions that can be examined in the service of creating and testing causal models. For example, whether hostile personality characteristics predict assaultive behavior and prior arrest history in homicide offenders is an empirical question. Likewise, the hypothesis that a motive of financial gain predicts unemployment and a history of delinquency in robbery offenders can be modeled and tested. By continuing to generate new ideas, and by transforming the clinical observations made in practice into testable research hypotheses, profiling practitioners can contribute greatly to bridging the gap between profiling science and practice and to ultimately improving law enforcement investigations.

Limitations of the Scientific Model of Profiling for Practice

Although profiling practice continues to evolve in tandem with a science of profiling, it is important to consider the current limitations of profiling knowledge and identify boundaries for profiling expertise. First, as previously discussed, profiling predictions should be presented to law enforcement as working hypotheses rather than conclusive statements. The logic of these profiling predictions should be clearly communicated to law enforcement agents, and it should be made clear that these predictions may change in the face of new information or contrary research findings. Second, profiling practitioners should become familiar with the most current offender literature and incorporate research findings into their practice whenever possible. In the same way that observations from practice can inform research studies, the findings from these studies should in turn be applied to profiling practice. Profiling practitioners should be clear to law enforcement agents about which aspects of their predictions are informed by research and which are based on clinical or logical inferences. Third, profiling expertise should be offered only in the investigation phase of criminal offenses, to generate leads and assist law enforcement agents in narrowing down the field of potential suspects. The state of the profiling research literature limits the expertise that profiling practitioners have to offer, in that it is not currently possible to express profiling predictions as certainties, or to even assert the strength of the causal relationships that are at the heart of these profiling predictions. This limitation to current profiling knowledge should not prohibit practitioners from suggesting new avenues for investigation or strategies (e.g., recommending the use of the three-tier model) for organizing evidence and behavioral information. It may even be possible for practitioners to suggest strategies for interrogation, such as a consideration of the types of questioning styles that might be more likely to elicit responses from offenders with particular sets of personality characteristics. Beyond investigation, however, in phases of the criminal justice system that are focused on establishing the guilt of a particular offender through prosecution and the levying of punishment through sentencing, profiling practitioners should refrain from characterizing their predictions as expertise, and profiling inferences should not be offered as proof to demonstrate the truth of any particular version of crime events or offender actions. There is currently no evidence in the offender literature to support the conclusive matching of an offender to a hypothesized crime reconstruction or set of offender characteristics, and there are no current indicators to suggest that profiling practitioners can or should apply hypotheses about second-level behaviors to individual suspects in the context of demonstrating guilt. Although it might be an appropriate risk to make certain investigative decisions, such as following a potential lead, on the basis of profiling predictions that may or may not be correct, the risks involved at the prosecution stage of a crime, to both victims and alleged offenders, are substantial. Providing potentially inaccurate information at trial, in the guise of expertise, could have devastating consequences. Profiling practitioners should therefore take great care to clearly state the limits of their expertise and refrain from participating in the phases of the criminal justice system for which they have no expertise to offer.

THE ART AND SCIENCE OF CRIMINAL PROFILING

There is today both a long-standing art and emerging science of criminal profiling. Although the continued development of a science of profiling may seem at first to be a gradual process of departing from the nonscientific profiling practices criticized in Part I of this book, it is in fact an effort to strengthen profiling by providing evidence for its truths and identifying and refuting its weaknesses. There would be no science of profiling without the vision of the early profilers, and it is the promise of applying scientific findings to investigation that gives the scientific model of profiling its current purpose. With this in mind, we hope that profiling scientists and practitioners will collaborate in an effort to secure funding and resources for conducting the comprehensive research that is so needed in the profiling field and will carry out empirical studies of the hypotheses that have emerged from profiling practice. Armed with these findings, profilers will have a substantial and sustained contribution to make to criminal investigations.

REFERENCES

Ahlmeyer, S., Kleinsasser, D., Stoner, J., & Retzlaff, P. (2003). Psychopathology of incarcerated sex offenders. *Journal of Personality Disorders, 17,* 306–318.

Alison, L., Bennell, C., & Mokros, A. (2002). The personality paradox in offender profiling: A theoretical review of the processes involved in deriving background characteristics from crime scene actions. *Psychology, Public Policy, and Law, 8,* 115–135.

Alison, L., & Canter, D. (1999a). Professional, legal and ethical issues in offender profiling. In D. Canter & L. Alison (Eds.), *Offender profiling series: II. Profiling in policy and practice* (pp. 21–54). Aldershot, England: Ashgate.

Alison, L., & Canter, D. (1999b). Profiling in policy and practice. In D. Canter & L. Alison (Eds.), *Offender profiling series: II. Profiling in policy and practice* (pp. 1–19). Aldershot, England: Ashgate.

Allport, G. W. (1961). *Pattern and growth in personality.* New York: Holt, Rinehart & Winston.

American Psychiatric Association. (1994). *Diagnostic and statistical manual of mental disorders* (4th ed.). Washington, DC: Author.

American Psychiatric Association. (2000). *Diagnostic and statistical manual of mental disorders* (4th ed., text rev.). Washington, DC: Author.

Annon, J. S. (1995). Investigative profiling: A behavioral analysis of the crime scene. *American Journal of Forensic Psychology, 13*(4), 67–75.

Asher, H. B. (1983). *Causal modeling.* Newbury Park, CA: Sage.

Axberger, G. (1973). Arson and fiction: A cross-disciplinary study. *Psychiatry, 36,* 244–265.

Barbaree, H., Seto, M., Serin, R., Amos, N., & Preston, D. (1994). Comparisons between sexual and nonsexual rapist subtypes. *Criminal Justice and Behavior, 21,* 95–114.

Becker, J. (1998). What we know about the characteristics and treatment of adolescents who have committed sexual offenses. *Child Maltreatment, 3,* 317–329.

Becker, J., Harris, C., & Sales, B. (1993). Juveniles who commit sexual offenses: A critical review of research. In G. C. Nagayama Hall, R. Hirschman, J. Graham, & M. Zaragoza (Eds.), *Sexual aggression: Issues in etiology, assessment, and treatment* (pp. 215–228). New York: Taylor & Francis.

Bem, D. J., & Allen, A. (1974). On predicting some of the people some of the time: The search for cross-situational consistencies in behavior. *Psychological Review, 81,* 506–520.

Bijleveld, C., & Hendriks, J. (2003). Juvenile sex offenders: Differences between group and solo offenders. *Psychology, Crime & Law, 9,* 237–245.

Block, J. (1971). *Lives through time.* Berkeley, CA: Bancroft Books.

Boon, J. C. W. (1997). The contribution of personality theories to psychological profiling. In J. L. Jackson & D. A. Bekarian (Eds.), *Offender profiling: Theory, research and practice* (pp. 43–59). Chichester, England: Wiley.

Bourget, D., & Bradford, J. M. (1987). Fire fetishism, diagnostic and clinical implications: A review of two cases. *Canadian Journal of Psychiatry, 32*, 459–462.

Bowers, K. (1973). Situationism in psychology: An analysis and a critique. *Psychological Review, 80*, 307–336.

Bozman, R. (Producer), & Demme, J. (Director). (1991). *The silence of the lambs* [Motion picture]. United States: MGM/UA Video.

Bradford, J. M. (1982). Arson: A clinical study. *Canadian Journal of Psychiatry, 27*, 188–193.

Bradford, J. M., Bloomberg, D., & Bourget, D. (1988). The heterogeneity/homogeneity of pedophilia. *Psychiatric Journal of the University of Ottawa, 13*, 217–226.

Brantingham, P. J., & Brantingham, P. L. (1981). *Environmental criminology.* Prospect Heights, IL: Waveland Press.

Bronfenbrenner, U. (1979). *The ecology of human development.* Cambridge, MA: Harvard University Press.

Bruck, M., & Ceci, S. J. (1995). Amicus brief for the case of State of New Jersey versus Margaret Kelly Michaels presented by the Committee of Concerned Social Scientists. *Psychology, Public Policy, and Law, 1*, 272–322.

Brussel, J. (1968). *Casebook of a crime psychiatrist.* New York: Bernard Geis Associates.

Burgess, A., Groth, A., & Holmstrom, L. (1978). *Sexual assault of children and adolescents.* Lexington, MA: Lexington Books.

Burgess, A. W., Douglas, J. E., & Burgess, A. G. (1997). Classifying homicides and forensic evaluations. *Crisis Intervention, 3*, 199–215.

Burgess, A. W., Hartman, C. R., Ressler, R. K., Douglas, J. E., & McCormack, A. (1986). Sexual homicide: A motivational model. *Journal of Interpersonal Violence, 1*, 251–272.

Butcher, J., Dahlstrom, W., Graham, J., Pellegen, B., & Kaemer, B. (1989). *MMPI–2: Manual for administration and scoring.* Minneapolis: University of Minnesota Press.

Canter, D. (1988). To catch a rapist. *New Society,* 14–15.

Canter, D. (1994). *Criminal shadows.* London: HarperCollins.

Canter, D. (1995). Psychology of offender profiling. In R. Bull & D. Carson (Eds.), *Handbook of psychology in legal contexts* (pp. 343–355). New York: Wiley.

Canter, D. (2000). Offender profiling and criminal differentiation. *Legal and Criminological Psychology, 5*, 23–46.

Canter, D., Coffey, T., Huntley, M., & Missen, C. (2000). Predicting serial killers' home base using a decision support system. *Journal of Quantitative Criminology, 16*, 457–478.

Canter, D., & Fritzon, K. (1998). Differentiating arsonists: A model of firesetting actions and characteristics. *Journal of Criminal and Legal Psychology, 3,* 73–96.

Canter, D., & Gregory, A. (1994). Identifying the residential location of rapists. *Journal of the Forensic Science Society, 34,* 169–175.

Canter, D., & Heritage, R. (1990). A multivariate model of sexual offense behaviour: Developments in "offender profiling" I. *Journal of Forensic Psychiatry, 1,* 185–212.

Canter, D., Hughes, D., & Kirby, S. (1998). Paedophilia: Pathology, criminality or both? The development of a multivariate model of offence behaviour in child sexual abuse. *Journal of Forensic Psychiatry, 9,* 532–555.

Canter, D., & Larkin, P. (1993). The environmental range of serial rapists. *Journal of Environmental Psychology, 13,* 63–69.

Carpenter, D. R., Peed, S. F., & Eastman, B. (1995). Personality characteristics of adolescent sexual offenders: A pilot study. *Sexual Abuse: A Journal of Research and Treatment, 7,* 195–202.

Carr, C. (1994). *The alienist.* New York: Random House.

Carr, C. (1997). *The angel of darkness.* New York: Random House.

Carter, C. (Producer). (1993). *The X-files* [Television series]. United States: 20th Century Fox.

Carter, C. (Producer). (1996). *Millenium* [Television series]. United States: 20th Century Fox.

Cattell, R. B., Cattell, A. K., & Cattell, H. E. P. (1993). *16 Personality Factors Questionnaire* (5th ed.). Champaign, IL: Institute for Personality and Ability Testing.

Cattell, R. B., & Cattell, M. D. L. (1969). *Handbook for the high school personality questionnaire.* Champaign, IL: Institute for Personality and Ability Testing.

Cervone, D., & Shoda, Y. (1999). Beyond traits in the study of personality coherence. *Current Directions in Psychological Science, 8,* 27–32.

Chantry, K., & Craig, R. J. (1994). Psychological screening of sexually violent offenders with the MCMI. *Journal of Clinical Psychology, 50,* 430–435.

Cheek, J. M. (1982). Aggregation, moderator variables, and the validity of personality tests: A peer-rating study. *Journal of Personality and Social Psychology, 43,* 1254–1269.

Chisum, W. J., & Rynearson, J. M. (1997). *Evidence and crime scene reconstruction* (5th ed.). Redding, CA: National Crime Scene Investigation and Training.

Cleckley, H. (1976). *The mask of sanity* (5th ed.). St. Louis, MO: Mosby.

Cohen, L. J., McGeoch, P. G., Watras-Gans, S., Acker, S., Poznansky, O., Cullen, K., et al. (2002). Personality impairment in male pedophiles. *Journal of Clinical Psychiatry, 63,* 912–919.

Coid, J., Wilkins, J., & Coid, B. (1999). Fire-setting, pyromania and self-mutilation in female remanded prisoners. *Journal of Forensic Psychiatry, 10,* 119–130.

Collins, W. (1985). *The woman in white*. New York: Bantam. (Original work published 1862)

Collins, W. (1994). *The moonstone*. London: Penguin. (Original work published 1868)

Cornish, D. B., & Clarke, R. V. (1986). *The reasoning criminal: Rational choice perspectives on offending*. New York: Springer-Verlag.

Curnoe, S., & Langevin, R. (2002). Personality and deviant sexual fantasies: An examination of the MMPI's of sex offenders. *Journal of Clinical Psychology, 58*, 803–815.

Cutler, B. L., & Penrod, S. D. (1995). *Mistaken identification: The eyewitness, psychology, and the law*. Cambridge, England: Cambridge University Press.

Dale, A., Davies, A., & Wei, L. (1997). Developing a typology of rapists' speech. *Journal of Pragmatics, 27*, 653–669.

Davies, A., Wittebrood, K., & Jackson, J. L. (1997). Predicting the criminal antecedents of a stranger rapist from his offence behavior. *Science and Justice, 37*, 161–170.

Davis, G. E., & Leitenberg, H. (1987). Adolescent sex offenders. *Psychological Bulletin, 101*, 417–427.

Davis, J. A. (1985). *The logic of causal order*. Newbury Park, CA: Sage.

Dean, C. W., Brame, R., & Piquero, A. (1996). Criminal propensities, discrete groups of offenders, and persistence in crime. *Criminology, 34*, 547–575.

Dietz, P. E., Hazelwood, R. R., & Warren, J. (1990). The sexually sadistic criminal and his offenses. *Bulletin of the American Academy of Psychiatry and Law, 18*, 163–178.

Digman, J. M., & Inouye, J. (1986). Further specification of the five robust factors of personality. *Journal of Personality and Social Psychology, 50*, 116–123.

Douglas, J. E., Burgess, A., Burgess, A., & Ressler, R. (1992). *Crime classification manual*. New York: Lexington.

Douglas, J. E., & Olshaker, M. (1995). *Mindhunter*. New York: Scribner's.

Douglas, J. E., & Olshaker, M. (1997). *Journey into darkness*. New York: Scribner's.

Douglas, J. E., & Olshaker, M. (1998). *Obsession*. New York: Scribner's.

Douglas, J. E., & Olshaker, M. (1999). *The anatomy of motive*. New York: Scribner's.

Douglas, J. E., & Olshaker, M. (2000). *The cases that haunt us*. New York: Scribner's.

Douglas, J. E., Ressler, R., Burgess, A., & Hartman, C. (1986). Criminal profiling from crime scene analysis. *Behavioral Sciences and the Law, 4*, 401–421.

Doyle, A. (1992). *The complete Sherlock Holmes*. New York: Barnes & Noble Books. (Original work published 1892–1927)

Dudycha, G. J. (1936). An objective study of punctuality in relation to personality and achievement. *Archives of Psychology, 204*, 1–319.

Duncan, O. D. (1966). Path analysis: Sociological examples. *American Journal of Sociology, 72*, 1–16.

Dutton, D. G. (1988). Profiling of wife assaulters: Preliminary evidence for a trimodal analysis. *Violence and Victims, 3*, 5–29.

Edwards, A. (1959). *Edwards Personal Preference Schedule*. New York: The Psychological Corporation.

Erickson, W. D., Luxenberg, M. G., Walbek, N. H., & Seely, R. K. (1987). Frequency of MMPI two-point code types among sex offenders. *Journal of Consulting and Clinical Psychology, 55*, 566–570.

Eysenck, H. J. (1973). *Eysenck on extraversion*. New York: Wiley.

Falkenhain, M. A., Duckro, P. N., Hughes, H. M., Rossetti, S. J., & Gfeller, J. D. (1999). Cluster analysis of child sexual offenders: A validation with Roman Catholic priests and brothers. *Sexual Addiction & Compulsivity, 6*, 317–336.

Farrington, D. P., & Lambert, S. (1994). Differences between burglars and violent offenders. *Psychology, Crime & Law, 1*, 107–116.

Fazel, S., Hope, T., O'Donnell, I., & Jacoby, R. (2002). Psychiatric, demographic and personality characteristics of elderly sex offenders. *Psychological Medicine, 32*, 219–226.

Feshbach, S. (1964). The function of aggression and the regulation of aggressive drive. *Psychological Review, 71*, 257–272.

Fiedler, J. (Producer), & Amiel, J. (Director). (1995). *Copycat* [Motion picture]. United States: Warner Studios.

Finkelhor, D., & Araji, S. (1986). Explanations of pedophilia: A four factor model. *Journal of Sex Research, 22*, 145–161.

Fisher, G. (1969). The psychological needs of heterosexual pedophiliacs. *Diseases of the Nervous System, 30*, 419–421.

Fras, I. (1997). Firesetting (pyromania) and its relationship to sexuality. In L. B. Schlesinger & E. Revitch (Eds.), *Sexual dynamics of antisocial behavior* (pp. 188–196). Syracuse: State University of New York Upstate Medical Center.

Fritzon, K. (2001). An examination of the relationship between distance travelled and motivational aspects of firesetting behavior. *Journal of Environmental Psychology, 21*, 45–60.

Gingrich, T. N., & Campbell, J. B. (1995). Personality characteristics of sexual offenders. *Sexual Addiction & Compulsivity, 2*, 54–61.

Godwin, G. M., & Canter, D. V. (1997). Encounter and death: The spatial behavior of US serial killers. *Policing: An International Journal of Police Strategy and Management, 20*, 24–38.

Gottfredson, M. R., & Hirschi, T. (1990). *A general theory of crime*. Stanford, CA: Stanford University Press.

Gough, H. G. (1957). *California Psychological Inventory: Manual*. Palo Alto, CA: Consulting Psychologists Press.

Gratzer, T., & Bradford, J. M. W. (1995). Offender and offense characteristics of sexual sadists: A comparative study. *Journal of Forensic Sciences, 40*, 450–455.

Graves, R. B., Openshaw, D. K., Ascione, F. R., & Ericksen, S. L. (1996). Demographic and parental characteristics of youthful sexual offenders. *International Journal of Offender Therapy and Comparative Criminology, 40,* 300–317.

Grossman, L. S., Haywood, T. W., & Wasyliw, O. E. (1992). The evaluation of truthfulness in alleged sex offenders' self-reports: 16PF and MMPI validity scales. *Journal of Personality Assessment, 59,* 264–275.

Groth, A., Burgess, A., & Holmstrom, L. (1977). Rape: Power, anger and sexuality. *American Journal of Psychiatry, 134,* 1239–1243.

Grove, W. M., & Meehl, P. E. (1996). Comparative efficiency of informal (subjective, impressionistic) and formal (mechanical, algorithmic) prediction procedures: The clinical–statistical controversy. *Psychology, Public Policy, and Law, 2,* 293–323.

Grubin, D. (1995). Offender profiling. *Journal of Forensic Psychiatry, 6,* 259–263.

Hagan, M. P., & Cho, M. E. (1996). A comparison of treatment outcomes between adolescent rapists and child sexual offenders. *International Journal of Offender Therapy and Comparative Criminology, 40,* 113–122.

Hall, G. C. N., Maiuro, R. D., Vitaliano, P. P., & Proctor, W. C. (1986). The utility of the MMPI with men who have sexually assaulted children. *Journal of Consulting and Clinical Psychology, 54,* 493–496.

Hare, R. D. (1991). *Hare Psychopathy Checklist—Revised.* Toronto, Canada: Multi-Health Systems.

Hare, R. D. (1999). Psychopathy as a risk factor for violence. *Psychiatric Quarterly, 70,* 181–197.

Hare, R. D., Forth, A. E., & Hart, S. D. (1989). The psychopath as prototype for pathological lying and deception. In J. C. Yuille (Ed.), *Credibility assessment* (pp. 25–49). New York: Kluwer Academic/Plenum.

Harris, A. J. R., & Hanson, R. K. (1998, October). *Supervising the psychopathic sex deviant in the community.* Paper presented at the 17th Annual Research and Treatment Conference, Association for the Treatment of Sexual Abusers, Vancouver, British Columbia, Canada.

Harris, G. T., & Rice, M. E. (1984). Mentally disordered firesetters: Psychodynamic versus empirical approaches. *International Journal of Law and Psychiatry, 7,* 19–34.

Harris, T. (1991). *The silence of the lambs.* New York: St. Martin's Press.

Hathaway, S. R., & McKinley, J. C. (1983). *Minnesota Multiphasic Personality Inventory: Manual.* New York: Psychological Corporation.

Hazelwood, R., & Burgess, A. (2001). *Practical aspects of rape investigation: A multidisciplinary approach* (3rd ed.). Boca Raton, FL: CRC Press.

Herkov, M. J., Gynther, M. D., Thomas, S., & Myers, W. C. (1996). MMPI differences among adolescent inpatients, rapists, sodomists and sexual abusers. *Journal of Personality Assessment, 66,* 81–89.

Hill, R. W., Langevin, R., Paitich, D., Handy, L., Russon, A., & Wilkinson, L. (1982). Is arson an aggressive act or a property offence? A controlled study of psychiatric referrals. *Canadian Journal of Psychiatry, 27,* 648–654.

Hillbrand, M., Foster, H., & Hirt, M. (1990). Rapists and child molesters: Psychometric comparisons. *Archives of Sexual Behavior, 19,* 65–71.

Holmes, R., & DeBurger, J. (1985). Profiles in terror: The serial murderer. *Federal Probation, 49*(3), 29–34.

Holmes, R., & Holmes, S. (1992). Understanding mass murder: A starting point. *Federal Probation, 56*(1), 53–61.

Holmes, R., & Holmes, S. (1996). *Profiling violent crimes: An investigative tool.* Thousand Oaks, CA: Sage.

Homant, R. J., & Kennedy, D. B. (1998). Psychological aspects of crime scene profiling: Validity research. *Criminal Justice and Behavior, 25,* 319–343.

Horley, J. (1988). Cognitions of child sexual abusers. *Journal of Sex Research, 25,* 542–545.

Howells, K. (1979). Some meanings of children for pedophiles. In M. Cook & G. Wilson (Eds.), *Love and attraction: An international conference* (pp. 519–526). Oxford, England: Pergamon.

Hunter, J. A., & Figueredo, A. J. (2000). The influence of personality and history of sexual victimization in the prediction of juvenile perpetrated child molestation. *Behavior Modification, 24,* 241–263.

Hunter, J. A., Figueredo, A. J., Malamuth, N. M., & Becker, J. V. (2003). Juvenile sex offenders: Toward the development of a typology. *Sexual Abuse: A Journal of Research and Treatment, 15,* 27–48.

Hunter, J. A., Hazelwood, R. R., & Slesinger, D. (2000). Juvenile-perpetrated sex crimes: Patterns of offending and predictors of violence. *Journal of Family Violence, 15,* 81–93.

Jeffreys, D. (1995). *The bureau.* New York: Houghton Mifflin.

Kagan, J. (1984). *The nature of the child.* New York: Basic Books.

Kalichman, S. C. (1991). Psychopathology and personality characteristics of criminal sexual offenders as a function of victim age. *Archives of Sexual Behavior, 20,* 187–197.

Kalichman, S. C., Craig, M. E., Shealy, L., Taylor, J., Szymanowski, D., & McKee, G. (1989). An empirically derived typology of adult rapists based on the MMPI: A cross-validation study. *Journal of Psychology and Human Sexuality, 2,* 165–182.

Kalichman, S. C., Szymanowski, D., McKee, G., Taylor, J., & Craig, M. E. (1989). Cluster analytically derived MMPI profile subgroups of incarcerated adult rapists. *Journal of Clinical Psychology, 45,* 149–155.

Kaplan, M. S., Becker, J. V., & Cunningham-Rathner, J. (1988). Characteristics of parents of adolescent incest perpetrators: Preliminary findings. *Journal of Family Violence, 3,* 183–190.

Kaufman, K. L., Hilliker, D. R., Lathrop, P., & Daleiden, E. L. (1993). Assessing child sexual offenders' modus operandi: Accuracy in self-reported use of threats and coercion. *Annals of Sex Research, 6,* 213–229.

Kavoussi, R. J., Kaplan, M. S., & Becker, J. V. (1988). Psychiatric diagnosis in adolescent sex offenders. *Journal of the American Academy of Child and Adolescent Psychiatry, 27,* 241–243.

Kelly, G. A. (1955). *The psychology of personal constructs.* New York: Norton.

Kenrick, D. T., & Stringfield, D. O. (1980). Personality trait and the eye of the beholder: Crossing some traditional philosophical boundaries in the search for consistency in all the people. *Psychological Review, 87,* 88–104.

Keppel, R., & Walter, R. (1999). Profiling killers: A revised classification model for understanding sexual murder. *International Journal of Offender Therapy and Comparative Criminology, 43,* 417–434.

Kessler, R. (1993). *The FBI.* New York: Pocket Books.

Knight, R., & Prentky, R. (1987). The developmental antecedents and adult adaptations of rapist subtypes. *Criminal Justice and Behavior, 14,* 403–426.

Kocsis, R. N., & Cooksey, R. W. (2002). Criminal psychological profiling of serial arson crimes. *International Journal of Offender Therapy and Comparative Criminology, 46,* 631–656.

Kolko, D. J., & Kazdin, A. E. (1991). Motives of childhood firesetters: Firesetting characteristics and psychological correlates. *Journal of Child Psychology and Psychiatry and Allied Disciplines, 32,* 535–550.

Kolko, D. J., & Kazdin, A. E. (1992). The emergence and recurrence of child firesetting: A one-year prospective study. *Journal of Abnormal Child Psychology, 20,* 17–37.

Kolko, D. J., & Kazdin, A. E. (1994). Children's descriptions of their firesetting incidents: Characteristics and relationship to recidivism. *Journal of the American Academy of Child and Adolescent Psychiatry, 33,* 113–122.

Koson, D. F., & Dvoskin, J. (1982). Arson: A diagnostic survey. *Bulletin of the American Academy of Psychiatry and the Law, 10,* 39–49.

Kronish, S. (Producer). (1996). *Profiler* [Television series]. New York: National Broadcasting Corporation.

Krug, S. E. (1980). *Clinical Analysis Questionnaire manual.* Champaign, IL: Institute for Personality and Ability Testing.

Laflen, B., & Sturm, W. (1994). Understanding and working with denial in sexual offenders. *Journal of Child Sexual Abuse, 3*(4), 19–36.

Langer, W. C. (1972). *The mind of Adolf Hitler: The secret wartime report.* New York: Basic Books.

Langevin, R., Hucker, S. J., Ben-Aron, M. H., Purins, J. E., & Hook, H. J. (1985). Why are pedophiles attracted to children? Further studies of erotic preference in heterosexual pedophilia. In R. Langevin (Ed.), *Erotic preference, gender identity, and aggression in men.* Hillsdale, NJ: Erlbaum.

Langevin, R., Paitich, D., Freeman, L., Mann, K., & Handy, L. (1978). Personality characteristics and sexual anomalies in males. *Canadian Journal of Behavioral Sciences, 10*, 222–238.

Lanyon, R. I. (1993). Validity of MMPI sex offender scales with admitters and nonadmitters. *Psychological Assessment, 5*, 302–306.

Lewis, N. D. (1966). Pathological firesetting and sexual motivation. In R. Slovenko (Ed.), *Sexual behavior and the law.* Springfield, IL: Charles C Thomas.

Lewis, N. D., & Yarnell, H. (1951). Pathological fire-setting (pyromania). *Nervous and Mental Disease Monograph No. 82.* Nicholasville, KY: Coolidge Foundation.

Liebert, J. (1986). Contributions of psychiatric consultation in the investigation of serial murder. *International Journal of Offender Therapy and Comparative Criminology, 29*, 187–188.

Lilienfeld, S. O., Wood, J. M., & Garb, H. N. (2000). The scientific status of projective techniques. *Psychological Science in the Public Interest, 1*, 27–66.

Loeber, R., & LeBlanc, M. (1990). Toward a development of criminology. In M. Tonry (Ed.), *Crime and justice: An annual review of research* (pp. 375–473). Chicago: University of Chicago Press.

Loehlin, J. C. (1998). *Latent variable models: An introduction to factor, path, and structural analysis* (3rd ed.). Mahwah, NJ: Erlbaum.

Loftus, E. F. (1996). *Eyewitness testimony.* Cambridge, MA: Harvard University Press.

Losada-Paisey, G. (1998). Use of the MMPI–A to assess personality of juvenile male delinquents who are sex offenders and non-sex offenders. *Psychological Reports, 83*, 115–122.

Lundrigan, S., & Canter, D. (2001). Spatial patterns of serial murder: An analysis of disposal site location choice. *Behavioral Sciences and the Law, 19*, 595–610.

Mann, J., Stenning, W., & Borman, C. (1992). The utility of the MMPI–2 with pedophiles. *Journal of Offender Rehabilitation, 18*(3/4), 59–74.

McAdams, D. P. (1990). *The person.* San Diego, CA: Harcourt Brace Jovanovich.

McAnulty, R. D., Adams, H. E., & Wright, L. W. (1994). Relationship between MMPI and penile plethysmograph in accused child molesters. *Journal of Sex Research, 31*, 179–184.

McCrae, R. R., & Costa, P. T. (1987). Validation of the five-factor model of personality across instruments and observers. *Journal of Personality and Social Psychology, 52*, 81–90.

Meehl, P. E. (1996). *Clinical versus statistical prediction: A theoretical analysis and a review of the evidence.* Northvale, NJ: Jason Aronson. (Original work published 1954)

Miller, J. G. (1984). Culture and the development of everyday social explanation. *Journal of Personality and Social Psychology, 46*, 961–978.

Millon, T. (1982). *Manual for the MCMI* (2nd ed.). Minneapolis, MN: National Computer Systems.

Mischel, W. (1968). *Personality and assessment.* New York: Wiley.

Mischel, W., & Peake, P. K. (1982). Beyond deja vu in the search for cross-situational consistency. *Psychological Review, 89,* 730–755.

Moody, E. E., Brissie, J. E., & Kim, J. (1994). Personality and background characteristics of adolescent sexual offenders. *Journal of Addictions and Offender Counseling, 14,* 38–48.

Moos, R. H. (1973). Conceptualizations of human environments. *American Psychologist, 28,* 652–665.

Morey, L. C. (1991). *The Personality Assessment Inventory: Professional manual.* Odessa, FL: Psychological Assessment Resources.

Murray, H. A. (1943). *The Thematic Apperception Test: Manual.* Cambridge, MA: Harvard University Press.

Nagin, D. S., & Paternoster, R. (1993). Enduring individual differences and rational choice theories of crime. *Law and Society Review, 27,* 467–496.

National Institute of Justice. (1999). *Death investigation: A guide for the scene investigator* (NCJ 167568). Washington, DC: U.S. Department of Justice.

National Institute of Justice. (2000a). *Crime scene investigation: A guide for law enforcement* (NCJ 178280). Washington, DC: U.S. Department of Justice.

National Institute of Justice. (2000b). *Fire and arson scene evidence: A guide for public safety personnel* (NCJ 181584). Washington, DC: U.S. Department of Justice.

National Institute of Justice. (2000c). *Guide for explosion and bombing scene investigation* (NCJ 181869). Washington, DC: U.S. Department of Justice.

National Institute of Justice. (2001). *Electronic crime scene investigation: A guide for first responders* (NCJ 187736). Washington, DC: U.S. Department of Justice.

Nugent, P. M., & Kroner, D. G. (1996). Denial, response styles, and admittance of offenses among child molesters and rapists. *Journal of Interpersonal Violence, 11,* 475–486.

Okami, P., & Goldberg, A. (1992). Personality correlates of pedophilia: Are they reliable indicators? *Journal of Sex Research, 29,* 297–329.

Panton, J. H. (1979). MMPI profile configurations associated with incestuous and non-incestuous child molesting. *Psychological Reports, 45,* 335–338.

Paternoster, R. (1989). Decisions to participate in and desist from four types of common delinquency: Deterrence and the rational choice perspective. *Law and Society Review, 23,* 7–40.

Perrin-Walqvist, R., & Norlander, T. (2003). Firesetting and playing with fire during childhood and adolescence: Interview studies of 18-year-old male draftees and 18–19-year-old female pupils. *Legal and Criminological Psychology, 8,* 151–157.

Pinizzotto, A. J., & Finkel, N. J. (1990). Criminal personality profiling: An outcome and process study. *Law and Human Behavior, 14,* 215–233.

Piquero, A. (2000). Frequency, specialization, and violence in offending careers. *Journal of Research in Crime and Delinquency, 37,* 392–418.

Poe, E. A. (1982). The murders in the Rue Morgue. In *The tell-tale heart and other writings* (pp. 315–340). New York: Bantam Books. (Original work published 1814)

Porter, S., Fairweather, D., Drugge, J., Herve, H., Birt, A., & Boer, D. P. (2000). Profiles of psychopathy in incarcerated sexual offenders. *Criminal Justice and Behavior, 27,* 216–233.

Prins, H., Tennent, G., & Trick, K. (1985). Motives for arson (fire raising). *Medicine, Science and the Law, 25,* 275–278.

Quinsey, V. L., Arnold, L. S., & Pruesse, M. G. (1980). MMPI profiles on men referred for a pretrial psychiatric assessment as a function of offense type. *Journal of Clinical Psychology, 36,* 410–417.

Quinsey, V. L., Chaplin, T. C., & Upfold, D. (1989). Arsonists and sexual arousal to fire setting: Correlation unsupported. *Journal of Behavioral Therapy and Experimental Psychiatry, 20,* 203–209.

Quinsey, V. L., Harris, G. T., Rice, M. E., & Cormier, C. A. (2005). *Violent offenders: Appraising and managing risk* (2nd ed.). Washington, DC: American Psychological Association.

Quinsey, V. L., Rice, M. E., & Harris, G. T. (1995). Actuarial prediction of sexual recidivism. *Journal of Interpersonal Violence, 10,* 85–105.

Ressler, R. K., Burgess, A., & Douglas, J. (1988). *Sexual homicide: Patterns and motives.* New York: Lexington Books.

Ressler, R. K., Burgess, A. W., Douglas, J. E., Hartman, C. R., & D'Agostino, R. B. (1986). Sexual killers and their victims: Identifying patterns through crime scene analysis. *Journal of Interpersonal Violence, 1,* 288–308.

Ressler, R. K., Burgess, A. W., Hartman, C. R., Douglas, J. E., & McCormack, A. (1986). Murderers who rape and mutilate. *Journal of Interpersonal Violence, 1,* 273–287.

Ressler, R. K., & Shachtman, T. (1992). *Whoever fights monsters.* New York: St. Martin's Press.

Rice, M. E., & Harris, G. T. (1997). Cross-validation and extension of the Violence Risk Appraisal Guide for child molesters and rapists. *Law and Human Behavior, 21,* 231–241.

Ridenour, T. A., Miller, A. R., Joy, K. L., & Dean, R. S. (1997). "Profile" analysis of the personality characteristics of child molesters using the MMPI–2. *Journal of Clinical Psychology, 53,* 575–586.

Rider, A. (1980a). The firesetter: A psychological profile (Part 1). *FBI Law Enforcement Bulletin, 49*(6), 6–13.

Rider, A. (1980b). The firesetter: A psychological profile (Conclusion). *FBI Law Enforcement Bulletin, 49*(7), 12–17.

Rogers, R., & Dickey, R. (1991). Denial and minimization among sex offenders: A review of competing models of deception. *Annals of Sex Research, 4*(1), 49–63.

Rorschach, H. (1921). *Psychodiagnostik* [Psychodiagnostics]. Bern, Switzerland: Bircher.

Rossmo, D. K. (1995a). Geographic profiling. In J. Jackson & D. Bekerian (Eds.), *Offender profiling: Theory, research and practice* (pp. 159–175). London: Wiley.

Rossmo, D. (1995b). Place, space and police investigations: Hunting serial violent criminals. In J. E. Eck & D. Weisburd (Eds.), *Crime and place* (pp. 217–235). Monsey, NY: Criminal Justice.

Rossmo, D. K. (1997). Geographic profiling. In J. L. Jackson & D. A. Bekerian (Eds.), *Offender profiling: Theory, research, and practice* (pp. 159–175). Hoboken, NJ: Wiley.

Rossmo, D. K. (2000). *Geographic profiling*. Boca Raton, FL: CRC Press.

Rumbelow, D. (1975). *The complete Jack the Ripper*. New York: Little, Brown.

Saferstein, R. (2001). *Criminalistics: An introduction to forensic science* (7th ed.). Upper Saddle River, NJ: Pearson Prentice Hall.

Sakheim, G. A., & Osborn, E. (1999). Severe vs. nonsevere firesetters revisited. *Child Welfare, 78,* 411–434.

Sakheim, G. A., Vigdor, M., Gordon, M., & Helprin, L. (1985). A psychological profile of juvenile firesetters in residential treatment. *Child Welfare, 64,* 453–476.

Salfati, C. G., & Canter, D. (1999). Differentiating stranger murders: Profiling offender characteristics from behavioral styles. *Journal of Behavioral Sciences and the Law, 17,* 391–406.

Santilla, P., Canter, D., Elfgren, T., & Hakkanen, H. (2001). The structure of crime scene actions in Finnish homicides. *Homicide Studies, 5,* 363–387.

Santilla, P., Hakkanen, H., Alison, L., & Whyte, C. (2003). Juvenile firesetters: Crime scene actions and offender characteristics. *Legal and Criminological Psychology, 8,* 1–20.

Santilla, P., Hakkanen, H., Canter, D., & Elfgren, T. (2003). Classifying homicide offenders and predicting their characteristics from crime scene behavior. *Scandinavian Journal of Psychology, 44,* 107–118.

Schiffman, S. S., Reynolds, M. L., & Young, F. W. (1981). *Introduction to multidimensional scaling: Theory, methods & applications*. Burlington, MA: Academic Press.

Schwartzman, P., Stambaugh, H., & Kimball, J. (1994). *Arson and juveniles: Responding to the violence. A review of teen firesetting and interventions*. Emmitsburg, MD: U.S. Fire Administration.

Scott, R. L., & Stone, D. A. (1986). MMPI profile constellations in incest families. *Journal of Consulting and Clinical Psychology, 54,* 364–368.

Serin, R. C., Mailloux, D. L., & Malcolm, P. B. (2001). Psychopathy, deviant sexual arousal and recidivism among sexual offenders. *Journal of Interpersonal Violence, 16,* 234–246.

Serin, R. C., Malcolm, P. B., Khanna, A., & Barbaree, H. E. (1994). Psychopathy and deviant sexual arousal in incarcerated sexual offenders. *Journal of Interpersonal Violence, 9,* 3–11.

Shealy, L., Kalichman, S. C., Henderson, M. C., Szymanowski, D., & McKee, G. (1991). MMPI profile subtypes of incarcerated sex offenders against children. *Violence and Victims, 6,* 201–212.

Showers, J., & Pickrell, E. P. (1987). Child firesetters: A study of three populations. *Hospital and Community Psychiatry, 38*, 495–501.

Simon, L. M. J., Sales, B. D., Kaszniak, A., & Kahn, M. (1992). Characteristics of child molesters: Implications for the fixated–regressed dichotomy. *Journal of Interpersonal Violence, 7*, 211–225.

Slavkin, M. L., & Fineman, K. (2000). What every professional who works with adolescents needs to know about firesetters. *Adolescence, 35*(140), 759–773.

Smith, W. R., Monastersky, C., & Deisher, R. M. (1987). MMPI-based personality types among juvenile sex offenders. *Journal of Clinical Psychology, 43*, 422–430.

Snook, B., Canter, D., & Bennell, C. (2002). Predicting the home location of serial offenders: A preliminary comparison of the accuracy of human judges with a geographic profiling system. *Behavioral Sciences and the Law, 20*, 109–118.

Stevenson, R. L. (2000). *The strange tale of Dr. Jekyll and Mr. Hyde.* Retrieved September 9, 2003, from http://www.bartleby.com/1015 (Original work published 1886)

Swaffer, T., & Hollin, C. R. (1995). Adolescent firesetting: Why do they say they do it? *Journal of Adolescence, 18*, 619–623.

Turco, R. (1990). Psychological profiling. *International Journal of Offender Therapy and Comparative Criminology, 34*, 147–154.

Turvey, B. (1999). *Criminal profiling: An introduction to behavioral evidence analysis.* San Diego, CA: Academic Press.

Underwood, B., & Moore, B. J. (1981). Sources of behavioral consistency. *Journal of Personality and Social Psychology, 40*, 780–785.

U.S. Department of Justice. (2003). *2002 uniform crime report.* Retrieved November 4, 2005, from http://www.fbi.gov/ucr/02cius/htm

Varano, S. P., & Cancino, J. M. (2001). An empirical analysis of deviant homicides in Chicago. *Homicide Studies, 5*(1), 5–29.

Wade, C. (Ed.). (2003). *FBI handbook of forensic services.* Retrieved November 4, 2005, from http://www.fbi.gov/hq/lab/handbook/forensics.pdf

Wagner, G. (1974). On the motivation of incendiarism. *Psychiatrie, Neurologie und Medizinische Psychologie, 26*, 155–164.

Wasyliw, O. E., Grossman, L. S., & Haywood, T. W. (1994). Denial of hostility and psychopathology in the evaluation of child molestation. *Journal of Personality Assessment, 63*, 185–190.

Watson, P. (1978). *War on the mind: The military uses and abuses of psychology.* London: Hutchinson.

Werts, C. E., & Linn, R. L. (1970). Path analysis: Psychological examples. *Psychological Bulletin, 74*, 193–212.

Wilson, G. D., & Cox, D. N. (1983). Personality of paedophile club members. *Personality and Individual Differences, 4*, 323–329.

Worling, J. R. (1995). Adolescent sex offenders against females: Differences based on the age of their victims. *International Journal of Offender Therapy and Comparative Criminology, 39*, 276–293.

Worling, J. R. (2001). Personality-based typology of adolescent male sexual offenders: Differences in recidivism rates, victim-selection characteristics, and personal victimization histories. *Sexual Abuse: A Journal of Research and Treatment, 13*, 149–166.

Yesavage, J. A. (1983). Arson in mentally ill and criminal populations. *Journal of Clinical Psychiatry, 44*, 128–130.

AUTHOR INDEX

D'Agostino, R. B., 121, 188
Dahlstrom, W., 192
Dale, A., 188
Daleiden, E. L., 188
Davies, A., 188, 227
Davis, G. E., 189
Davis, J. A., 241
Dean, C. W., 91
Dean, R. S., 193
DeBurger, J., 17, 26
Deisher, R. M., 191
Demme, J., 3
Dickey, R., 103, 172
Dietz, P. E., 188
Digman, J. M., 165
Douglas, J. E., 11, 12, 13, 17, 18, 20, 21,
        23, 24, 25, 27, 28, 50, 54, 55,
        57–58, 60, 62, 63, 65, 66–68, 69,
        119, 120, 121, 122, 123, 128,
        129, 130, 136, 159, 164, 173,
        174, 175, 176, 177, 181, 188
Doyle, A., 5, 128
Duckro, P. N., 193
Dudycha, G. J., 204
Duncan, O. D., 158
Dutton, D. G., 164
Dvoskin, J., 174

Eastman, B., 190
Elfgren, T., 217, 219, 220, 221, 225,
        231
Ericksen, S. L., 189
Erickson, W. D., 193, 194
Eysenck, H. J., 164, 188

Falkenhain, M. A., 193, 200
Farrington, D. P., 159
Fazel, S., 198
Feshbach, S., 159
Fiedler, J., 3
Figueredo, A. J., 189, 190
Fineman, K., 176
Finkel, N. J., 164, 203
Finkelhor, D., 192, 194, 195
Fisher, G., 195
Forth, A. E., 103, 172
Foster, H., 198
Fras, I., 176
Freeman, L., 194

Fritzon, K., 83, 101, 103, 105, 106, 115,
        117, 159, 172, 177, 178, 179,
        181, 182, 183, 217, 244

Garb, H. N., 119, 167, 188
Gfeller, J. D., 193
Gingrich, T. N., 195, 198
Godwin, G. M., 107, 115, 217, 222–223,
        244
Goldberg, A., 196
Gordon, M., 27
Gottfredson, M. R., 91
Gough, H. G., 167, 191
Graham, J., 192
Gratzer, T., 188
Graves, R. B., 189
Gregory, A., 85, 188
Grossman, L. S., 197
Groth, A., 28, 44, 45, 53, 174
Grove, W. M., 250, 251, 252
Grubin, D., 164
Gynther, M. D., 190

Hagan, M. P., 189
Hakkanen, H., 177, 179, 180, 182, 183,
        217, 219, 220, 221, 225, 231
Hall, G. C. N., 193
Handy, L., 194
Hanson, R. K., 202
Hare, R. D., 103, 172, 201, 202
Harris, A. J. R., 202
Harris, C., 189
Harris, G. T., 174, 176, 202
Harris, T., 12
Hart, S. D., 103, 172
Hartman, C., 13, 18, 50, 119, 121, 128,
        136, 159, 188
Hathaway, S. R., 167, 188, 238
Haywood, T. W., 197
Hazelwood, R., 36, 121, 188, 189
Helprin, L., 27
Henderson, M. C., 193
Hendriks, J., 190, 192
Heritage, R., 101, 105, 106, 107, 115,
        117
Herkov, M. J., 190
Hill, R. W., 172, 175, 176
Hillbrand, M., 198
Hilliker, D. R., 188

Hirschi, T., 91
Hirt, M., 198
Hollin, C. R., 175
Holmes, R., 17, 25–36, 44, 50, 54, 55,
        56–57, 58, 59, 60–61, 62, 63, 66–
        68, 69, 76–77, 116, 119, 120,
        123, 129, 130, 136, 159, 164,
        174, 175, 176, 188, 196, 203,
        221, 250
Holmes, S., 17, 25–36, 44, 50, 54, 55,
        56–57, 58, 59, 60–61, 62, 63,
        66–68, 69, 76–77, 116, 119, 120,
        123, 129, 130, 136, 159, 164,
        174, 175, 176, 188, 196, 203,
        221, 250
Holmstrom, L., 28, 53
Hook, H. J., 194
Hope, T., 198
Horley, J., 196
Hormant, R. J., 17
Howells, K., 196
Hucker, S. J., 194
Hughes, D., 98
Hughes, H. M., 193
Hunter, J. A., 189, 190
Huntley, M., 217, 244

Inouye, J., 165

Jackson, J. L., 188, 227
Jacoby, R., 198
Jeffreys, D., 13, 17
Joy, K. L., 193

Kagan, J., 165
Kahn, M., 195
Kalichman, S. C., 193, 197, 198, 200
Kaplan, M. S., 189
Kaszniak, A., 195
Kaufman, K. L., 188
Kavoussi, R. J., 189
Kazdin, A. E., 27, 174, 175
Kelly, G. A., 195
Kennedy, D. B., 17
Kenrick, D. T., 204
Keppel, R., 36–41, 50, 53, 55, 57, 58,
        61, 62, 63, 65, 66–68, 120, 122,
        123

Kessler, R., 10, 11, 17
Khanna, A., 202
Kim, J., 190
Kimball, J., 175
Kirby, S., 98
Kleinsasser, D., 195
Knight, R., 28
Kocsis, R. N., 178, 179, 180, 181, 182,
        184, 243
Kolko, D. J., 27, 174, 175
Koson, D. F., 174
Kremer, B., 192
Kroner, D. G., 197
Kronish, S., 3

Laflen, B., 103
Lambert, S., 159
Langer, W. C., 7
Langevin, R., 194, 198
Larkin, P., 223, 244
Lathrop, P., 188
LeBlanc, M., 91
Leitenberg, H., 189
Lewis, N. D., 174, 175, 176
Liebert, J., 41
Lilienfield, S. O., 119, 167, 188
Linn, R. L., 158
Loeber, R., 91
Loehlin, J. C., 242
Loftus, E. F., 103
Losada-Paisey, G., 189
Lundrigan, S., 223, 244
Luxenberg, M. G., 193

Mailloux, D. L., 202
Maiuro, R. D., 193
Malamuth, N. M., 190
Malcolm, P. B., 202
Mann, J., 193
Mann, K., 194
McAdams, D. P., 164, 165
McAnulty, R. D., 194
McCormack, A., 121, 159, 188
McCrae, R. R., 165
McKee, G., 193, 197
McKinley, J. C., 167, 188, 238
Meehl, P. E., 250, 251, 252
Miller, A. R., 193
Miller, J. G., 165

Millon, T., 167, 188
Mischel, W., 165, 204
Missen, C., 217, 244
Mokros, A., 203, 228, 237
Monastersky, C., 191
Moody, E. E., 190
Moore, B. J., 204
Moos, R. H., 165
Murray, H. A., 166, 188
Myers, W. C., 190

Nagin, D. S., 91
National Institute of Justice, 137, 139, 140
Norlander, T., 172, 174, 175, 176
Nugent, P. M., 197

O'Donnell, I., 198
Okami, P., 196
Olshaker, M., 11, 12, 17, 69, 128, 129, 130
Openshaw, D. K., 189
Osborn, E., 175, 176

Paitich, D., 194
Panton, J. H., 194
Paternoster, R., 91
Peake, P. K., 204
Peed, S. F., 190
Pellegen, B., 192
Penrod, S. D., 103
Perrin-Walqvist, R., 172, 174, 175, 176
Pickrell, E. P., 174
Pinizzotto, A. J., 164, 203
Piquero, A., 91
Poe, E. A., 3–4, 128
Porter, S., 201
Prentky, R., 28
Preston, D., 202
Prins, H., 175
Proctor, W. C., 193
Pruesse, M. G., 194
Purins, J. E., 194

Quinsey, V. L., 176, 194, 202

Ressler, R., 13, 18, 27, 50, 57, 119, 128, 159, 173, 188
Ressler, R. K., 10–11, 12, 17, 22, 25, 72, 121, 129, 136, 159, 188, 203
Retzlaff, P., 195
Reynolds, M. L., 82
Rice, M. E., 174, 176, 202
Ridenour, T. A., 193
Rider, A., 27
Rogers, R., 103, 172
Rorschach, H., 166, 188
Rossetti, S. J., 193
Rossmo, D. K., 32, 203, 221, 222
Rumbelow, D., 6
Rynearson, J. M., 150, 152, 153, 155

Saferstein, R., 140, 142, 147, 148, 149, 150
Sakheim, G. A., 27, 175, 176
Sales, B. D., 189, 195
Salfati, C. G., 98, 101, 103, 105, 106, 107, 108, 109, 115, 117, 217, 218, 219, 221, 224, 225, 227, 243, 244
Santilla, P., 177, 178–179, 180, 182–183, 217, 219, 220, 221, 225, 231
Schachtman, T., 11, 17, 22, 129, 203
Schiffman, S. S., 82
Schwartzman, P., 175
Scott, R. L., 194
Seely, R. K., 193
Serin, R., 202
Seto, M., 202
Shealy, L., 193, 197
Shoda, Y., 204
Showers, J., 174
Simon, L. M. J., 195
Slavkin, M. L., 176
Slesinger, D., 189
Smith, W. R., 191, 192, 193, 200
Snook, B., 223, 227, 244
Stambaugh, H., 175
Stenning, W., 193
Stevenson, R. L., 90
Stone, D. A., 194
Stoner, J., 195
Stringfield, D. O., 204
Sturm, W., 103
Swaffer, T., 175
Szymanowski, D., 193, 197, 200

SUBJECT INDEX

Eysenck Personality Questionnaire, 188, 194–195

Family, offender's. *See* Parental factors
Family, victim's, 18
Family murders, 20
Fanatical behavior
    arson motivation, 173
    Douglas et al. model of homicide intent, 21
Fantastic thinking
    criminal motivation and, 23
    Keppel and Walter rape–murder typology, 37, 38, 40
FBI Handbook of Forensic Evidence, 140
Feathers, as evidence, 142
Federal Bureau of Investigation
    evolution of profiling efforts, 10–11, 12, 13
    inadequacy of current profiling efforts, 47, 72
    Investigative Support Unit, 10, 12
Fiber evidence, 143, 148
Fictional literature, 3–5
Fingerprints, 143
Firearms
    as evidence, 143
    gunshot residue, 144
First-level behaviors. *See* Inferred behaviors
Footprints, 18
Forensic analyses, 147–149
    medical, 6, 19
    performance evaluation of, 155–156
Functional evidence, 154
Future prospects, 14, 85

Genocide, 26
Geographic factors
    causal modeling and path analysis, 244–245, 247
    circle hypothesis, 223
    computer analysis, 33
    crime location, 32
    distance-decay hypothesis, 222
    Holmes and Holmes model, 26, 31–33, 56–57
    home range/criminal range, 85

interpersonal narratives theory and, 222, 225
    land use, 33
    offender travel patterns, 32
    physical boundaries, 33
    profiling research, 221–224
    in scientific model of profiling, 225–226
    serial killings, 26, 56
    spatial consistency of offender behavior, 84–85
    See also Neighborhood characteristics
Glass, evidence from, 143–144
Goals, profiling
    Canter model, 88–89
    common features of extant research, 128
    crime scene investigation, 128, 131, 253–254
    crime scene reconstruction, 131, 132
    Douglas et al. model, 50, 129
    Holmes and Holmes model, 50
    identifying specific suspect vs. identifying offender type, 129–130
    interrogation of suspect, 130
    Keppel and Walter rape–murder typology, 50
    limitations of nonscientific models, 49, 50–53, 54
    operationalizing, 130–131
    primary goal, 128
    proposed scientific model, 216
    scientific models, 73, 127, 255–256
    testability of profiling predictions, 132–133
    Turco model, 50
    Turvey model, 50, 129
Gunshot residue, 144

Habits of offender, 24
Hair as evidence, 144
Hallucinations, in serial killer typology, 26
Hartright, Walter, 4
Hero, would-be, 27
Hero killings, 20
Historical development of profiling
    early criminal investigations, 8–11
    early fictional portrayals, 3–5

procedures for use of, 62
scientific properties of, 122–123
shortcomings, 50, 53, 55–56, 57, 58, 62, 63, 65
Korean War, 7–8

Langer, Walter, 7
Law enforcement officers
profiler relationship, 133–134
training for evidence collection, 149
Limiting evidence, 153
Literature, 3–5
Location evidence, 153
Location of crimes
geographic profiling, 222
identifying, 136–137
significance of, 32, 33
See also Geographic factors
Lubricants, as evidence, 145

Mad Bomber case, 8–10
Malice aforethought, 46–47
Marital status of victim, 34
Mass murder, 20
Media, investigators' use of, 24
Media representations of profiling, 3
Meierhofer, David, 10–11
Mental disorders
crime scene patterns associated with, 10
Douglas et al. model of homicide intent, 20–21
pedophile typology, 30–31
Mercy killings, 20
Metallic evidence, 145
Metesky, George, 9–10
Military uses of profiling, 7–8
Millennium (TV Show), 3
Millon Clinical Multiaxial Inventory, 188, 190, 195, 198
Minnesota Multiphasic Personality Inventory, 188, 189, 190–191, 192–194, 197–198
Missing evidence, 154
Models of profiling
criteria for evaluating, 87
current state, 127
testability of profiling predictions, 132–133

See also Holmes and Holmes model;
Keppel and Walter rape–murder typology; Nonscientific approaches to profiling; Proposed model of profiling; Scientific approach to profiling; Turco model of profiling; Turvey model of profiling
Modus operandi behaviors
Canter's use, 75–76, 100
crime location characteristics, 32
definition, 54, 64
identifying in prosecution, 46
as inferred behavior, 168–169
shortcomings of nonscientific models in investigating, 64
signature behaviors and, 64, 169
Turvey model of profiling, 45, 46
Moonstone, The, 4–5
Motive, 14
arsonist classification, 27–28, 172–177
assessment methods, 166–167, 235–236, 245
challenges in identifying, 159–160
crime scene evidence–offender behavior–motive associations, 181–184
definition, 159
Douglas et al. model of investigation, 20–21, 23, 63
evolution of, 236
expressive, 159, 177
geographic profiling studies, 222
goals of profiling, 254–255
instrumental, 159, 177
intent and, 159, 160, 161–163
interpersonal-narratives theory and, 225
Keppel and Walter rape–murder typology, 36–37, 38–40, 63
legal context, 160
pathways, 160–163
person-directed vs. object-directed, 83, 177
personality–offender behavior–motive associations, 212–213
extant research, 216–227
rapist classification, 28–30
to regain lost power, 80

Relational evidence, 153–154
Research
    actuarial, 250–252
    arson motives, 172–180
    consideration of disconfirming
        evidence, 114–115
    convicted offenders as research
        subjects, 232–234
    limitations of Canter's model,
        101–109
    methods for scientific profiling,
        100–101
    motive, 171
        opportunities for improving, 163–
            164, 184–186
    motive–personality–behavior
        relationships, 216–227
    personality research needs, 187,
        203–206, 247–248
    sex offender personality, 188–197
    on success of crime scene investiga-
        tions, 155–156
    See also Data collection; Testing of
        profiling models
Ressler, Robert, 10–12
Revenge arson, 27, 173, 174–175
Revenge murders
    Douglas et al. model of homicide
        intent, 20
    Keppel and Walter rape–murder
        typology, 38–39
Risk of victimization
    Douglas et al. model of
        investigation, 21
    victim characteristics and, 34–35
Ritual behaviors, rapist's, 29
Rope, 150–151

Sadism
    pedophile typology, 31
    rapist characteristics, 29–30
Saliva, 141
Samson syndrome, 80
Scientific approaches to profiling
    application of research findings,
        249–252
    Canter's research and, 224–227
    consideration of disconfirming
        evidence, 114–115
    criteria for evaluating, 87

current state, 13–14, 71, 257–258
    description of procedures, 110–111
    discussion of models' limitations,
        116–117
    empirical validation, 112–114
    goals, 73, 127, 128
    limitations, 256–257
    in nonscientific models, 118–123
    origins and development, 11–13
    path analysis, 242–243
    practice application, 255–257
    rationale, 73
    recommendations for near-term
        implementation, 252–256
    research methods, 100–101, 239–244
    role of theory in, 87–88
    situational factors in, 227–230
    terminology of, 99
    Turvey on, 47
    See also Canter model of profiling;
        Proposed model of profiling
Search warrants, 13
Second-level behaviors
    assessment, 239
    goals of profiling, 254–255
    scientific model of profiling,
        213–216
    See also Predicted behaviors
Self-concept, offender, 79–82, 92–96
Self-control, offender, 91
Self-defense murders, 20
Self-reported data, 167, 233, 234
    behavior assessment, 238
    on motive, 172–177, 185–186, 233,
        235–236, 245
    personality characteristics, 205,
        236–237
    sex offender research, 188, 197
Semen
    evidence collection, 141
Sequential evidence, 153
Serial murder
    definition, 54, 55
        Douglas et al. model, 20, 57–58
    geographic factors, 26
    Holmes and Holmes typology, 26–
        27, 56
    motivation typology, 26–27, 56
Sexual acts
    arson motive, 176, 178
    criminal investigation, 19

ABOUT THE AUTHORS

Scotia J. Hicks, PhD, resides in Berkeley, California, where she is a student at the University of California, Boalt Law School. In addition to criminal profiling, Dr. Hicks's scholarly research and interests focus broadly on forensic identification, forensic assessment, and the use of expert evidence in legal decision making.

Bruce D. Sales, PhD, JD, is professor of psychology, sociology, psychiatry, and law at the University of Arizona, where he also directs its Psychology, Policy, and Law Program. Some of his other recent books are *Scientific Jury Selection* (with J. D. Lieberman, 2006); *Experts in Court: Reconciling Law, Science, and Professional Knowledge* (with D. Shuman, 2005); *More Than the Law: Behavioral and Social Facts in Legal Decision Making* (with P. W. English, 2005); *Family Mediation: Facts, Myths, and Future Prospects* (with C. J. A. Beck, 2001); and *Treating Adult and Juvenile Offenders With Special Needs* (coedited with J. B. Ashford & W. H. Reid, 2001). Professor Sales, the first editor of the journals *Law and Human Behavior* and *Psychology, Public Policy, and Law,* is a fellow of the American Psychological Association and the American Psychological Society and an elected member of the American Law Institute. He twice served as president of the American Psychology–Law Society. He received the Award for Distinguished Contributions to Psychology and Law from the American Psychology–Law Society, the Award for Distinguished Professional Contributions to Public Service from the American Psychological Association, and an honorary Doctor of Science degree from the City University of New York for being the "founding father of forensic psychology as an academic discipline."